I0810042

IMAGES
of America

OCEAN SHORES

On the Cover: This Del Mulkey photograph, loaned by the Aberdeen Museum of History, is a quintessential image of the new 1960s Ocean Shores real estate development during a time when cheesecake reigned. Teri Lee McDougal, a 1961 graduate and cheerleader of Aberdeen's Weatherwax High School, was chosen as the centerpiece between the two famous symbols of the oceanside community—the carved cedar razor clam and the sixties classic graphic sign. Teri modeled for both the Wolff and Weinstein's Department Stores in Aberdeen. Terri moved to Los Angeles, California, immediately after graduating from high school and did some modeling and appeared in television commercials for shampoo, toothpaste, and so on form three or four years. She married a man from South America and the couple lived in Beverly Hills and had two daughters. They also had a home in Santa Barbara. Teri now lives in Indonesia. She's been there for about 20 years or more, but she has maintained her ties with her Grays Harbor friends. (Aberdeen Museum of History.)

IMAGES
of America

OCEAN SHORES

Gene Woodwick

ARCADIA
PUBLISHING

ISBN 978-0-7385-8045-6

Published by Arcadia Publishing
Charleston, South Carolina

Library of Congress Control Number: 2009940084

For all general information contact Arcadia Publishing at:
Telephone 843-853-2070
Fax 843-853-0044
E-mail sales@arcadiapublishing.com
For customer service and orders:
Toll-Free 1-888-313-2665

Visit us on the Internet at www.arcadiapublishing.com

Contents

ACKNOWLEDGMENTS

The photographs used in this book are a portion of a 50-year collection of Ocean Shores history gathered for personal enjoyment, not for publishing a book. Many photographs in the collection were taken by the author. The origins and photographers of those that weren't are identified whenever possible. For those not identified, the author offers a personal apology.

Jeff Dukes's help has been invaluable. Others who made the book possible were Russ Riffenburg; Dann Sears of the Aberdeen Museum of History; James Derigamore; and Nancy Cuyne, John Larson, and Scott Lucas of the Polson Museum. Thorn Ward and Tom Quigg helped in identifying photographs. It never could have been accomplished without Larry Woodwick, whose help was beyond compare. Over the years many other people contributed to the stories and information collected about this city of dreams.

Images courtesy of the following entities are abbreviated as follows:

AMH Aberdeen Museum of History
CHSGWC Coastal Heritage Services, Gene Woodwick Collection
MFP Minard Family Photograph
NCN North Coast News
PM Polson Museum

Introduction

As the place called Ocean Shores, Washington, enters its 50-year anniversary, it is important to recall that the Point Brown Peninsula of northern Grays Harbor has always been a place of dreams. The year 2010 is only the continuation of the longtime dreams of those developers who, in 1960, paid a cattle rancher, Ralph Minard, $1 million to give up his dream of a ranch encompassing the six-mile point of land jutting into the Pacific Ocean. No matter what era the dreamers began dreaming, their constants always centered on the *Siliqua patula*, the razor clam.

The "time before dreaming," as the Native Americans referred it to, was promoted by the abundance of life's necessities, especially the abundance of the razor clam. Misunderstood by those who later settled the area, this long peninsula was Oyehut, the place of crossing over, used by many of the 32 Native American bands of present day Grays Harbor and Pacific Counties. It was home for the largest, permanent camp of the Chepalis (Copalis) people. It was usual and accustomed ground of those who became the Consolidated Tribes of the Quinault Nation and for the northern Oregon Chinook people who had a provisioning camp on the land. The North Bay that Lt. Charles Wilkes called "Useless Bay" added the abundance of all species of salmon, steelhead, and 23 species of other fish to the provisions and trade items. The land supported a vast array of game birds and animals as well as the all important cedar, yew, and grasses.

The dream of the settlers was not just land ownership, but to become entrepreneurs and make money from the land and resources. The most successful of these was Albert Olson (A. O.) Damon of Olympia, who gained ownership of first peninsula settler Matthew McGee's cattle and land to become a merchant; a port dock location for entry into the North Beach and southern Clallam County, western Jefferson County, the Queets, and Quinault country; and a holder of a variety of local offices whose enumeration boosted his financial holdings that eventually became the reality of McGee's dream—that of a large, long-lived cattle ranch.

Damon's success drew the other pioneers to dream of industrial manufacturing, logging, clamming, fishing, and hunting, which furthered the Point Brown Peninsula's reputation for resource-based recreational activities. The U.S. Government's involvement in building a jetty system (1904–1916) to protect maritime trade activities surrounding the peninsula was brought to the forefront with the arming of the peninsula during World War II. After the war ended, it was time for Ralph Minard, the grandson of A. O. Damon, to fulfill his dream to own the entire peninsula as a cattle ranch. The time of the Native Americans had ended, and the time of the cowboys began.

For many folks, the Great Depression was the end of their dreams, but the saying was true on the coast, "When the tide is out the table is set." Urban folks who had lost jobs, the bluebills who were the seasonal workers of the Washington Coast, and the migrant fruit and field workers all found refuge at Jetty Camp, Big Root Camp Sampson Johns, Oyehut, and Illahee with long strongholds of the Native Americans, the Finns, and other Scandinavians. All were havens for the dispossessed, the hard workers, or the scoundrels who survived by living off the beach. If that failed, there was always bootlegging, some cattle rustling, and other borderline ways to jingle a few coins in their pockets. By the time Minard consolidated his holdings, the peninsula sported a fair-sized population squatting on his land. Minard solved the problem by personally moving all the beach shacks up to his north pasture area, creating the present day Oyehut.

A new bunch of dreamers came home from World War II. They "had seen the elephant" of far away places. They knew how quickly a person's world could end. They were risk takers, and most of all, they were dreamers—big dreamers. Their dream was to obtain the Point Brown Peninsula and set upon it a California style of development, where clamming, hunting, fishing, golfing, and a multitude of other recreational activities would be available to the common Joe, the kind of guy who had served in the war and now worked for corporations and who could enjoy life at the ocean, hobnob with Hollywood, and, incidentally, make the developer rich.

Selling real estate began in earnest when MacPherson Realty was named the exclusive sales office for the new Ocean Shores Estates, Inc., which had 1,200 lots to be developed on the $1 million hunk of land purchased on June 20, 1960. The first lots sold for $595 from a trailer parked at the beach. By the time the realtor moved into the Executive Villa, folks were buying lots sight unseen from maps in the salesmen's hands. Ted Adams, Elmer Huhta (a former Washington State University football star and state legislator), and Don Eastvold (newly retired Washington state attorney general) negotiated the sale of land with Ralph Minard. Murdock MacPherson, owning equal shares with Don Eastvold and his law partner, Moksha Smith, began an aggressive campaign to sell Ocean Shores lots. Eventually the stockholders included Dr. Allen Adams, Howard McGowan (special assistant to Sen. Warren Magnuson), Edward D. Telise, Ruskin and Fisher (engineers), Glen Corning (road builder), Howard Ker, Cliff Mortensen, Dr. Henry Landberg, and Mike Banks. In 1961, Ole Bardahl was elected president of Ocean Shores Estates.

The stunning success of the Ocean Shores development depended upon the unparalleled public relations work of Robert "Bob" Nevin Ward, a Seattle newspaper man hired to make sure the new place on the Pacific Ocean would be on the lips of folks around the world. He and his son, Thorn, in 1961, developed the house organ, the *Sandpaper*, later rolling it into the *Observer* to keep those global buyers and owners abreast of all the hijinks and latest news. Bob's fertile mind dreamed unforgettable celebrations that grabbed media attention, celebrations he himself had no shame in promoting or enjoying. A consummate newsman, he understood the risk takers and blue-collar folks to which he pitched the California-style Shangri-la, and he was totally fearless in approaching the elite in helping promote the real estate venture. It is no wonder that Thorn has spent most of his adult life involved in the real estate his dad made so desirable. Bob served on the city council, good experience for a guy whose glider plane had been shot down over Germany and who had worked as a crop duster. Anyone remembering Bob does so with a chuckle and admiration.

Those who have made this place of dreams come true knew one thing: If you are going to dream, dream big. It is better to fail at a dream than to never have the courage and imagination to dream big. And some dreams fell flat. But that is all the more reason for the future citizens to keep on dreaming about what lies ahead in the next 50 years for the people who have the courage and civility to stay behind and build on those dreams. And, what the heck? You can always dig razor clams.

One

The Time before Dreaming

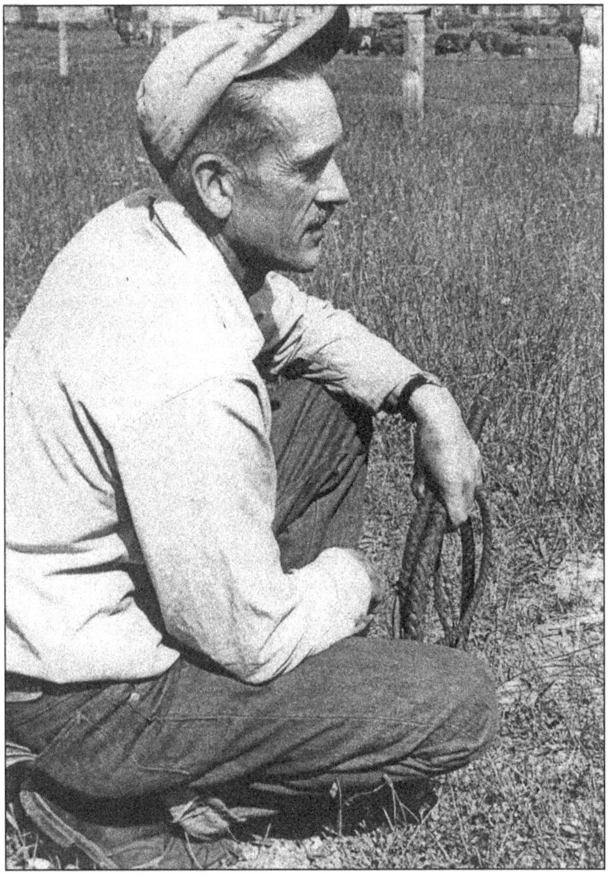

Ralph Minard sacrificed his dream of a cattle ranch for the developers' dream of a city of the future. Minard sold 1,200 acres, including accreted tidelands, to Ocean Shores Estates. The family had owned the land since 1878. (MFP.)

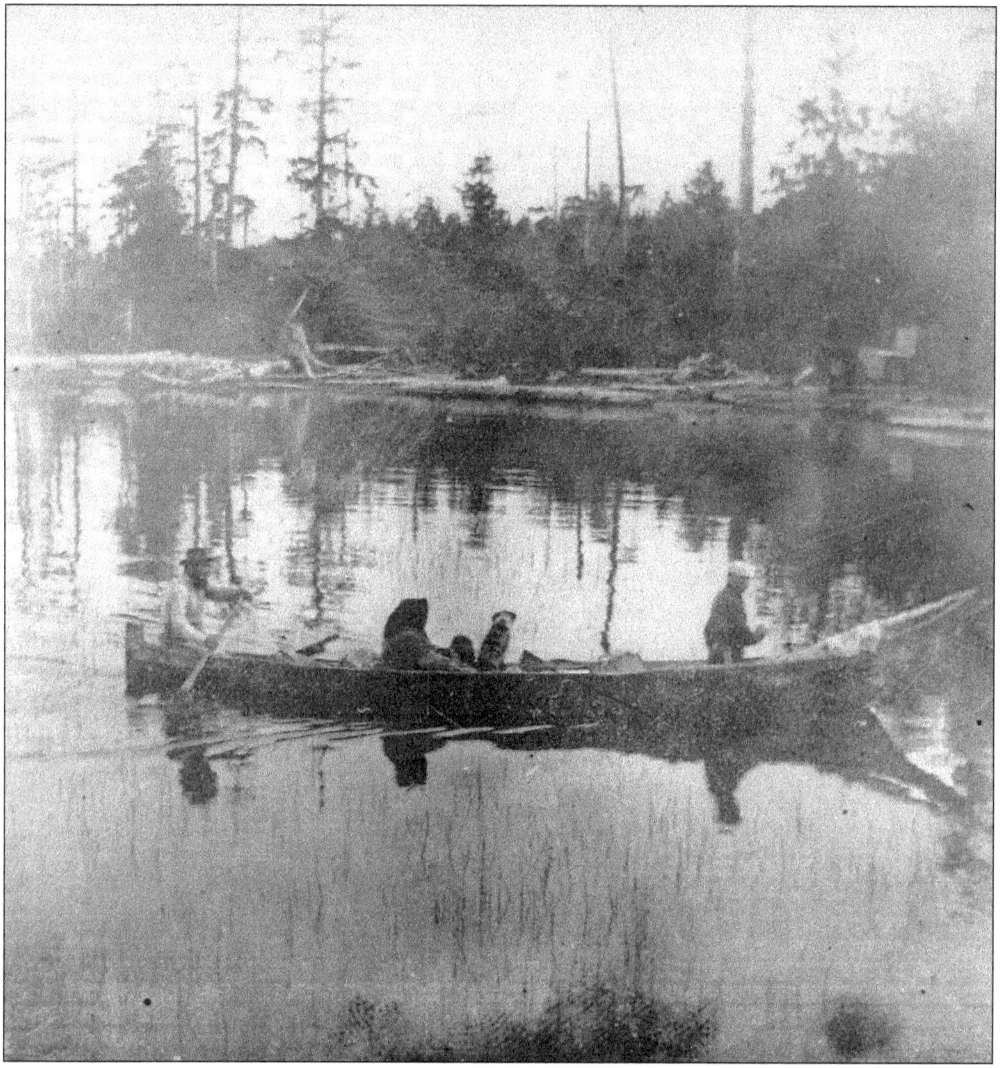

The serenity of the Point Brown Peninsula swales made travel across the Oyehut area pleasant and safe. The Southwest swale systems led to a canoe drag. Native American travelers from the Columbia River could avoid the dangerous river bars of both the Columbia and Grays Harbor by traversing swales and river systems to the South Beach peninsula of Grays Harbor. They could cross the bay, portage across the narrow neck of Point Brown Peninsula swale, and continue their northward Pacific Ocean journeys to visit coastal Olympic Peninsula and Canadian tribes. (PM; Cliff Summerlin.)

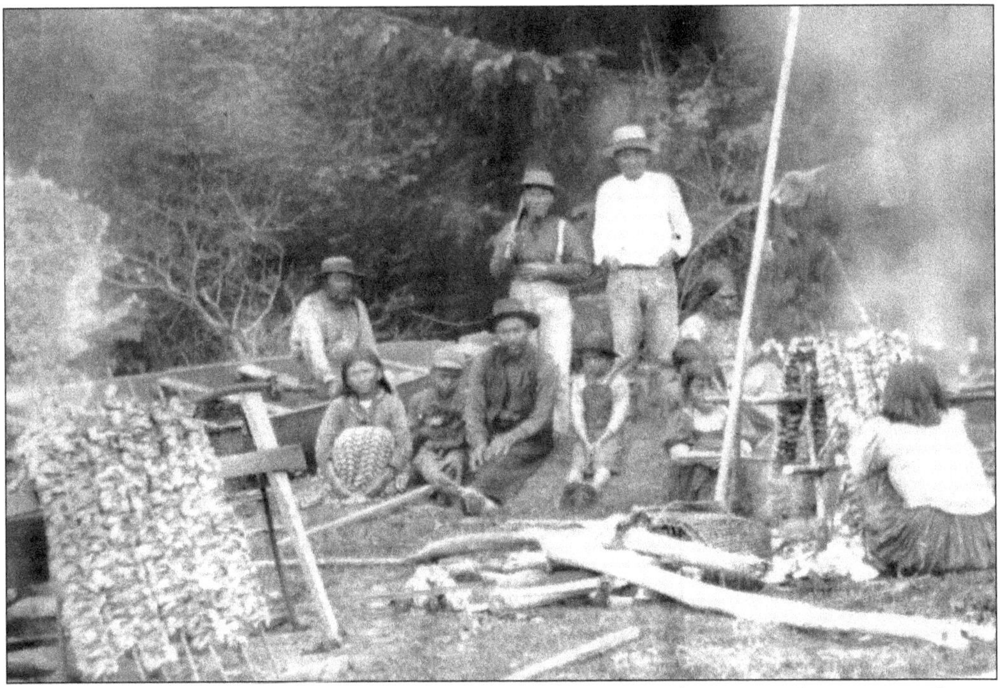

The largest of the Copalis Indian camps was near the present-day S.R. 115 curve into Ocean Shores. The importance of the razor clam is shown by the huge drying racks at work in this photograph. It is believed that the man in the canoe is Old Man Pope, holding the rifle is Johnny Johns with his brother, and Sampson Johns is seated in front of his brother. The other persons are not identified. The Johns brothers first received life-saving medals and large land awards for the rescue of sailors from the *Lillie Grace* and for other late-1800s shipwrecks. (MFP.)

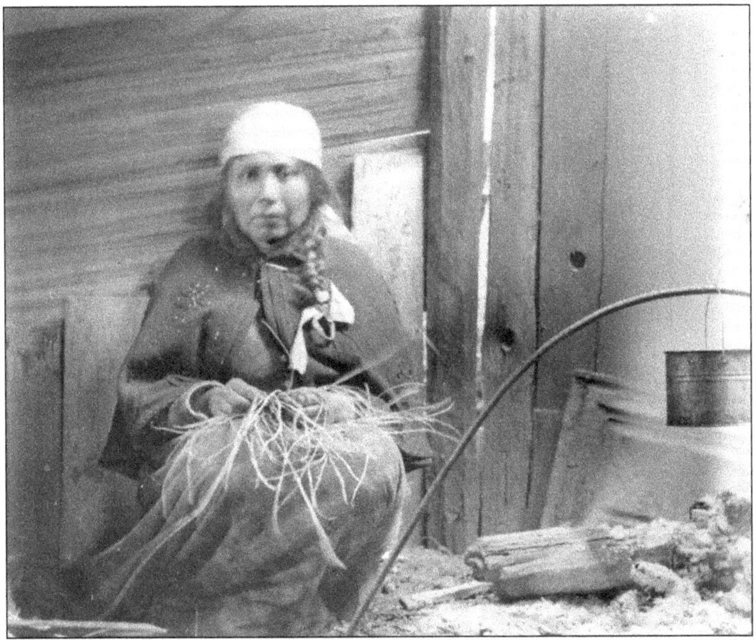

Basketry as an art form and as a utilitarian purpose was greatly admired by early ethnographers and served as trade items between the tribes, explorers, settlers, and the early coastal tourists. Some of today's Quinault Nation basket makers are related to this Copalis artisan. (MFP.)

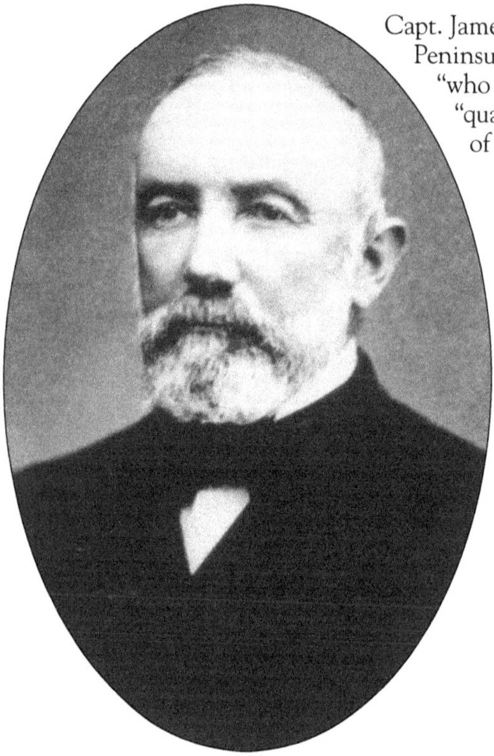

Capt. James Swan, who traveled through the Point Brown Peninsula, wrote in an 1852 diary about Caslah'han "who lived on the North side of the Bay" and how "quahogs" could be "plucked from the banks" of the creeks and swales. (CHSGWC.)

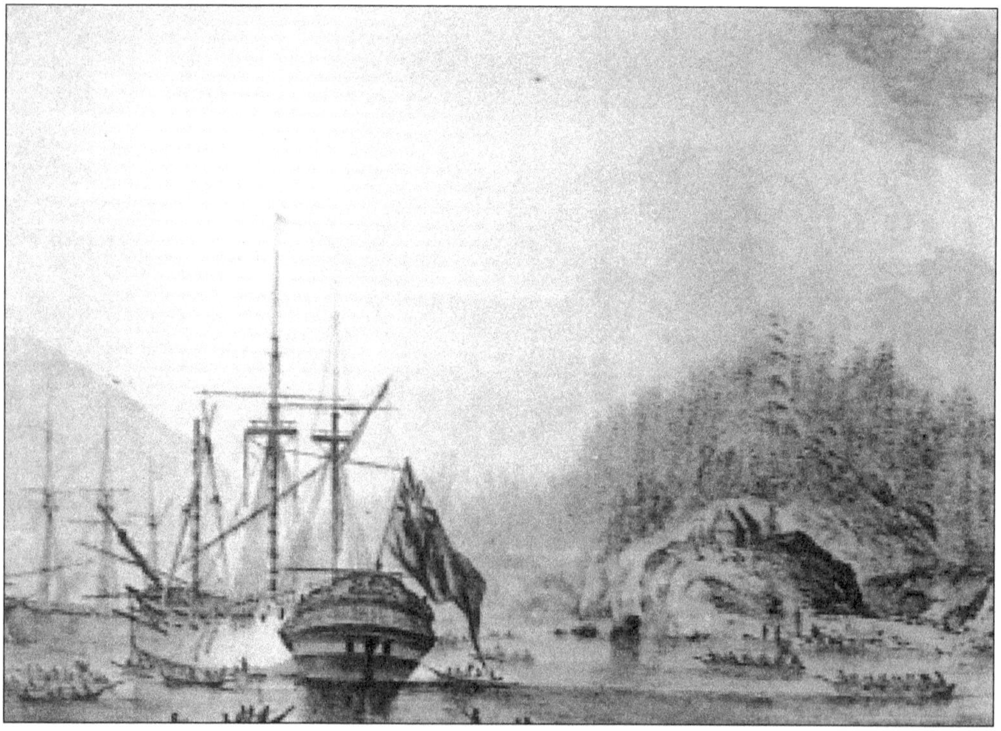

Capt. Robert Gray, the intrepid Boston sea captain, was the first American to enter Grays Harbor on May 7, 1792. (CHSGWC.)

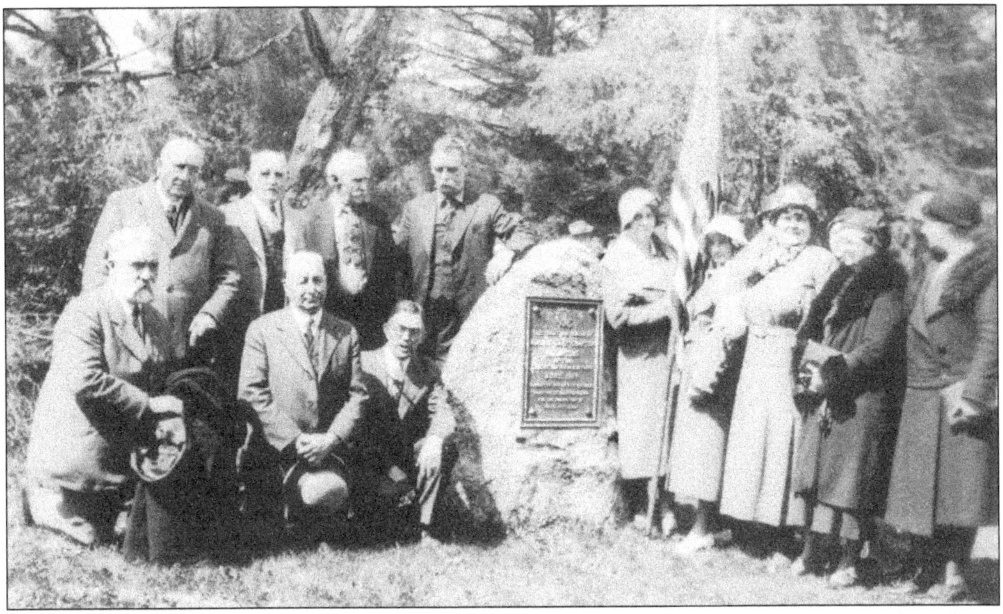

The Lone Tree that stood near the mouth of Grays Harbor is often, erroneously, thought to have guided Captain Gray across the bar. The Robert Gray Chapter of the Daughters of the American Revolution (DAR) placed a bronze marker commemorating Gray's achievement at the site. The marker was saved by the Minard family when the Lone Tree was eroded in 1921. The marker was then placed at the junction of U.S. 109 and S.R. 115 in a small triangular park. Ocean Shores Development Company donated land to the west of the Beach Club (now Community Club) where the marker is now located. (CHSGWC.)

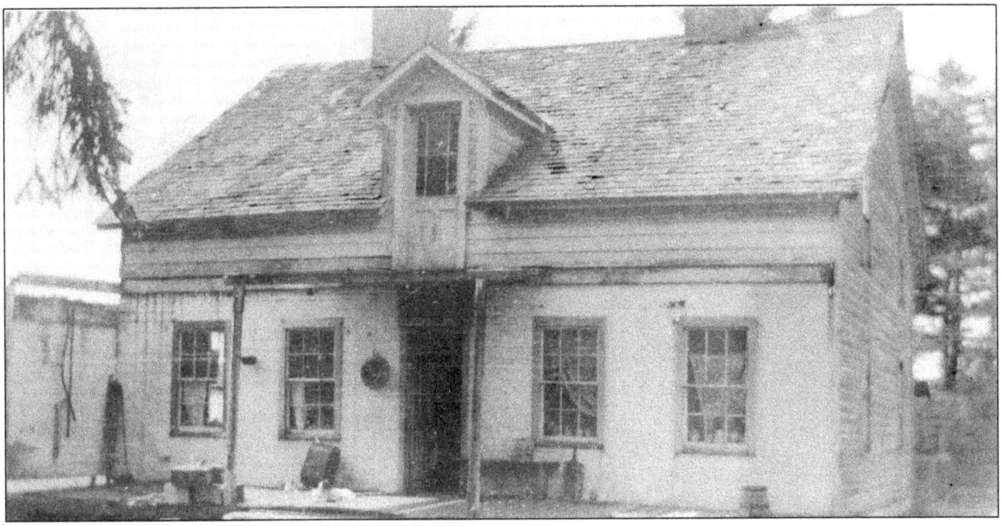

Matthew McGee, the first settler on the Peninsula, paid fellow sea otter hunters in whiskey to tear down an officer's home and one of the barracks from U.S. Army Fort Chehalis on the South Peninsula, raft it across the harbor, and to help build his new abode. His four-bedroom home with a great room, kitchen, and storage had a fireplace in each room, but there was no furniture to be purchased. Still it served as the first overnight accommodation for travelers to the North County. It was later home for the A. O. Damons and several other families. When Ocean Shores was developed remains of an orchard were still seen near the Community Club. (CHSGWC.)

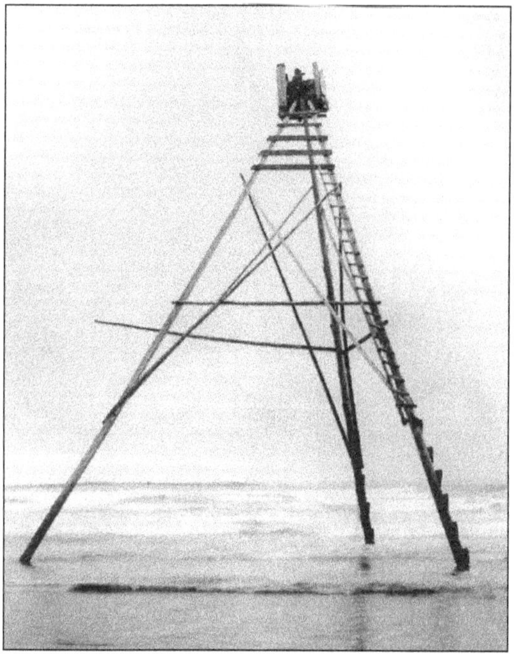

Tripod sea otter hunting towers lined the North Beaches from October through April each year; one tower was located near the present Ocean Lake Way beach approach. Hunters marked their bullets, thus identifying their prey when it washed in on the tide. The last of the old otter hunters was Charlie McIntyre. The last commercially hunted sea otter was killed in 1923. (CHSGWC.)

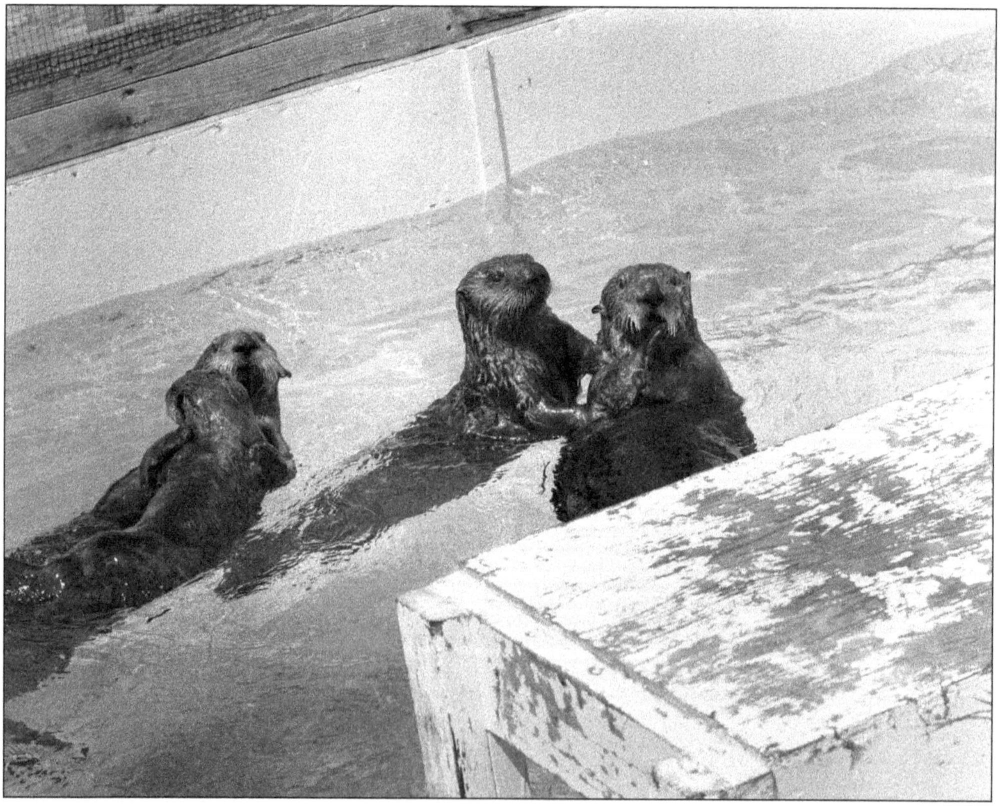

Sea otter restoration efforts were carried out locally in 1972 by the Washington State Department of Game. These three otters, shown aboard a ship, were part of the California denizens brought to the area in the transplanting efforts. (CHSGWC.)

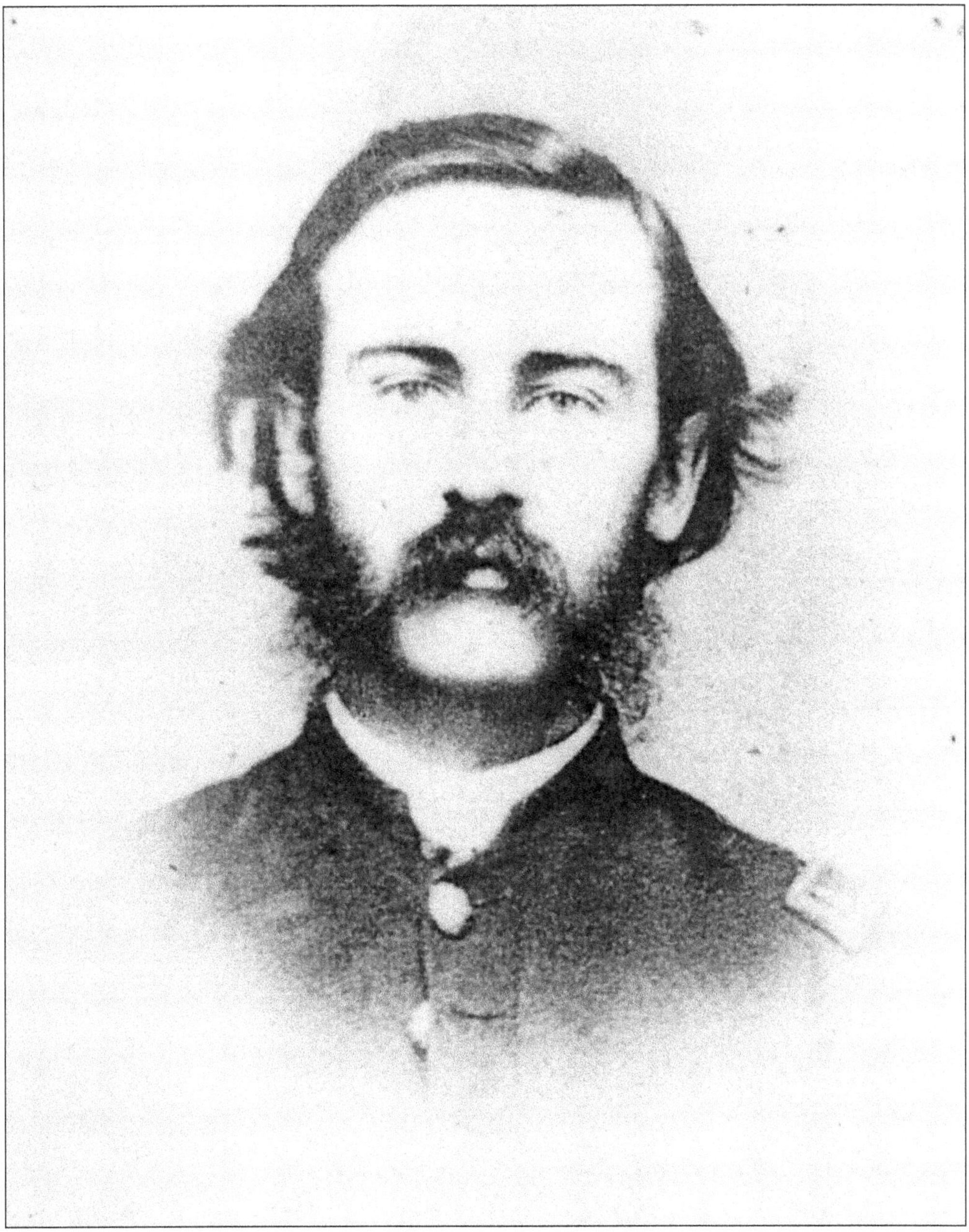

The dream of the settlers was not just land ownership, but to become entrepreneurs and make money from the land and resources. The most successful of these was Albert Olson (A. O.) Damon, an Olympia businessman who held a mortgage on acreage and the home of Matthew McGee and called in the loan, forcing a bankruptcy. In 1879, he had purchased 1,400 acres of land from McGee for $2,953 in gold coins and built a trading post near the present eastern outskirts of the city. "He was always looking for a way to make money and increase his investments," said his granddaughter, Emma Minard Tanner. The 1956 purchase of 1,200 acres, including accreted tidelands for 38¢ a foot, completed the holdings for the cattle ranch Minard sold to developers in 1960. (MFP.)

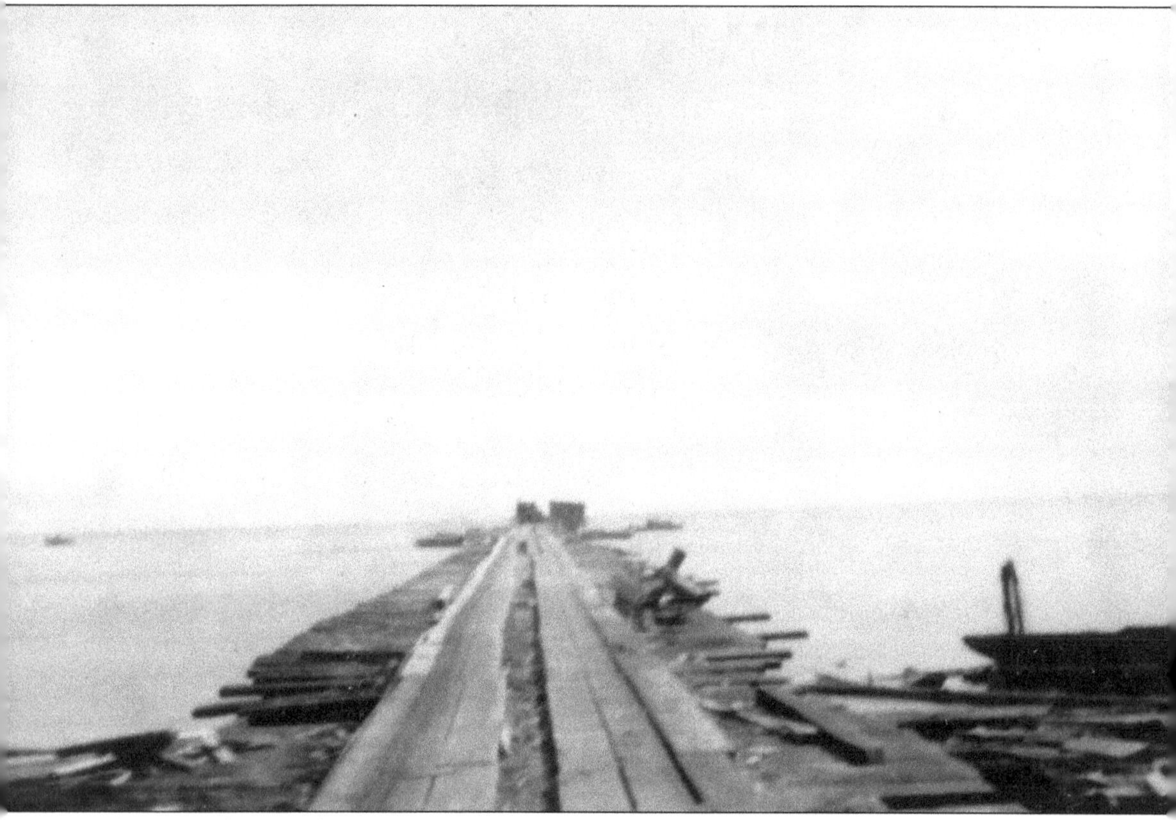

This 1920 photograph shows the freight building at the tip of Damon's dock where passengers could escape the wet Grays Harbor weather. Passengers and freight, including cattle, collected at the dock for transport to and from the North Grays Harbor beaches. (CHSGWC.)

Two

IN PREPARATION OF THE DREAM

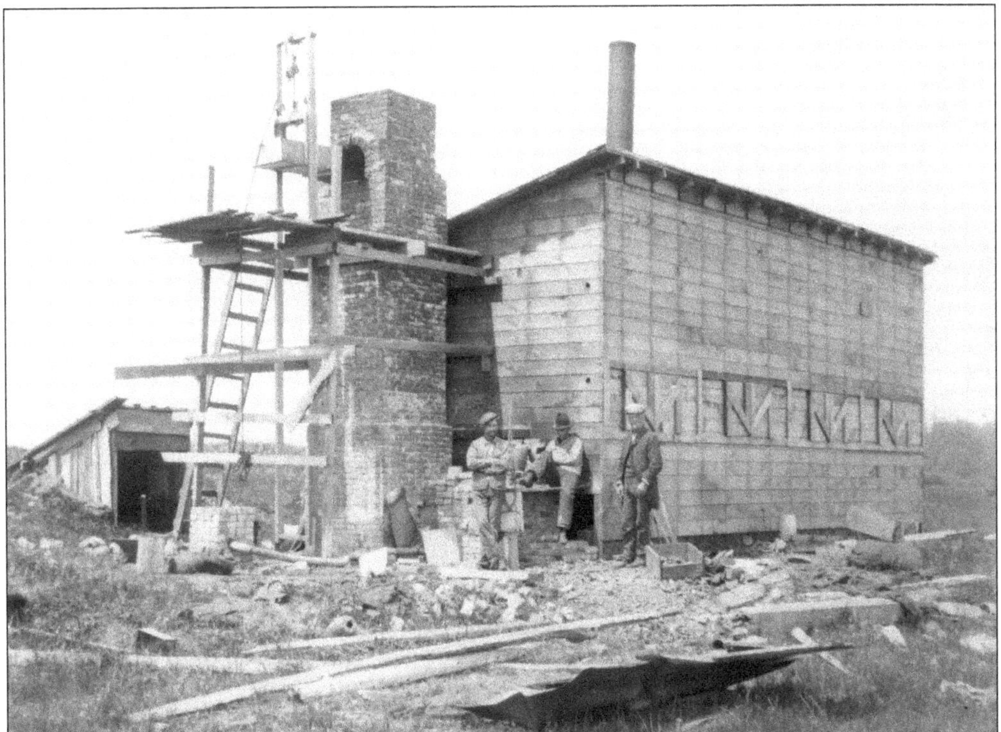

J. H. Barnett began building the steel mill (also termed the pig iron plant) near the recent concrete plant in December 1905. It went into operation in January 1906 to produce steel from the black sands of the area but proved to be economically unfeasible. (CHSGWC.)

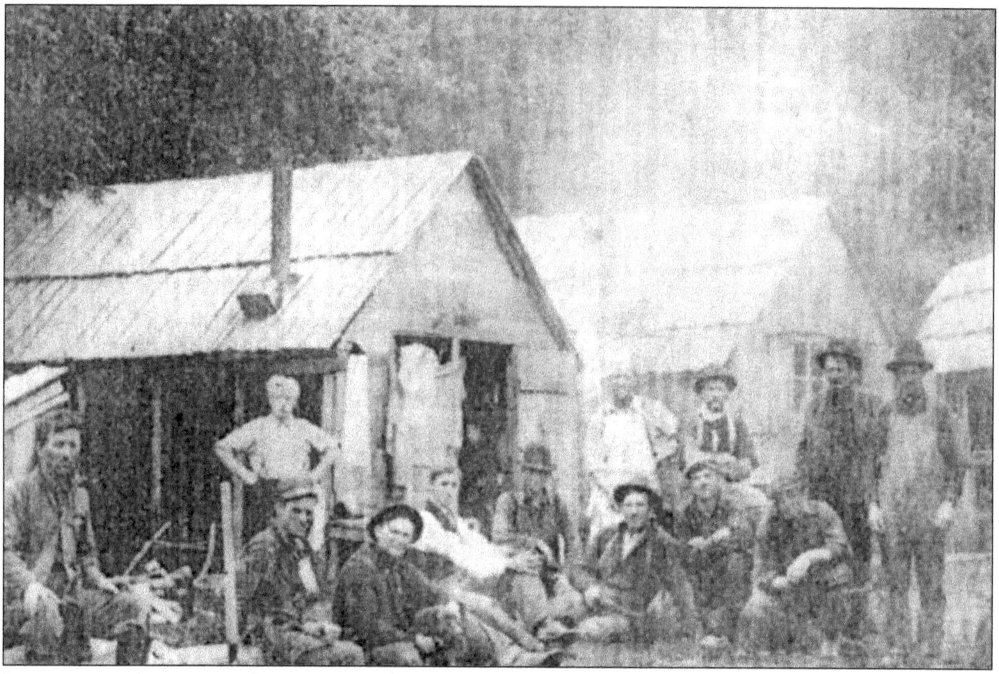

Logging on the peninsula was carried out in 1909 by this crew from Curtis Logging. Later the Greenwood Logging Company, owned by Bill Boeing Sr., purchased a strip of land down the center of the five-mile peninsula as a part of his holdings. Boeing used the proceeds from his Grays Harbor Company to begin the Boeing Airplane Company. (CHSGWC.)

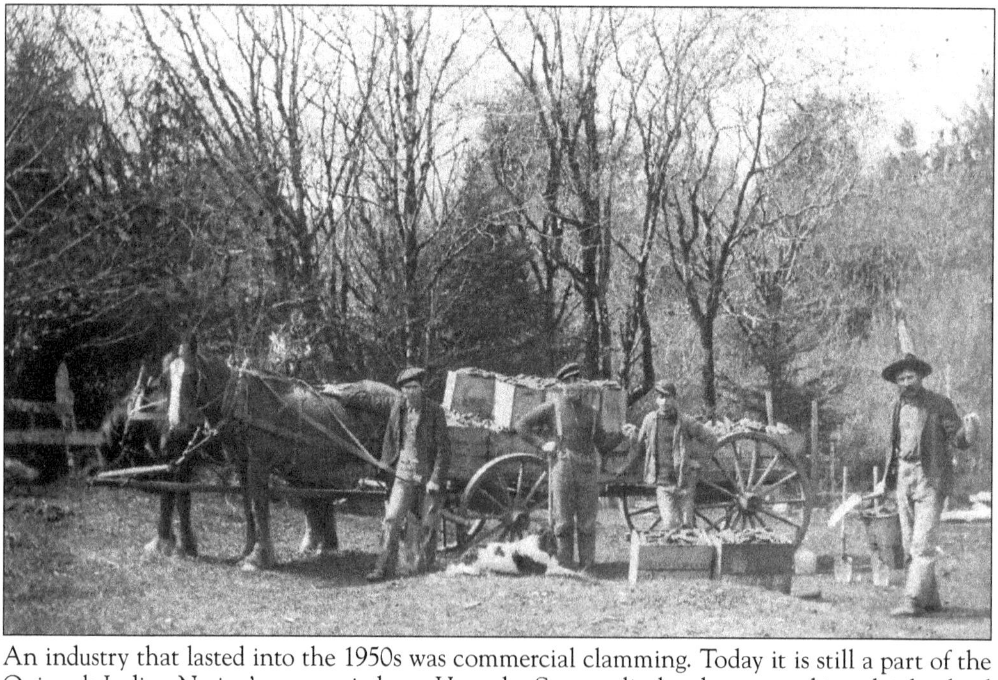

An industry that lasted into the 1950s was commercial clamming. Today it is still a part of the Quinault Indian Nation's economic base. Here the Summerlin brothers are taking this big load of clams across the Oyehut for scowing to canneries in Aberdeen and Hoquiam in 1911. (PM; Cliff Summerlin.)

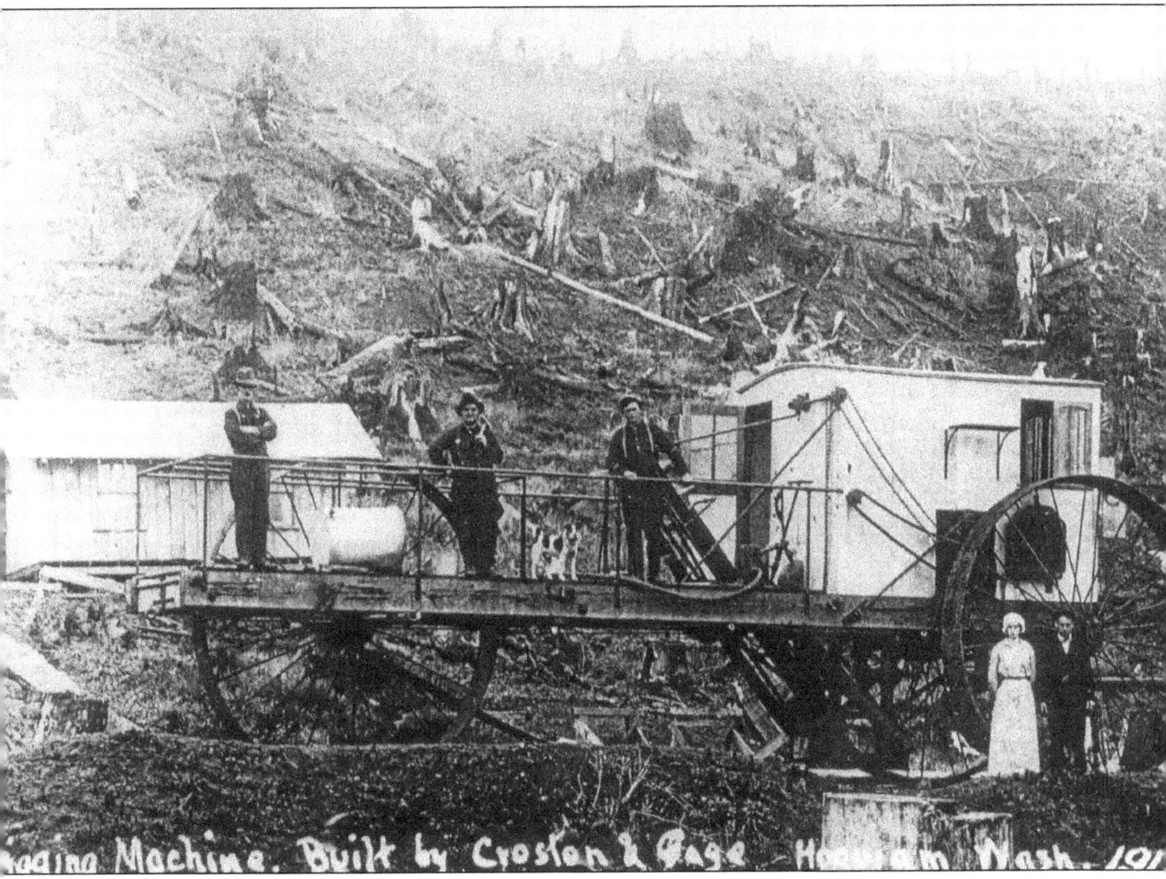

Grays Harbor loggers are among the most inventive people in the world; witness this massive razor clam digging machine built by Croston and Gauge Logging Company of Hoquiam in 1910. It worked, too. Eventually it was found to be too cumbersome to transport to the beaches for the clam harvests. (PM.)

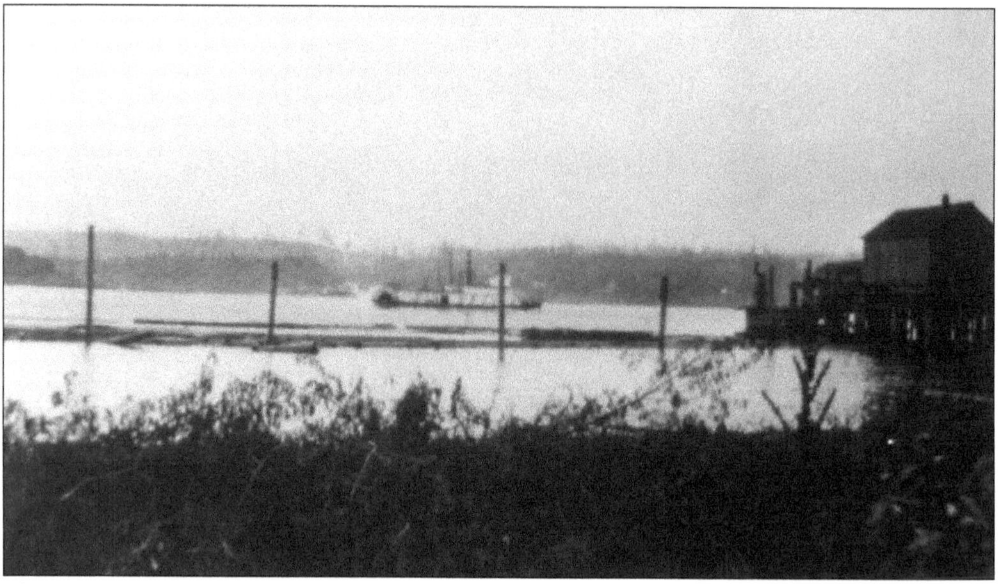

The Damon dock, funded by the federal government, stretched into the North Bay's Oyehut Channel to carry passengers and freight via sail-driven Native American dugouts, sternwheelers, steamers, and small freighters. (CHSGWC.)

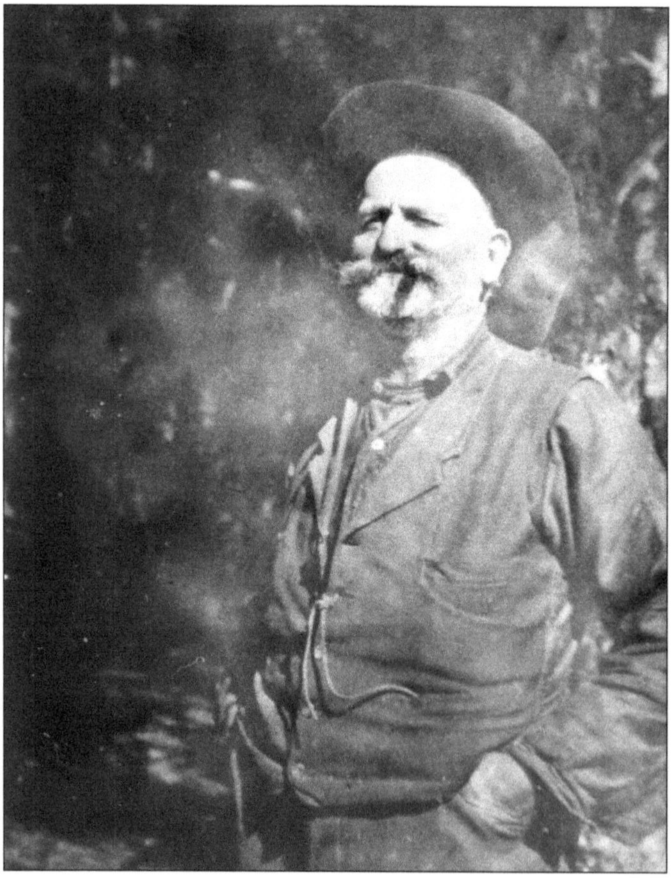

Ben Grigsby, much loved by the North Beach folks, hauled mail, freight, and passengers from Taholah to Damon's dock. His Copalis home was famous for holiday picnics, especially Fourth of July, and its front room served as a school until the first schoolhouses were built on the North Beach. His fellow freighter of many years was Charlie McIntyre, who eventually platted the town of Copalis. (CHSGWC.)

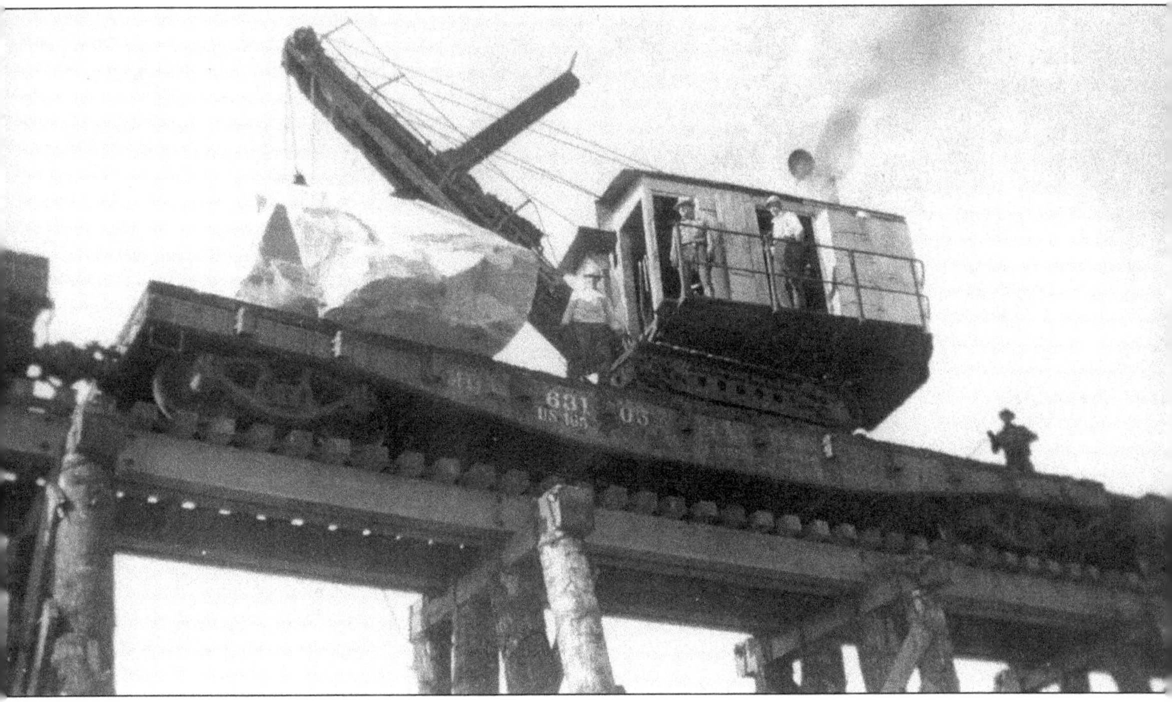

Increased shipping over the dangerous Grays Harbor bar led to congress funding jetty wings on both sides of the bar. Tom Murphy stands at the left of the door to his steam shovel while working on the North Jetty. Joining him was Ralph Matthews, fireman. Murphy built both the North and South Grays Harbor Jetties. This *c.* 1915 photograph shows no indication of the raging winter storms that often washed waves over the equipment. Such an event swept young Earl Ingram to his death. His body was never recovered. (CHSGWC.)

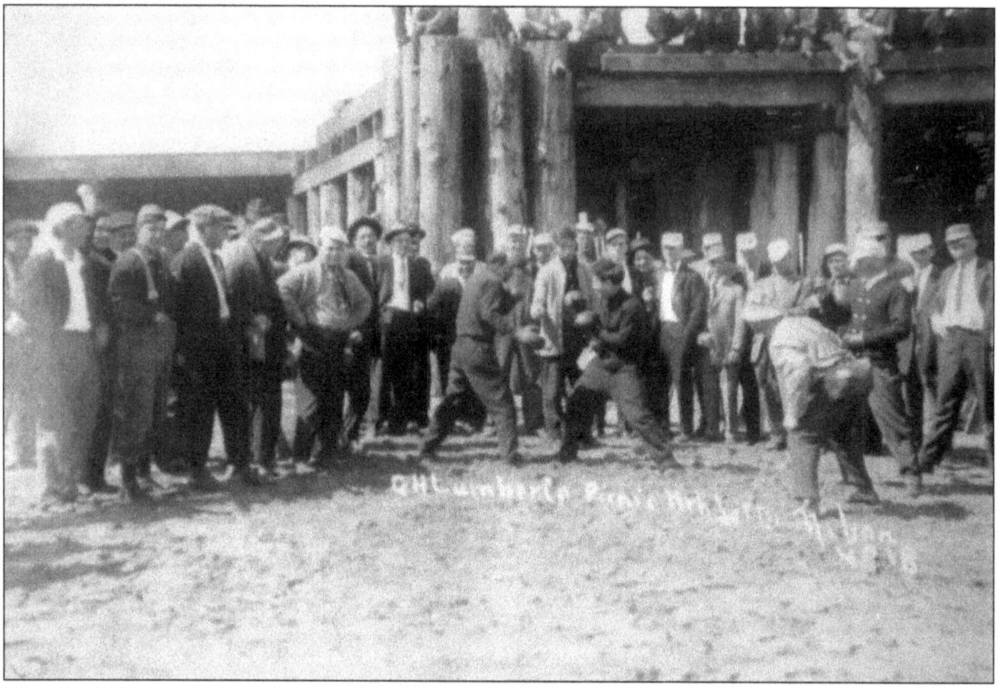

The North Jetty construction project was a favorite site for family and company picnics. This group of Grays Harbor Lumber Company workers had a grand time (minus their womenfolk) eating prodigious amounts of food, quaffing a brew, and enjoying an impromptu prizefight. (CHSGWC.)

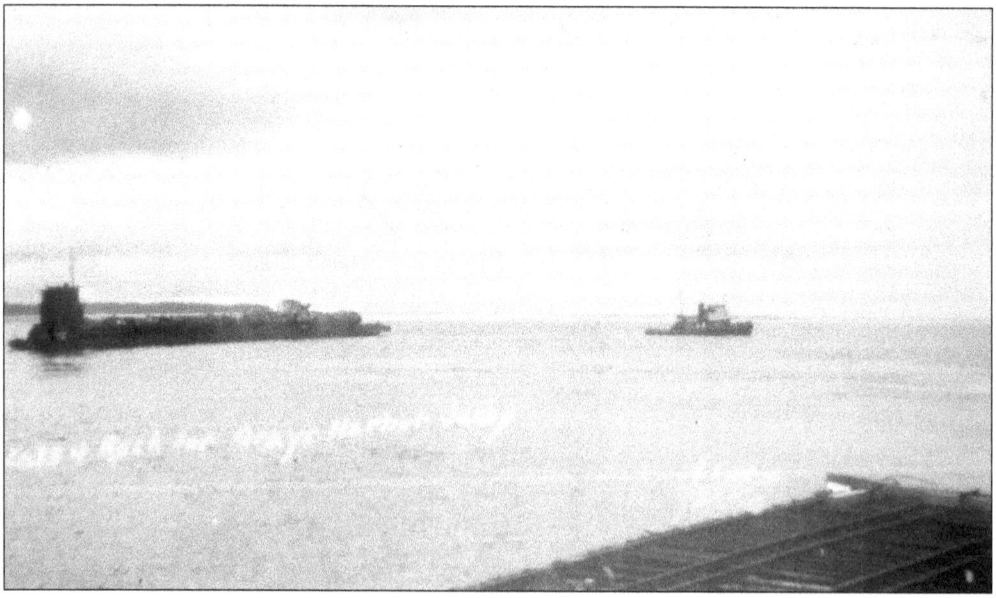

The first trainload of rock in 1904 was offloaded from the rails in Aberdeen onto the barge bound for the Lone Tree North Jetty construction site. The 1,000 feet of rock built five feet high in 1904–1910 was extended in 1911–1916 by 7,000 feet. The jetty system was restored in 1935–1942, 1975, 1999, and 2000 under congressional order. Since the 1942 rebuild, the entrance channel has been self-scouring, allowing for deep-draft vessels. (AMH.)

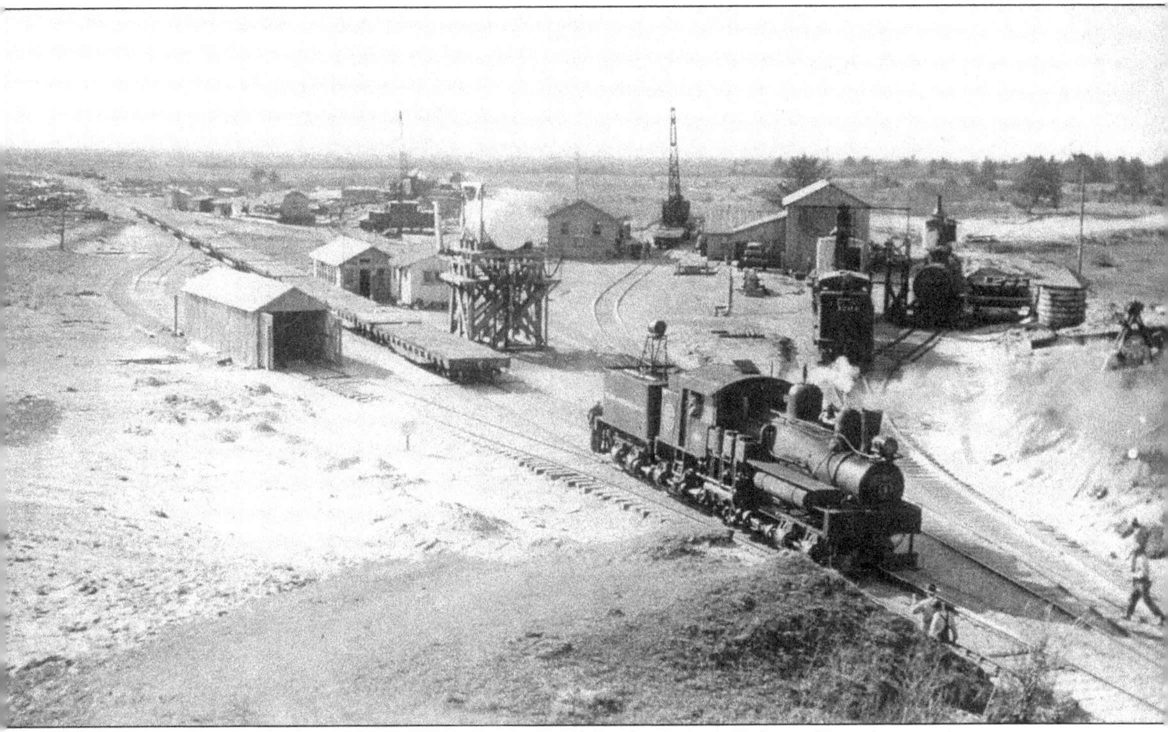

The town of Lone Tree occupied land, now eroded, that extended south and east of Armstrong Bay. The town had its own post office, stores, homes, boardinghouses, rail system, and a huge swamp works. (CHSGWC.)

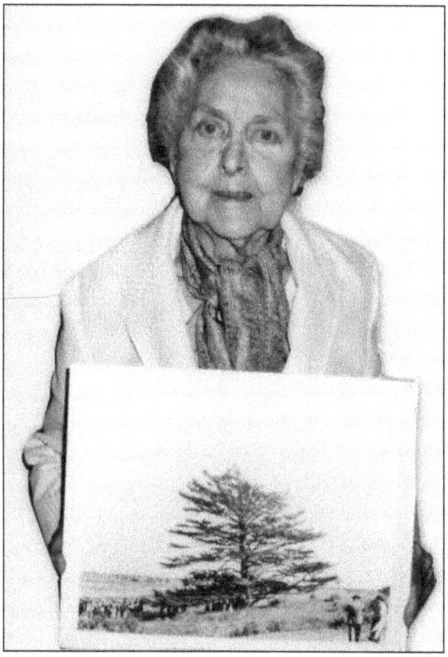

Agnes "Aggie" Taylor, age 83, holds a photograph of the iconic Lone Tree, which she used as a guide into the Oyehut Channel to offload supplies and passengers from the steamer *Irene* at Lone Tree and Damon's. The steamer had been built by her father at his boat works on Grass Creek. Aggie had been taught to operate the steamer at the age of 12 and piloted the craft from Aberdeen and Hoquiam to the North Beach during her teenage years. (CHSGWC.)

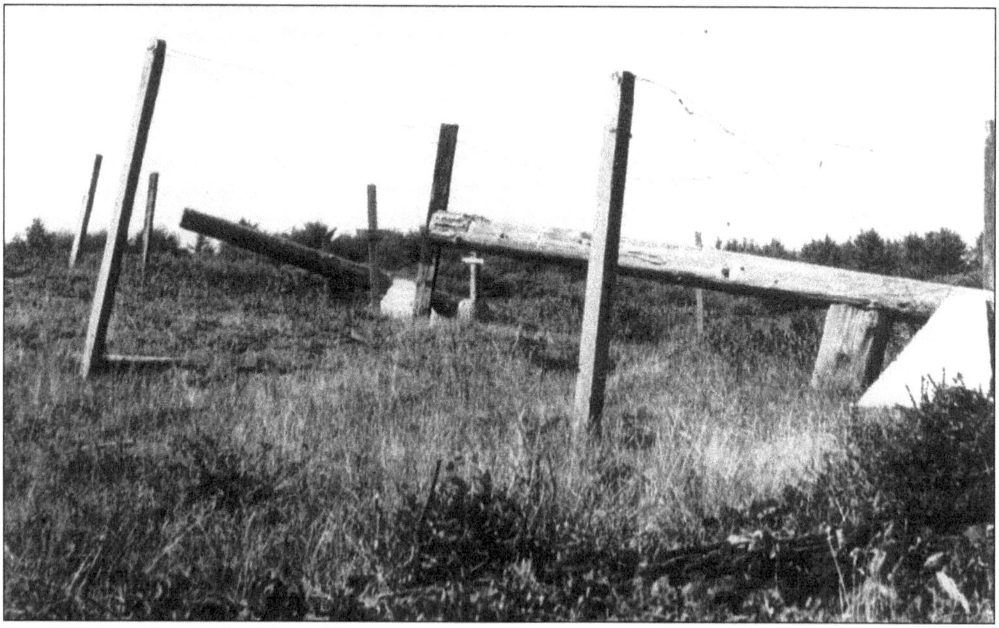

Pearl Harbor thrust the United States into World War II, and troops were immediately sent to guard the entrance of Grays Harbor. Kyle Smith, owner of Tacoma's Smith Western Company, was one of the soldiers snatched into a canvas-topped truck, still in his dance band suit, and sent to guard the Point Brown Peninsula with a broomstick in lieu of a gun. Logs were painted and propped up like phony cannons to ward off the enemy. Smith later served in the 7th U.S. Infantry as part of the 3rd Division in North Africa, then with the 7th Army in Sicily. As a photographer, his most famous shot was of the hanging of dictator Benito Mussolini taken on a *Stars & Stripes* jaunt with Bill Mauldin. Since he was not supposed to be in that area, he did not receive credit for the photograph. (MFP.)

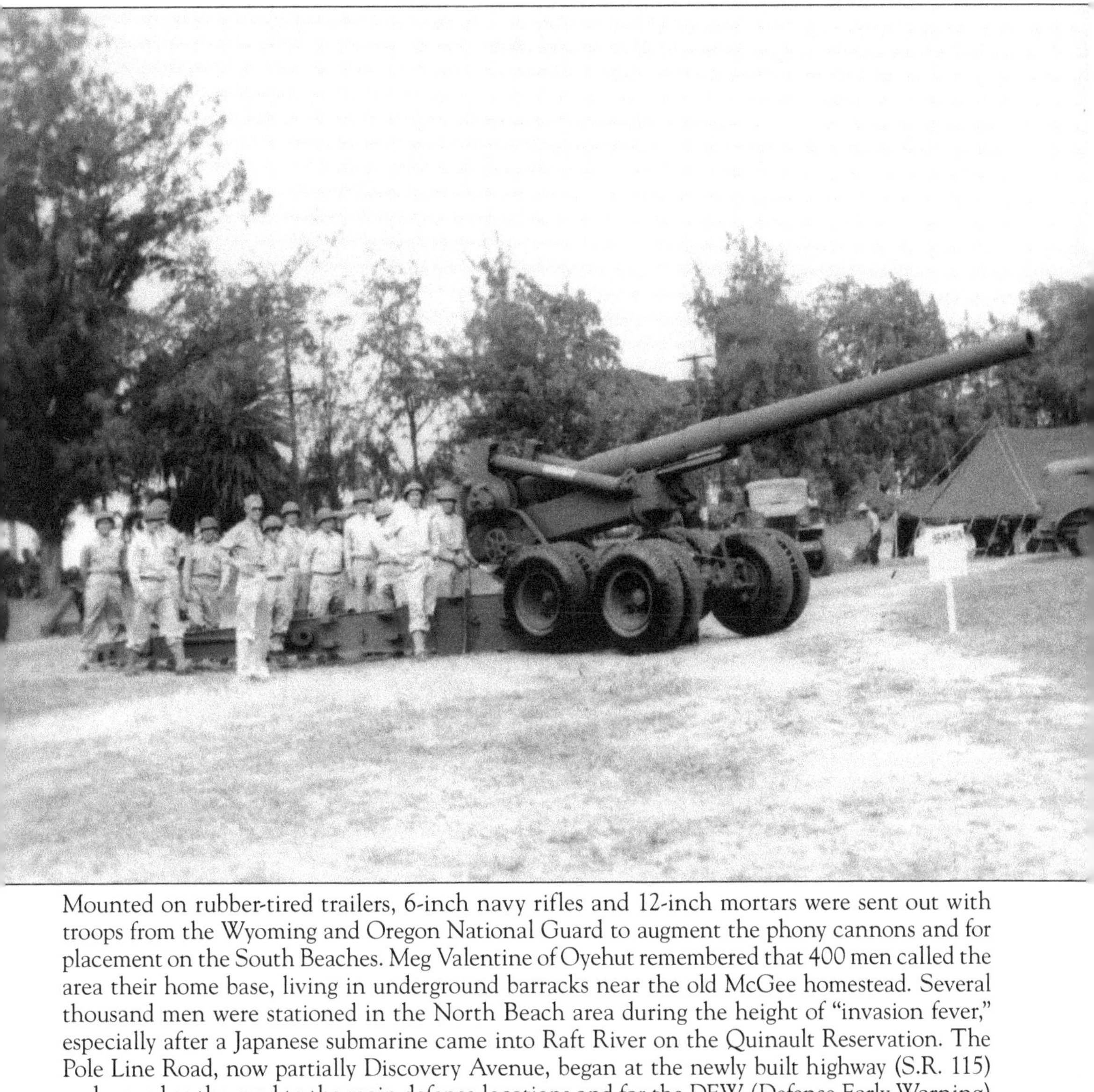

Mounted on rubber-tired trailers, 6-inch navy rifles and 12-inch mortars were sent out with troops from the Wyoming and Oregon National Guard to augment the phony cannons and for placement on the South Beaches. Meg Valentine of Oyehut remembered that 400 men called the area their home base, living in underground barracks near the old McGee homestead. Several thousand men were stationed in the North Beach area during the height of "invasion fever," especially after a Japanese submarine came into Raft River on the Quinault Reservation. The Pole Line Road, now partially Discovery Avenue, began at the newly built highway (S.R. 115) and served as the road to the main defense locations and for the DEW (Defense Early Warning) Line from Alaska across the bay to the South Beaches. Observation towers were located within the present Discovery Avenue to eastern Duck Lake. Submarine nets stretched across the mouth of the Harbor. The U.S. Coast Guard patrolled the beaches from Damon to Queets looking for unexploded mines on the beach. The last mine that popped to the surface was found in 1982 in the bay. World War II was not the only time invasion fever took hold. The Russian fleet of trawlers poised offshore during the 1960s Cold War era was close enough to see the crewmen's faces, which kept coast folks uneasy. Russian submarines were often spotted off Damon Point in 1985. (CHSGWC.)

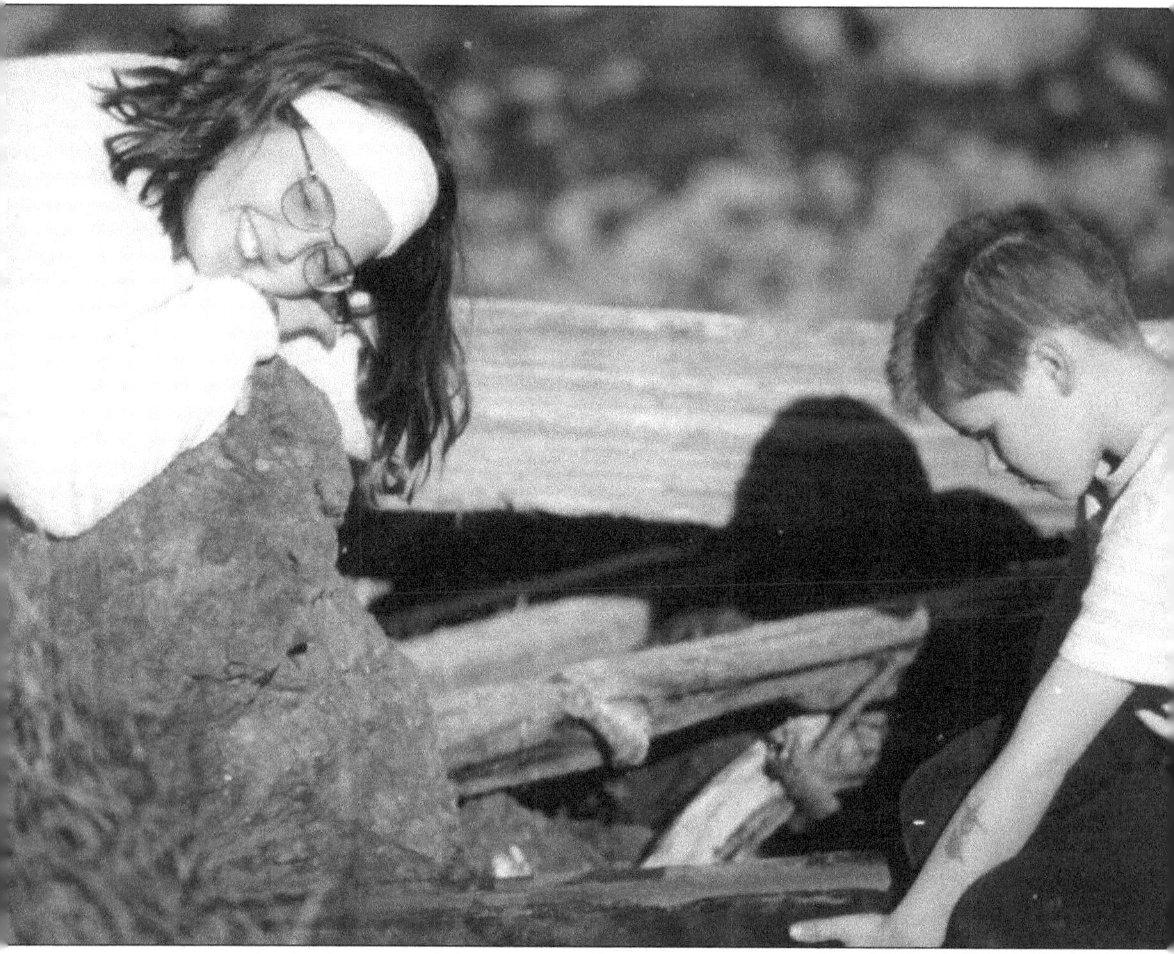

Four trainloads of 75mm and 155mm field artillery guns were moved in by the 18th, 56th, and 249th Coast Guard Artillery to be placed around Armstrong Bay and other coastal forts. Don Cramer, who grew up in the old McGee house, recalled sliding down the gun barrels for fun when he delivered newspapers to the soldiers. The railroad mortar pads placed in the dunes were removed following the war. Here, in 1995, Stephanie and Cody Church of Woodland, Washington, inspect remainders of the gun emplacement mortar rail system bulldozed when the developers built the Marina. (CHSGWC.)

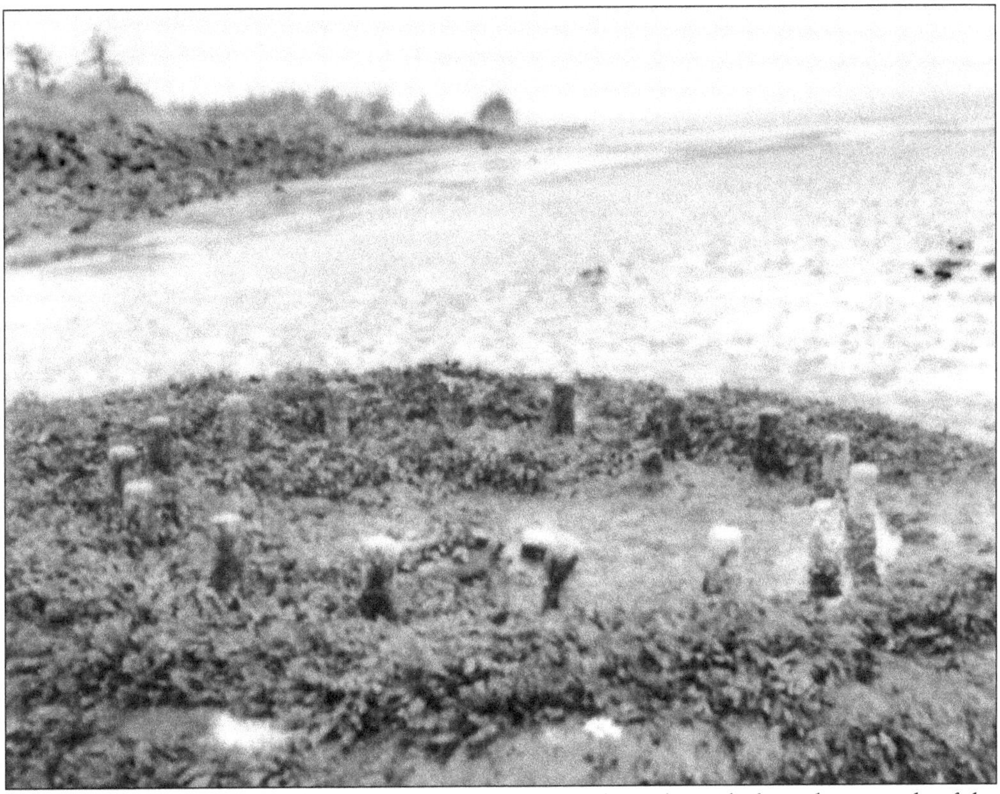

The remains of one gun emplacement pad can be seen today at low tide from the east side of the marina groin revetment. (CHSGWC.)

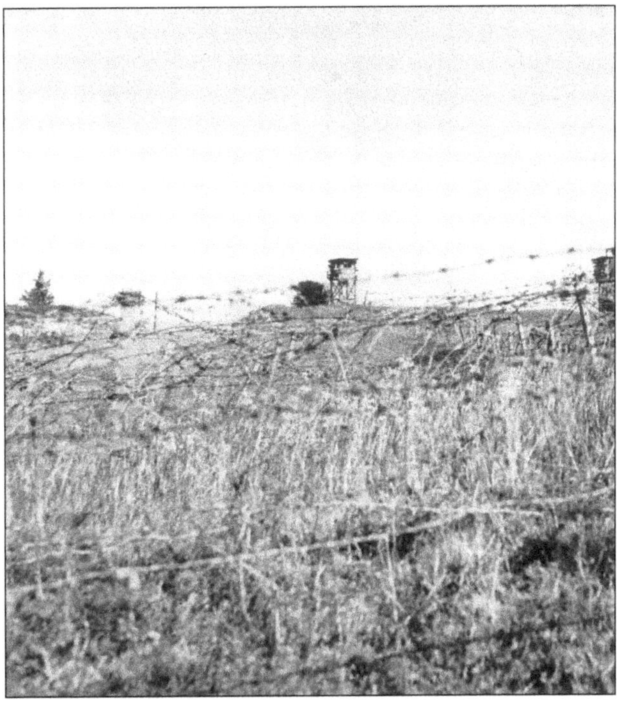

Barbed wire lay in windrows along the bay shore of the peninsula. A machine gun tower stands in the back of the dunes. Cliff Todd of Ocean Shores remembered when he was stationed at Point Brown in 1942 and sent to Warrington, Oregon, to harvest Russian beach grass. It was trucked back to the peninsula and planted in rows to conceal the barbed wire. The observation and machine gun towers faced Bowerman Basin. (MFP.)

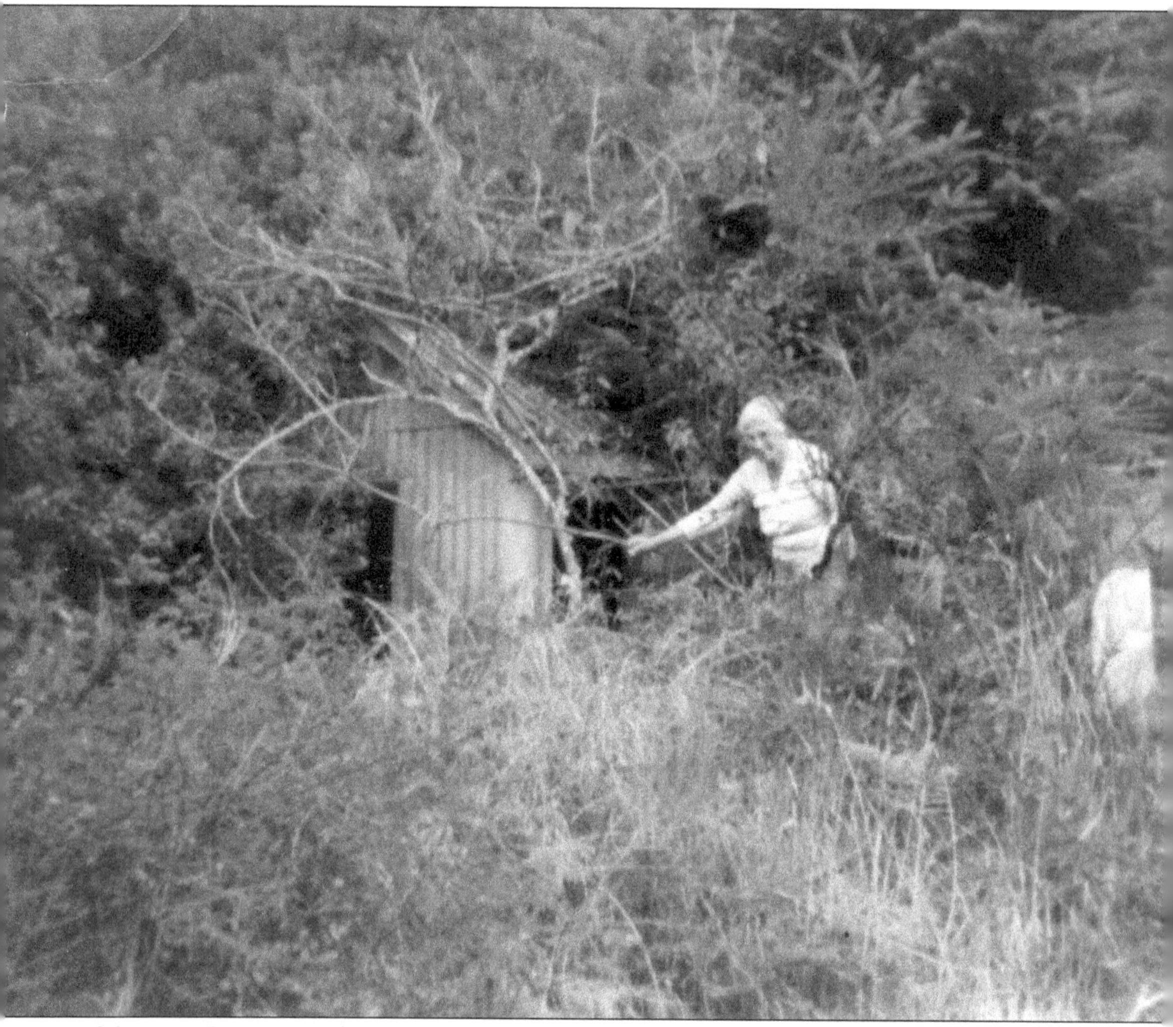

Margaret Rasmussen, local Ocean Shores chronicler, stands in front of a concrete battery storage shed located at Battery Court and Discovery Avenue in this 1985 photograph. It was subsequently bulldozed. The huge Klieg searchlight was located at Blaine Court and Catala Avenue. (CHSGWC.)

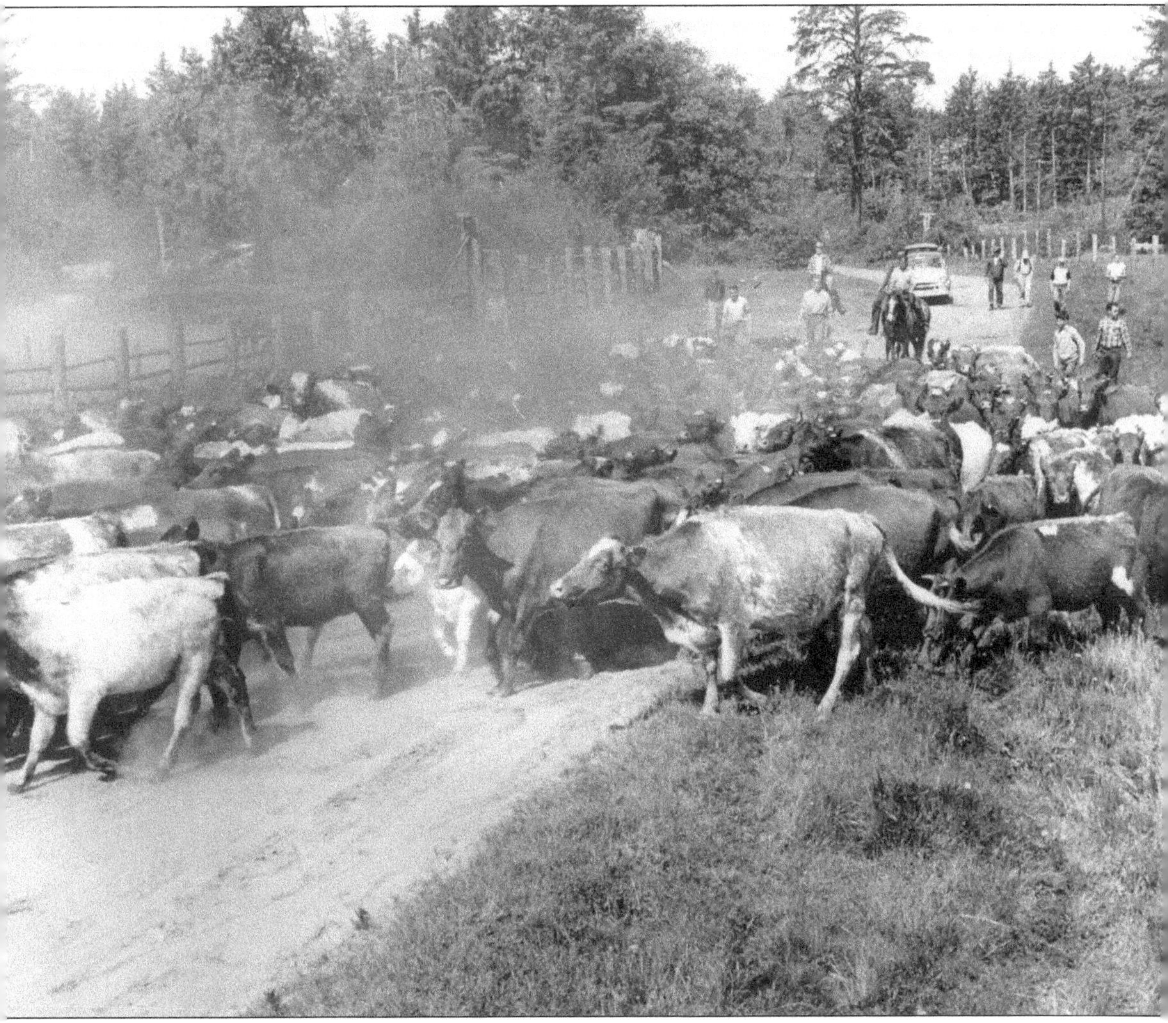

After the war, many folks have fond memories of being a wrangler for the day at the Minard ranch when the spring drive herded short-horned Durham cattle down the Oyehut road to the Damon homestead barn from the north and west pastures to be branded and separated for market. (MFP.)

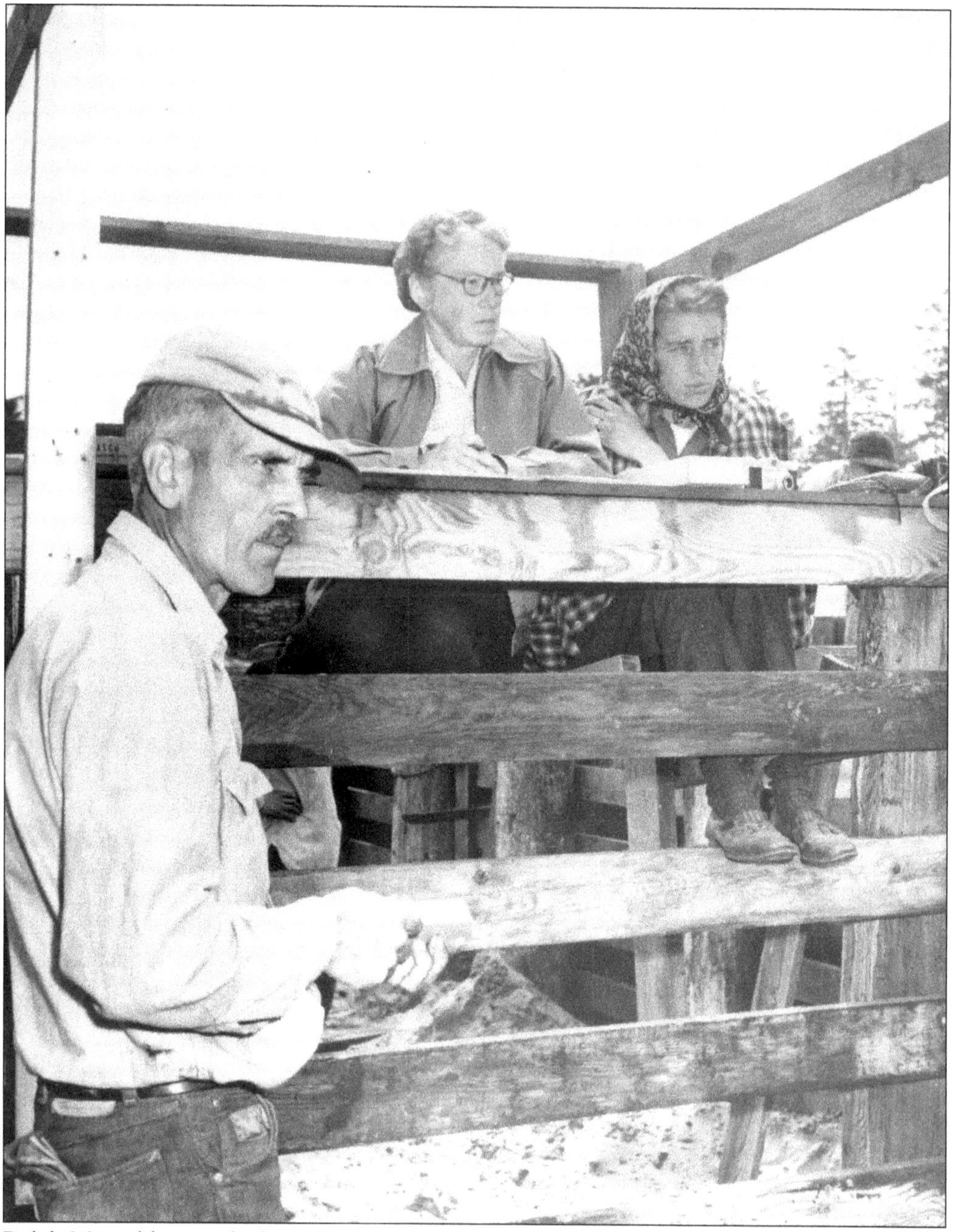

Ralph Minard keeps a lookout on the volunteer wranglers as Clara and Patty Minard Seaman tally the cattle. (MFP.)

Three

DECADE OF DREAMS

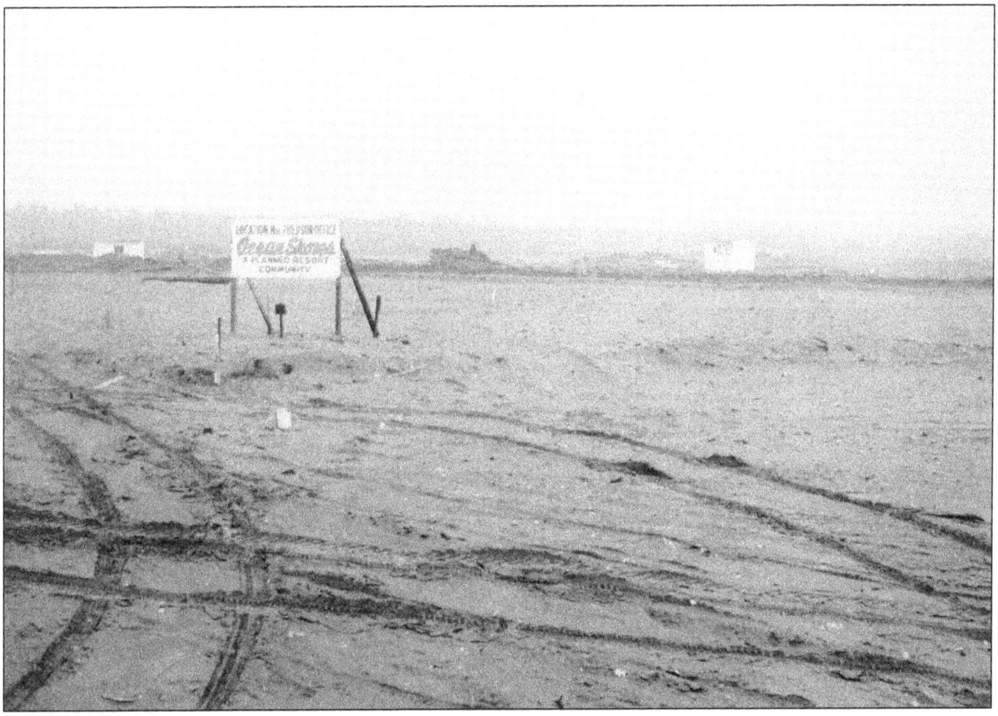

This stretch of sand, now the Chance la Mer Boulevard beach approach, holds a sign proudly proclaiming that McPherson Realty will soon be offering lots to the new phase of Ocean Shores. The land was sold as the "Palm Springs of the West" with the slogan, "Where the sun nearly always shines." Notice the commercial clam diggers lined up at the clam shacks to sell their tide's harvest. Ted Adams, an initial owner of the sales division, was foremost in promoting the MacPherson Real Estate Company as a sales organization. William (Bill) and Murdock MacPherson owned equal shares in the Ocean Shores venture with Don Eastvold, former Washington State attorney general, and his law partner, Moksha Smith. Eventually the stockholders included Dr. Allen Adams, Howard McGowan (special assistant to Sen. Warren Magnuson), Edward D. Telise, Ruskin and Fisher (engineers), Glen Corning (road builder), Howard Ker, Cliff Mortensen, Dr. Henry Landberg and Mike Banks. In 1961, Ole Bardahl, an investor in the Ocean Spray Motel was elected president of Ocean Shores Estates. (AMH.)

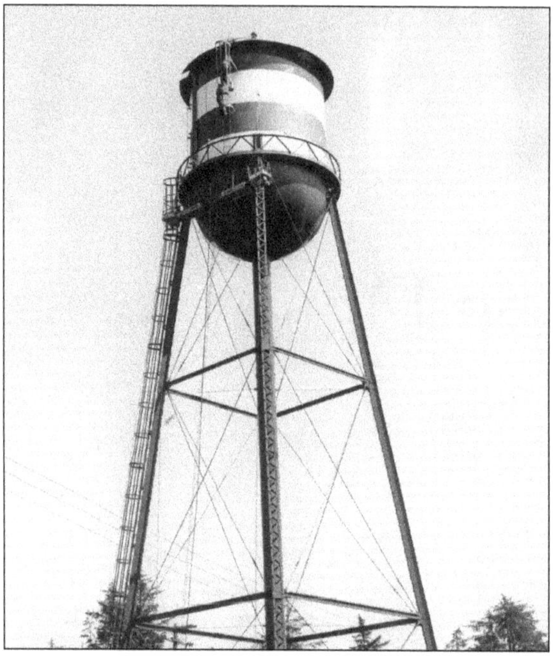

Sunshine Mining Company struck out with oil well site No. 1, but the effort did not go to waste. The drill well was plugged at the 700 level to become the first water tower in 1963, looming over the land now holding the city's public works yard. Service ended in 1984. (CHSGWC.)

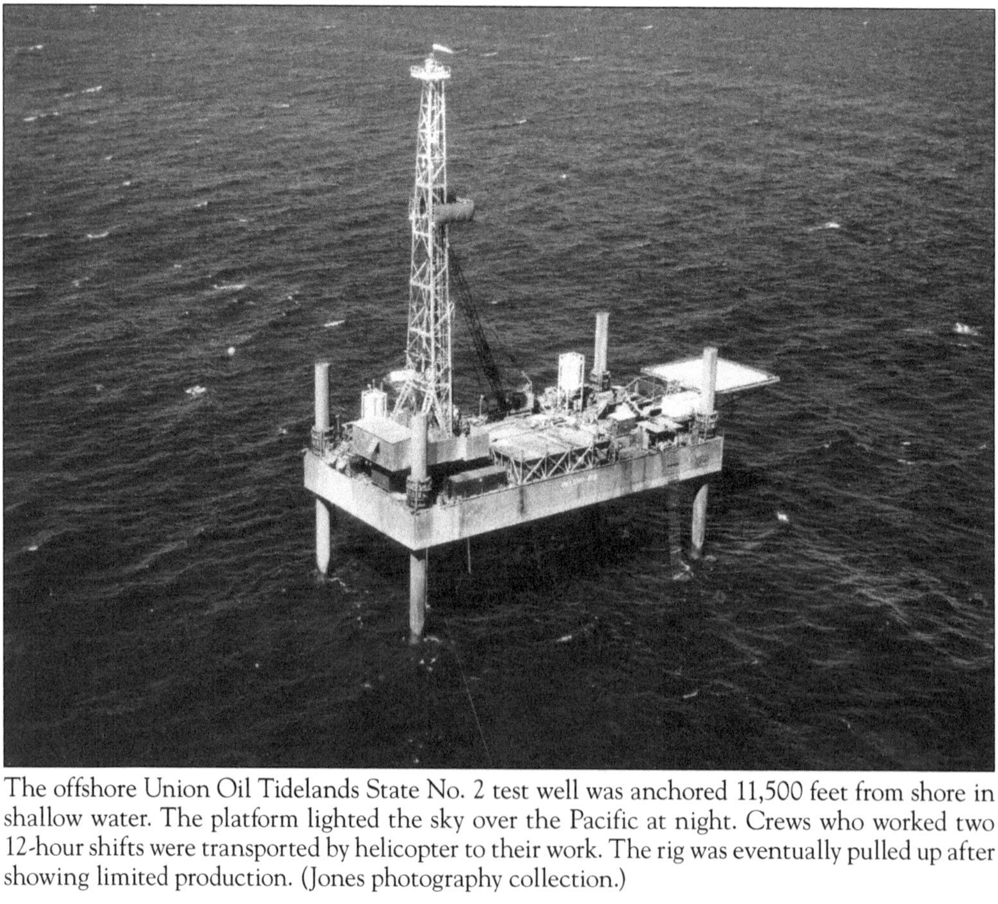

The offshore Union Oil Tidelands State No. 2 test well was anchored 11,500 feet from shore in shallow water. The platform lighted the sky over the Pacific at night. Crews who worked two 12-hour shifts were transported by helicopter to their work. The rig was eventually pulled up after showing limited production. (Jones photography collection.)

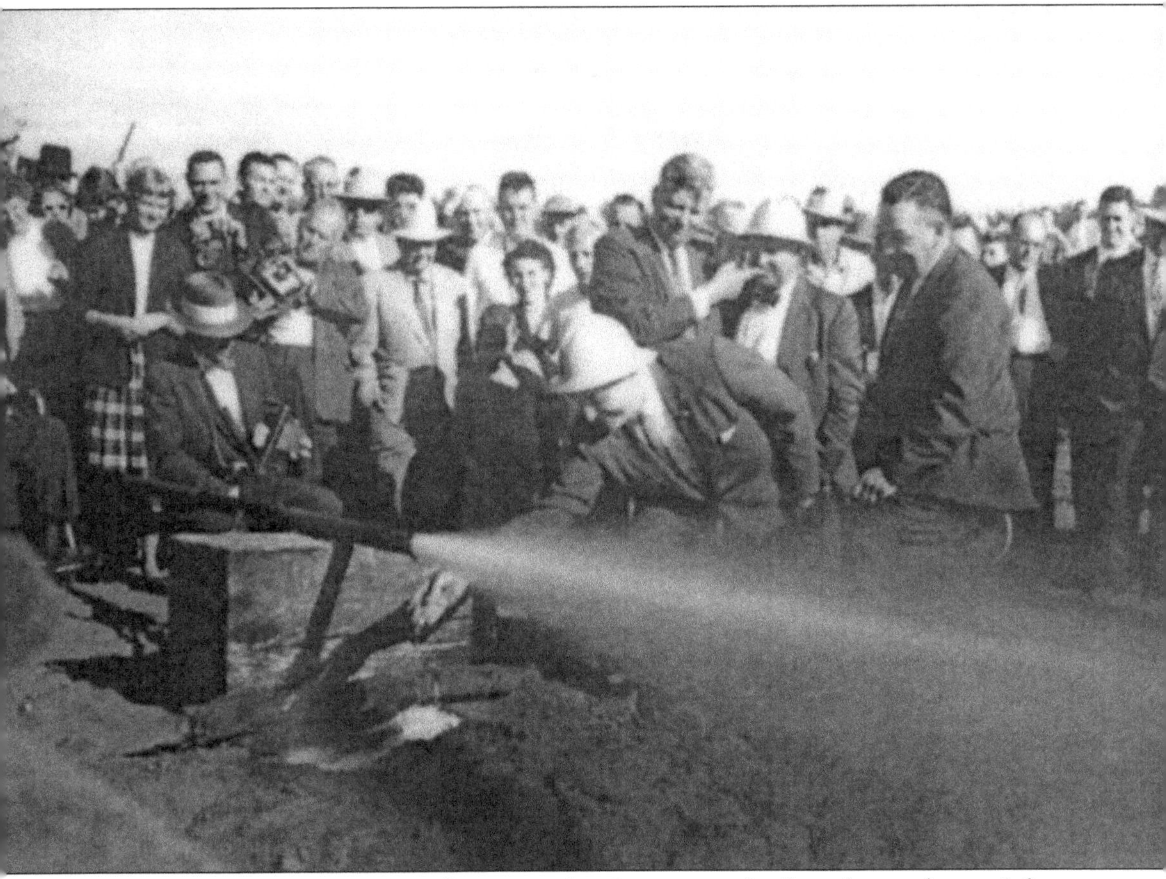

Washington State's Governor Rossellini was on hand to turn on the flow of gas at the state's first commercial production well at Ocean City. Natural gas from the exploration site lighted torches for the Ginny Simms Restaurant and served as kitchen grill backup during the numerous winter power outages. (PM.)

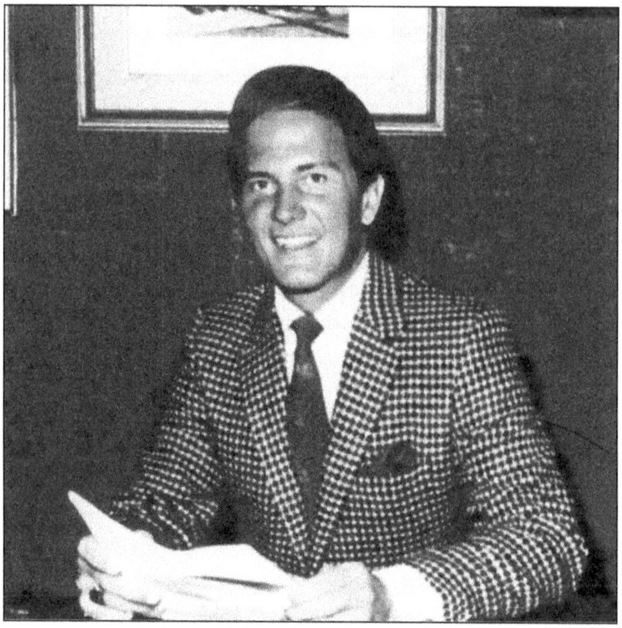

In 1966, Pat Boone became one of the stockholders in the Wendell-West Corporation, which held the first Pat Boone Golf Classic the following year. By 1969, media had dubbed the development the state's "Richest Little City" with an assessed evaluation of $35 million, although it only had 900 year-round residents. More than 8,000 families had purchased lots, not a bit worried about the proposed nuclear facility to be built at Roosevelt Beach. Landowners were more than happy in 1973 when the state decreed guaranteed unlimited public access to all navigable waters within the state boundaries. (CHSGWC.)

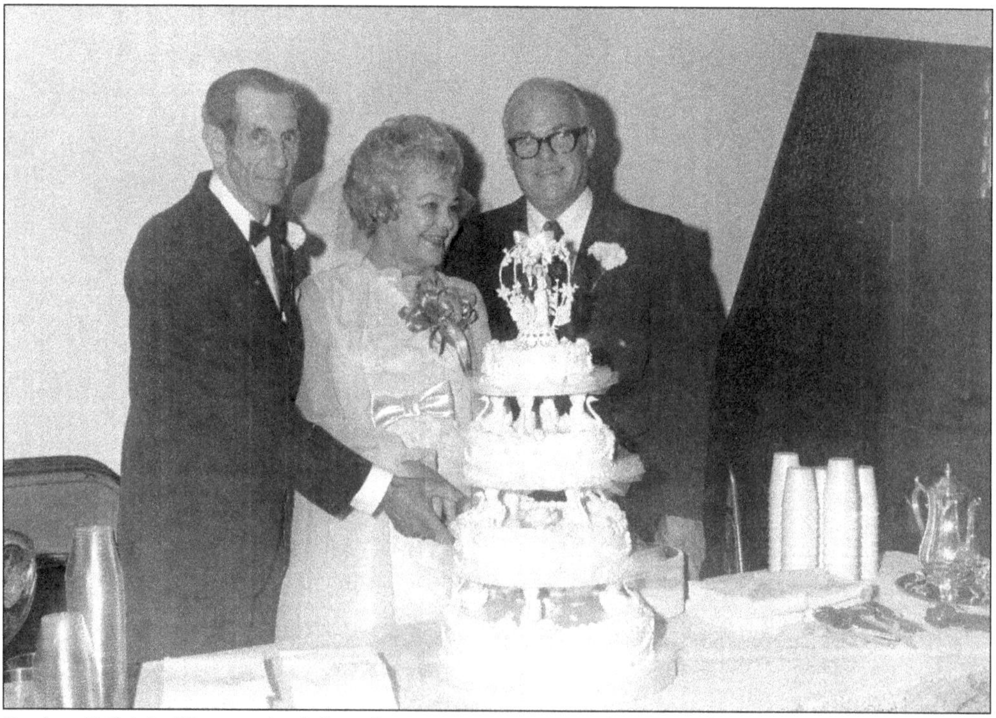

Realtor Bill MacPherson (right) took part in community doings with as much verve as he sold lots. Here he helps Alice Liles, Beacon Burger owner, and Russell Gross celebrate their June 1972 wedding. Gross, a true character from Shelton, bought the Union Gas Station on May 10, 1965. He had been one of the first 15 state patrol officers in the state. Gross was known for his love of women, practical jokes, and hauling folks out of sand traps on the beach, taking watches, wedding rings, and even a dog in lieu of cash. McPherson Realty handled the first sales of the new development and later developed Oregon's Crooked River development. (CHSGWC.)

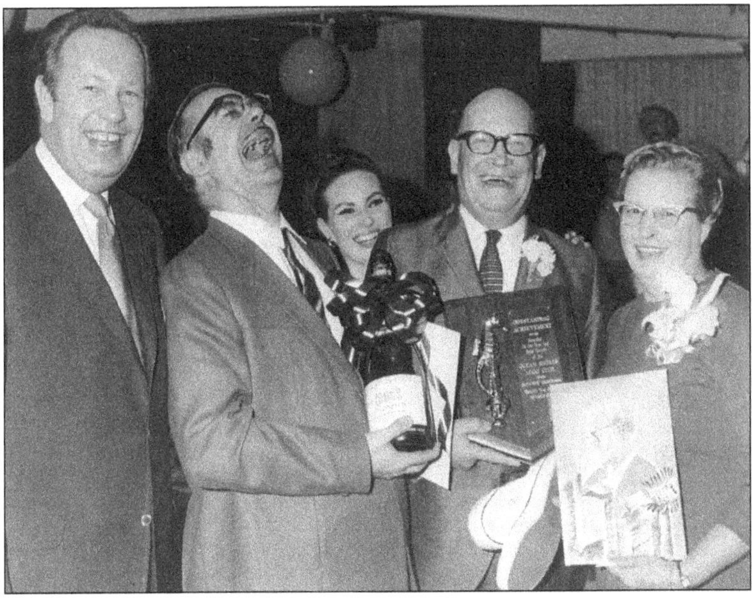

Salespeople were in it not just for the money, but also for fun. Winning some hooch and a plaque for selling 1,000 lots made Andy Anderson very happy. From the left to right are Dick Hagar, Mark Grubisich, and Andy and Nita Ford. (CHSGWC.)

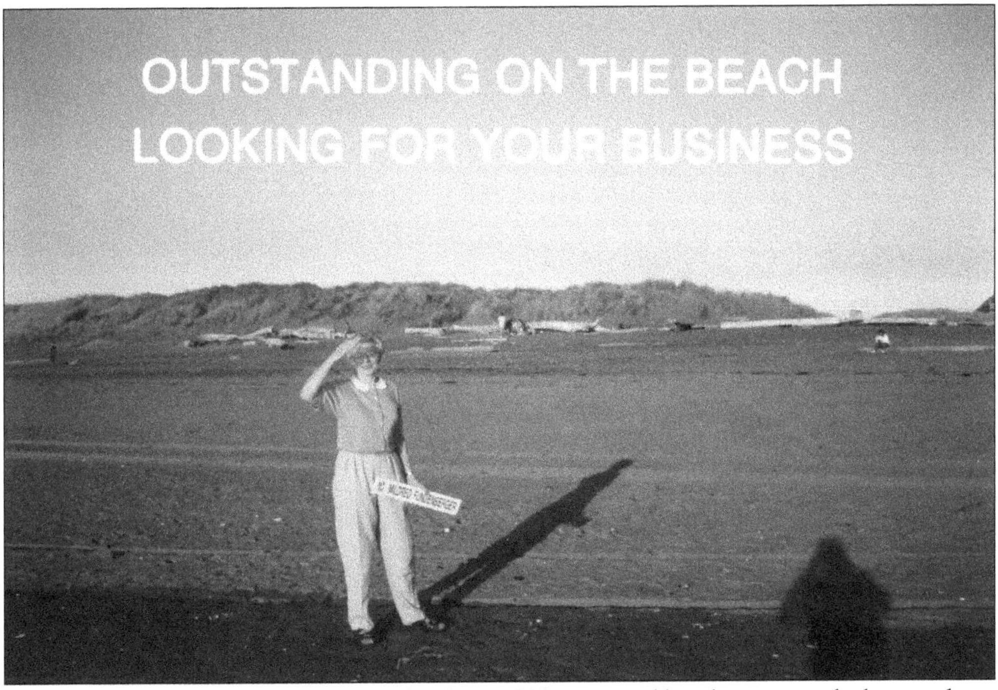

Mildred Fundenburger won so many sales she could have paved her driveway with them and was still top salesperson at the age of 85. An active believer in the community of Ocean Shores, she was married over 67 years to Glen, a former councilman and mayor. They were instrumental in building the Galilean church, the Galilean Retreat Center, the Ocean Shores Food Bank, the Senior Center, the second airport facilities, and the Lion's Club complex. (CHSGWC.)

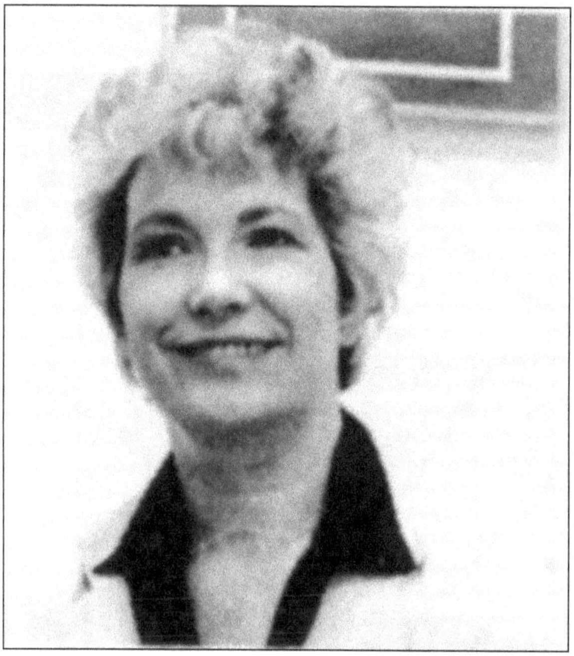

Marge McBride, shown here as a salesperson for Ford Wilgus's Ocean Investment Realty, came to town with the first wave of salespeople, later owning Marjuli's Gallery, famous on the West Coast as a showcase for well-known watercolor artists. Her mantra for years was Ocean Shores deserves beautification. She was always the first to donate to any cause for the betterment of the city as a community. (NCN.)

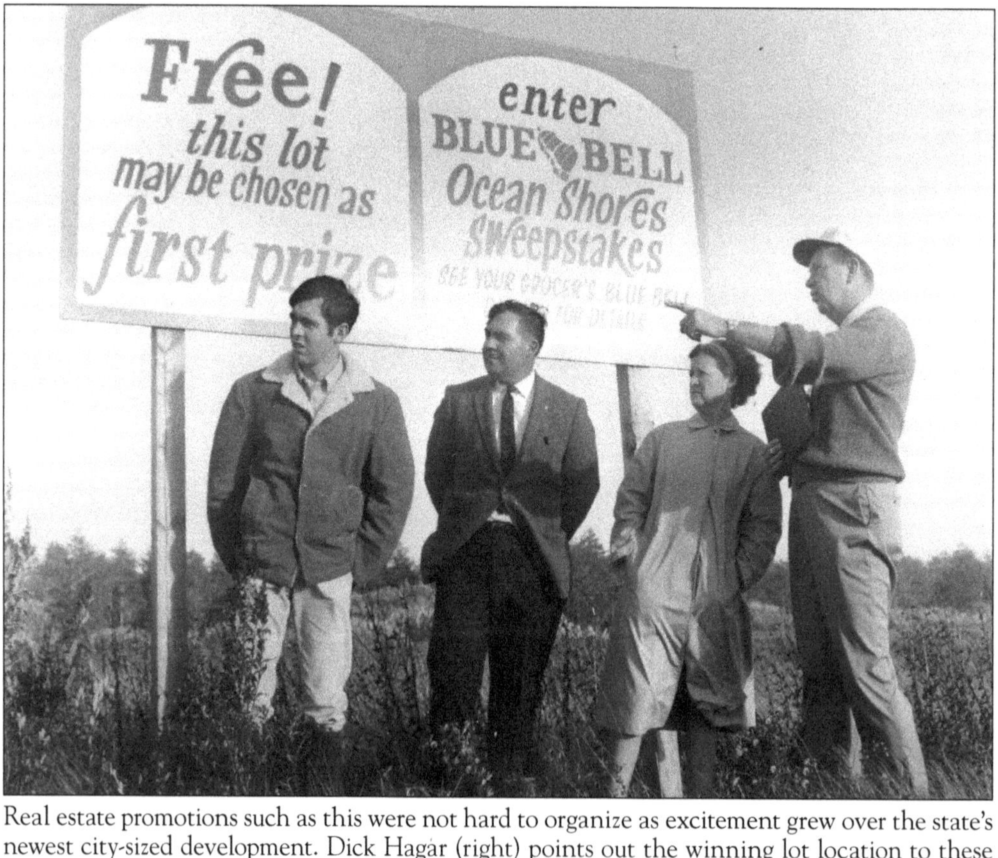

Real estate promotions such as this were not hard to organize as excitement grew over the state's newest city-sized development. Dick Hagar (right) points out the winning lot location to these unidentified visitors. (CHSGWC.)

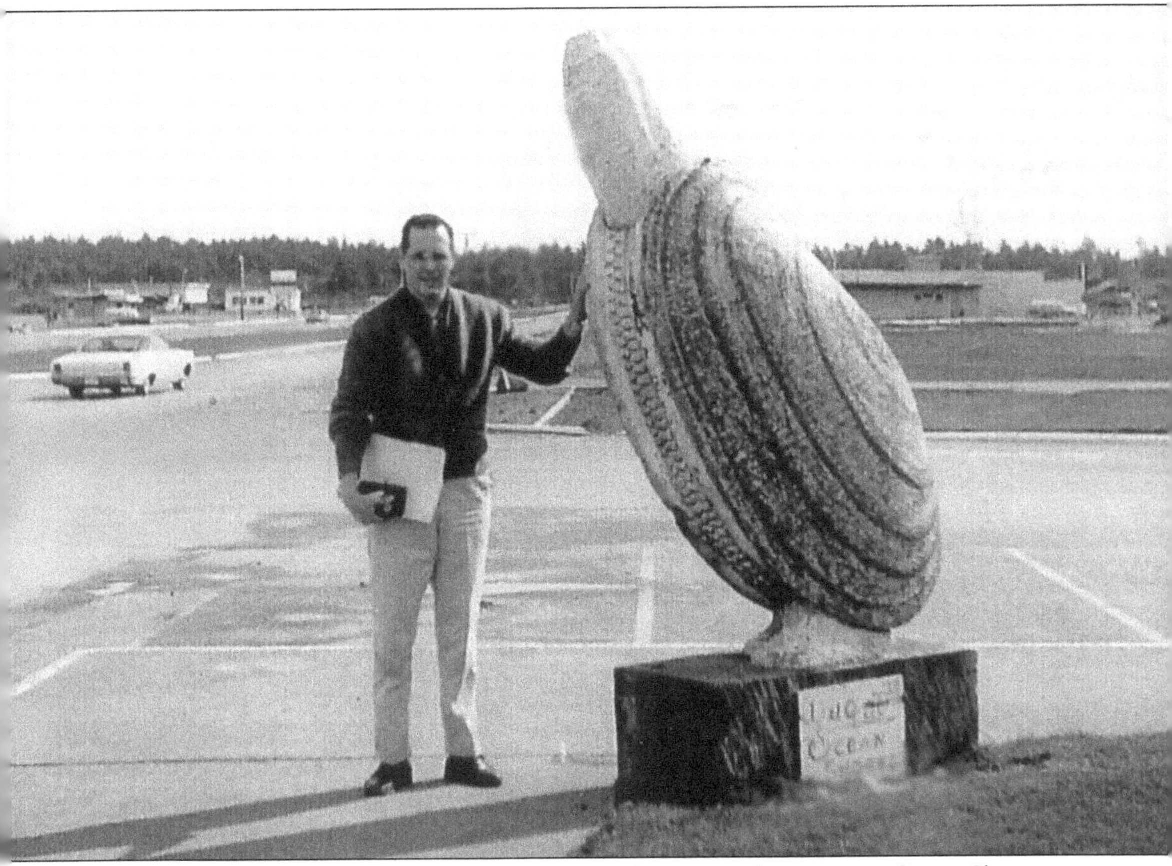

Larry Woodwick proudly holds the papers declaring him a new lot owner in Ocean Shores as he poses in front of the famous carved cedar clam donated by Tommer Construction Company, which graced the front of the Executive Villa sales office at the corner of Ocean Shores Avenue and Chance la Mer Boulevard. The clam is the town's mystery, as it disappeared, and speculation still exists as to its probable kidnappers or demise via a street crew. (CHSGWC.)

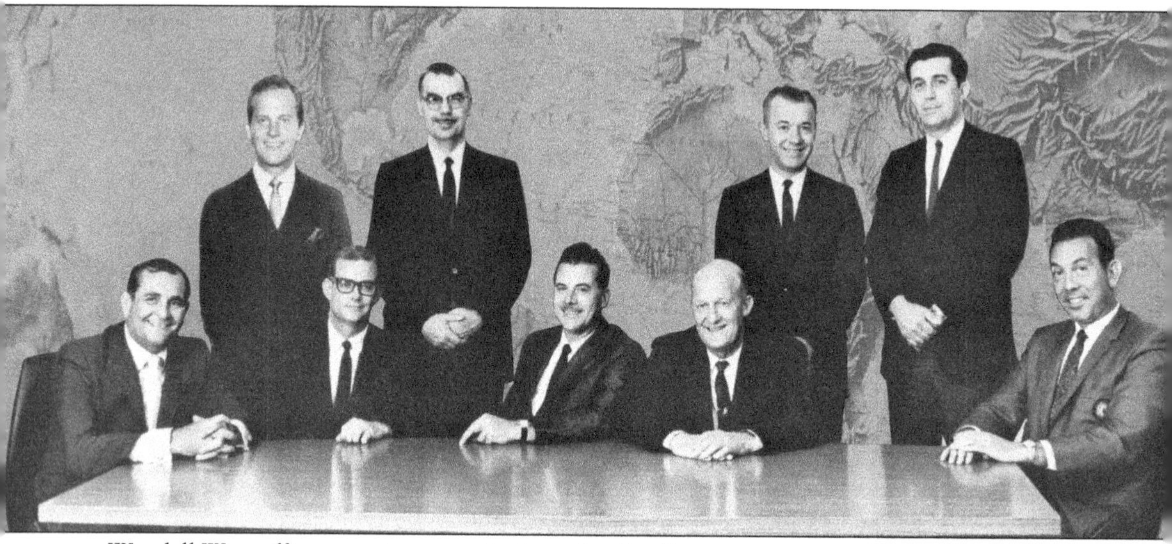

Wendell West officers are, in no particular order, Pat Boone, internationally known entertainer and vice president of the Ocean Shores Development Corporation; Mark Grubisich, former purchasing agent for the Olympic Steamship Company, vice president of the corporation, and head of direct sales and services; Moksha Smith, development corporation president who served five years with the Washington State Office of Attorney General; Lawrence C. Angell, vice president and director of the Development Corporation with a background of law and insurance, active in legal and administration, and general manager of public relations; A. J. Hutton Jr., secretary and director of the Development Corporation, previous assistant state attorney general serving as general legal advisor and director of governmental relations; Patrick H. Cox, general sales and promotional director of the firm with 16 years professional experience in commercial and real estate; Glen Corning, chief development consultant with a diverse business background holding major interests in firms that built the city, including Tommer Construction Company, Glen Corning Logging Company, Ludke Hauling Company, Pacific Dump Trucks, Inc., and Corning-Ludke Equipment Company; and James Magnus, treasurer, who served the Bank of California in the real estate division. (CHSGWC.)

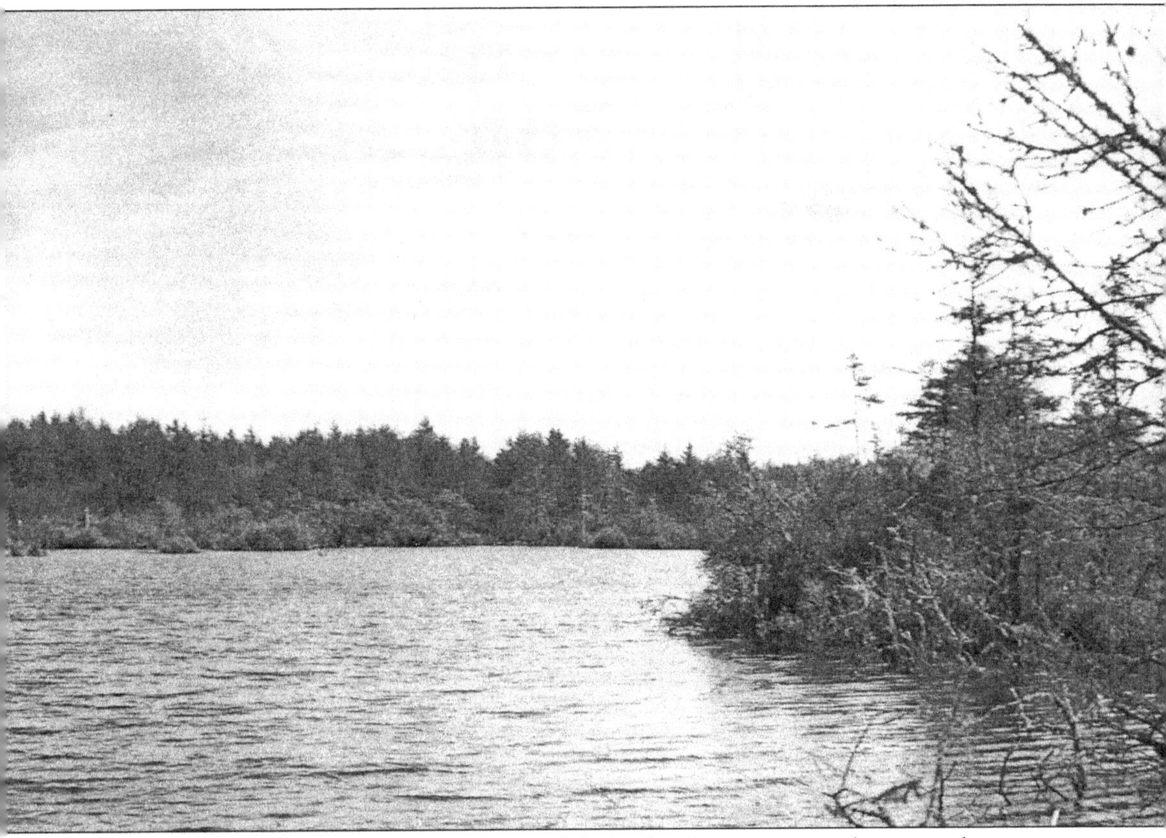

A 1958 view of Snider Lake prior to the Duck Lake development was taken near the present Weatherwax Trail location. (MFP.)

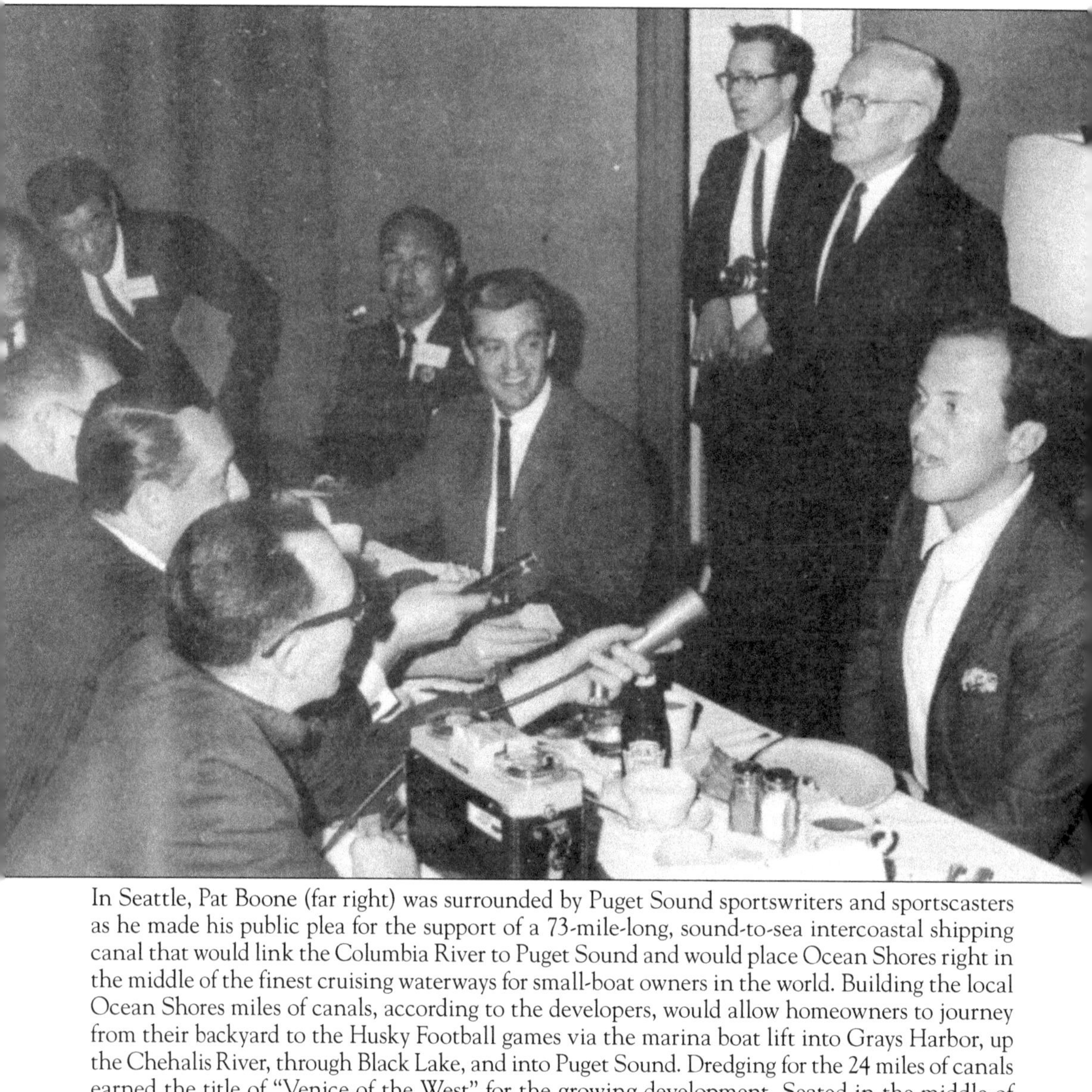

In Seattle, Pat Boone (far right) was surrounded by Puget Sound sportswriters and sportscasters as he made his public plea for the support of a 73-mile-long, sound-to-sea intercoastal shipping canal that would link the Columbia River to Puget Sound and would place Ocean Shores right in the middle of the finest cruising waterways for small-boat owners in the world. Building the local Ocean Shores miles of canals, according to the developers, would allow homeowners to journey from their backyard to the Husky Football games via the marina boat lift into Grays Harbor, up the Chehalis River, through Black Lake, and into Puget Sound. Dredging for the 24 miles of canals earned the title of "Venice of the West" for the growing development. Seated in the middle of the photograph is Craig Breedlove, holder of the world's land speed record. To the left of Boone is Royal Brougham, sportswriter and president of the group. (Ocean Shores News Bureau.)

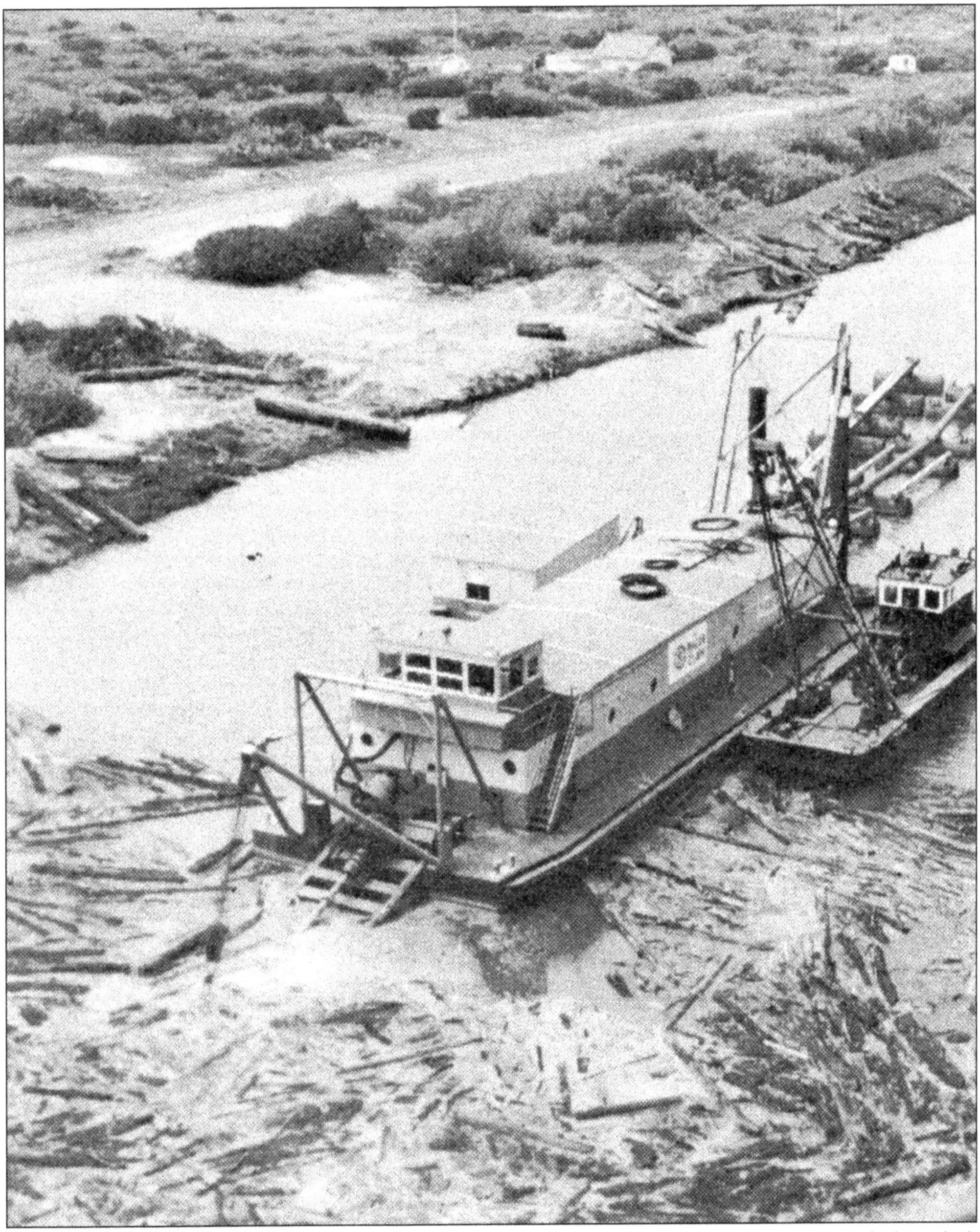

In a massive, never-to-be-done-again effort, the landscape of Ocean Shores was scraped, shoveled, and dredged in a manner precluded by today's environmental laws. Later, on August 15, 1984, Quigg Brothers-McDonald, Inc. dredged 300,000 cubic yards of sand that had sloughed into the canals and Duck Lake to provide fill for the bayside location of the present airport. (CHSGWC.)

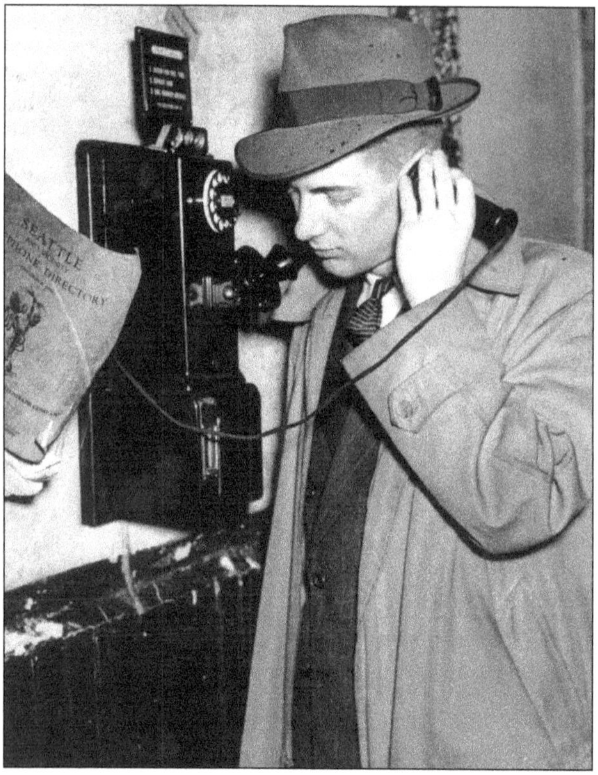

A true ringmaster for the huge, California-style development, the irrepressible Bob Ward is seen working the phone for a Seattle newspaper story prior to becoming the all-time promoter of Ocean Shores. (Thorn Ward.)

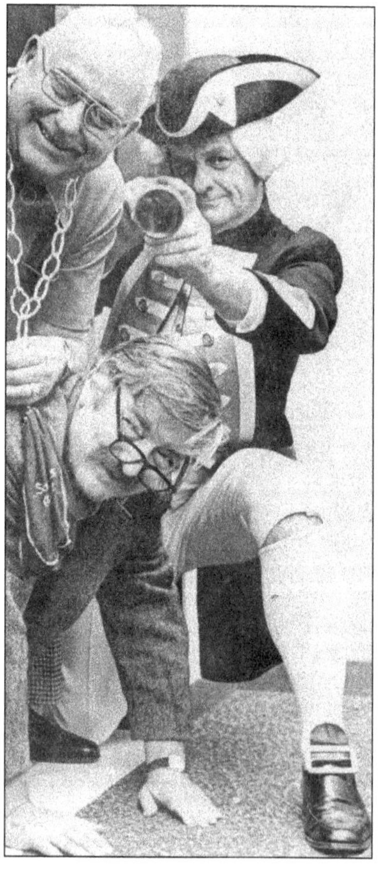

Ward (kneeling) peeks around the door at the photographer as he shares this photograph with Mayor Bun Lewis and Harvie Rourke, dressed as Capt. George Vancouver to promote Ward's imaginative Undiscovery Day celebration, which gained media attention around the world. (Thorn Ward.)

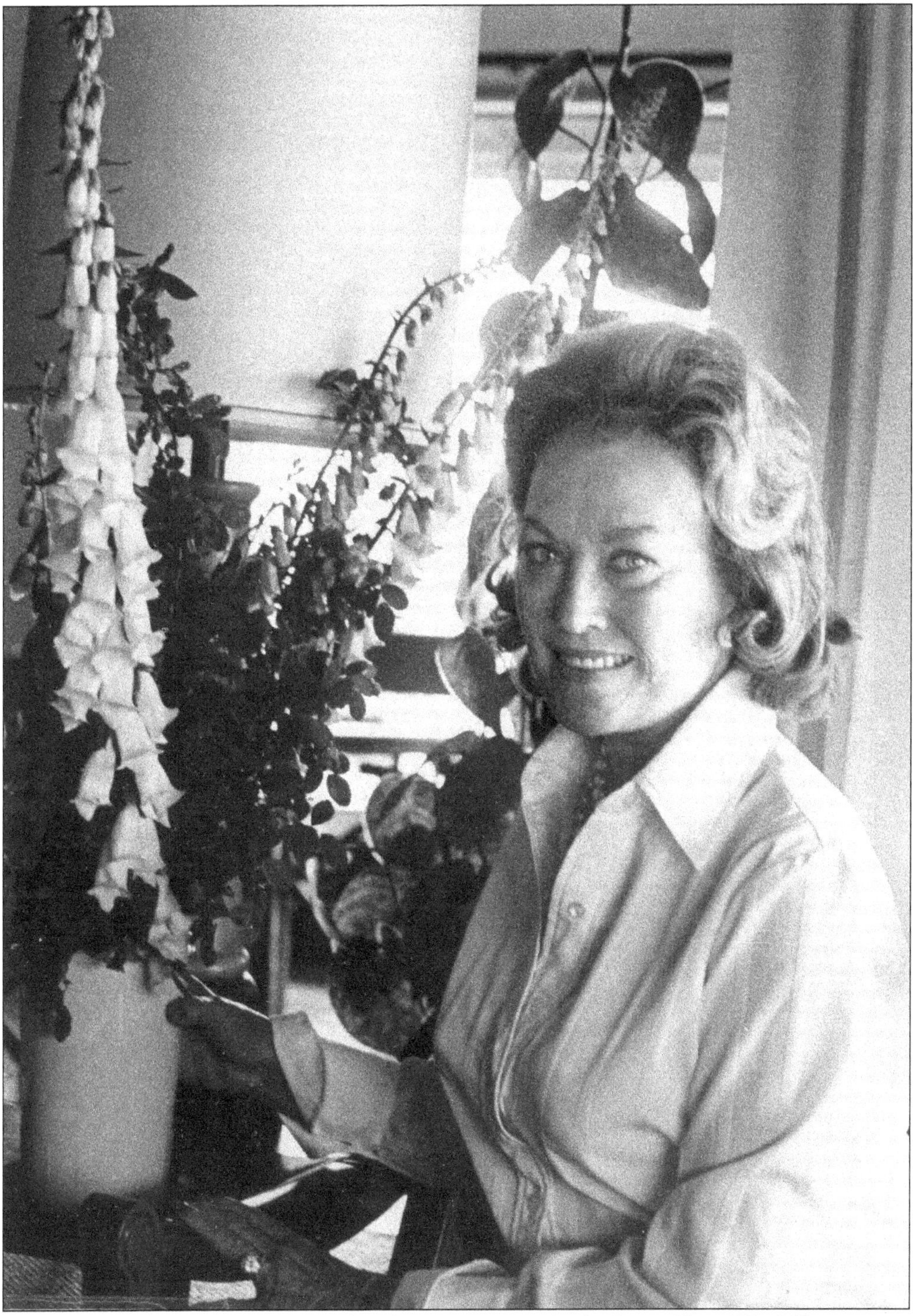

Ginny Simms, star of Hollywood films from 1939 to 1950, for James Kern "Kay" Kyser, singer during the Big Band era famed for 11 hit songs, loaned her name to the Mortensen Restaurant that became known as the Ginny Simms Restaurant by the Sea, later renamed the Ocean Shores Inn. (CHSGWC.)

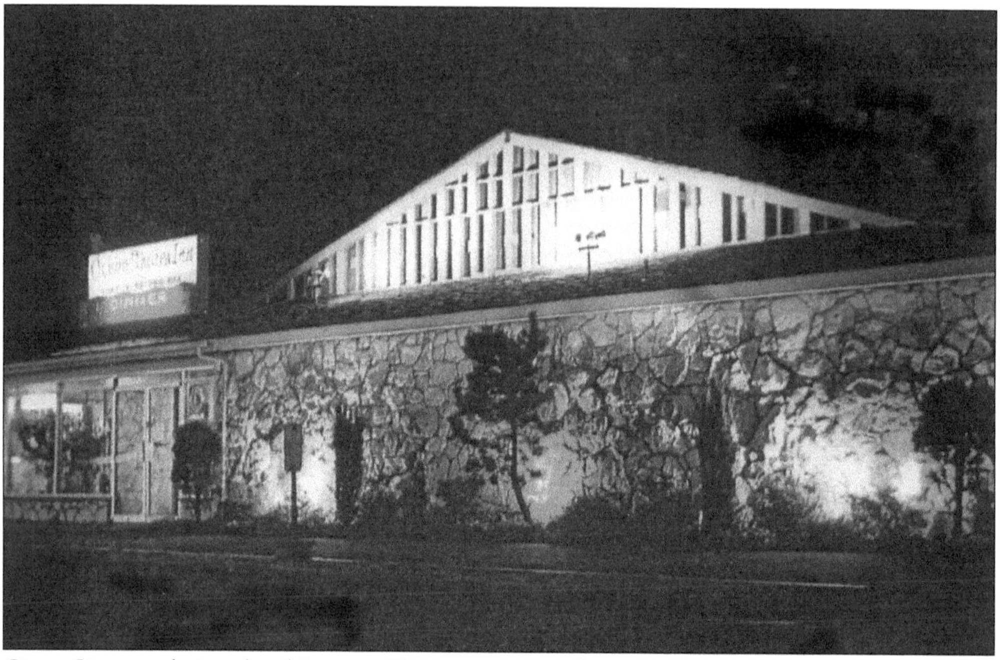

Ginny Simms redesigned and decorated her restaurant to the tune of $400,000. The doorway opened to a classy gold and charcoal interior with silver wallpaper and fire engine–red banquettes. The grand opening drew stars such as Jane Powell, Patrice Wymore, Lee Anderson, Hugh O'Brien (Wyatt Earp), Charlie Chan, Ginger Rogers, Walter Winchell, and Luella Parsons. As the stars landed at Bowerman Basin Airport in Hoquiam, 11,000 people were on hand to greet them. (CHSGWC.)

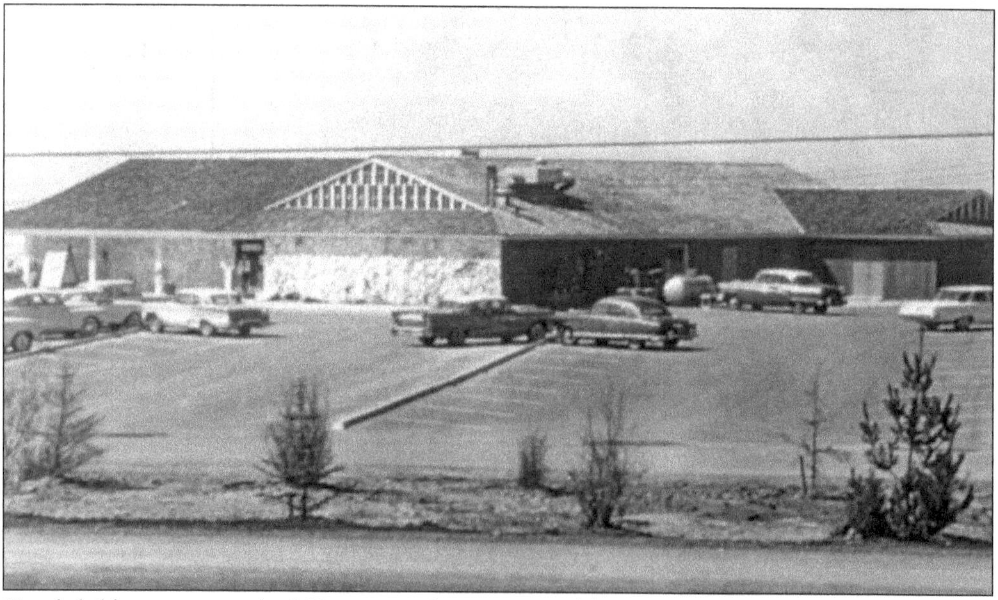

Good children eating in the 300-capacity dining room of the Ginny Simms Restaurant by the Sea were rewarded with a toy from a wooden pirate's chest. Fifteen years after the Ocean Shores Inn came into being, Ginny, with her husband, Don Eastvold, returned to Ocean Shores and developed the Ginny Simms Chalet Village, a condominium apartment complex. The Beachcomber Inn, with 194 luxury apartment and motel units, was built on the adjoining property. (CHSGWC.)

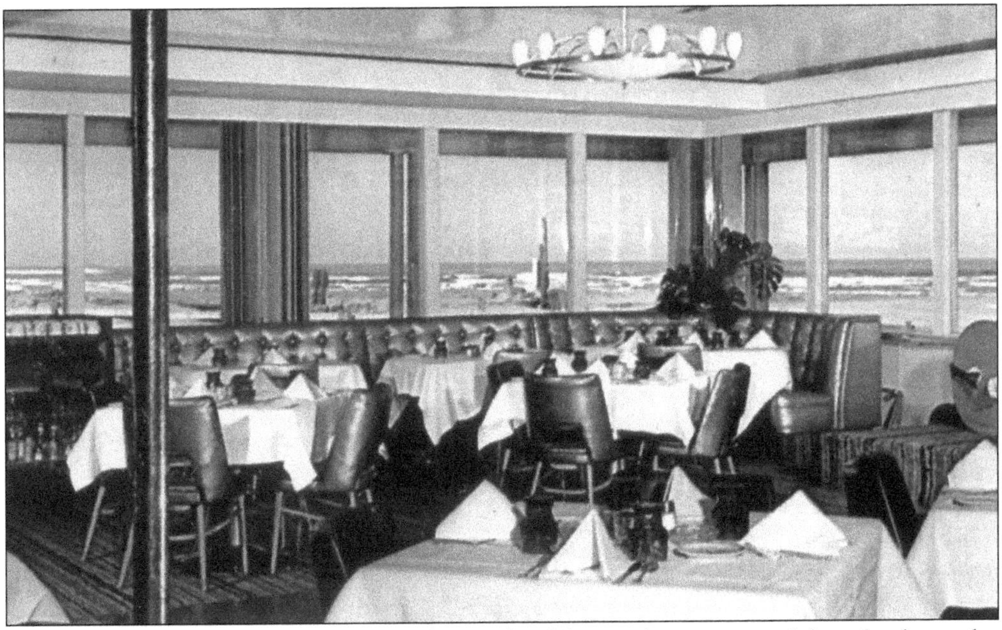

The 360-degree view of the beach directly outside of the windows was a real draw for those who dined in the Horizon Room during the day. The Skylark Lounge, with its floor to ceiling windows overlooking the Pacific, was a favored nightspot where the Guadalajara Boys held sway with live music on Tuesday through Sunday evenings. Daily menu prices included lobster tail thermidor for $1.85, salmon fillet for $1.85, and half a cracked Dungeness crab priced at $1.50. (CHSGWC.)

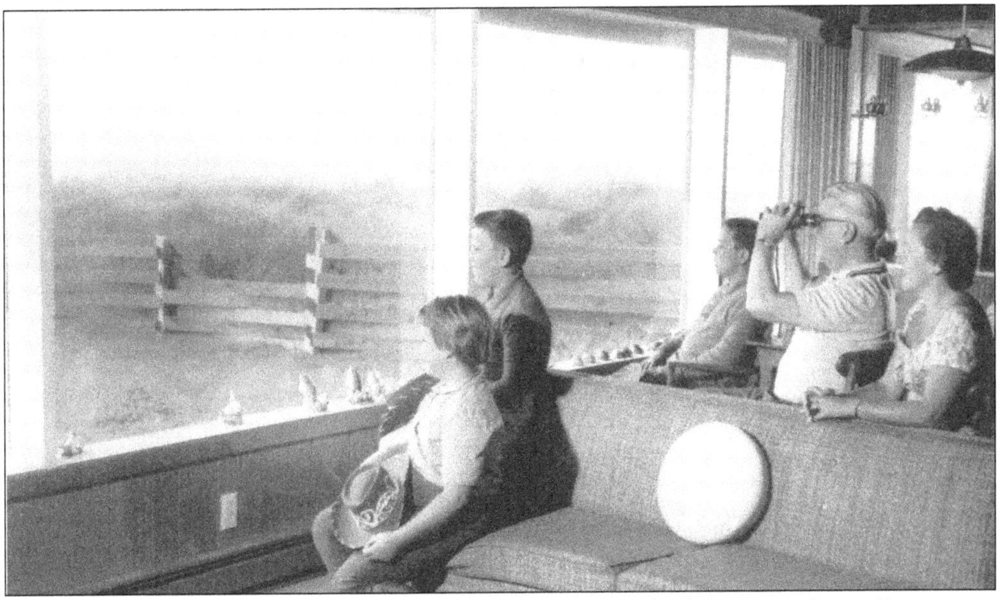

Families were more than welcome at the Ginny Simms Inn north of the Ginny Simms Restaurant. Mom could sit in an easy chair and watch the kids cavorting on the sandy beach right outside the window. The 65 units were priced at $6.50 a night with features such as fireplaces, kitchens, mezzanines, decks, and balconies. Courtesy cars from the Hoquiam airport were provided to prospective lot owners who had flown the 40 minutes from Seattle. The inn was sold and renamed the Beachcomber and was totally renovated in 1976. (CHSGWC.)

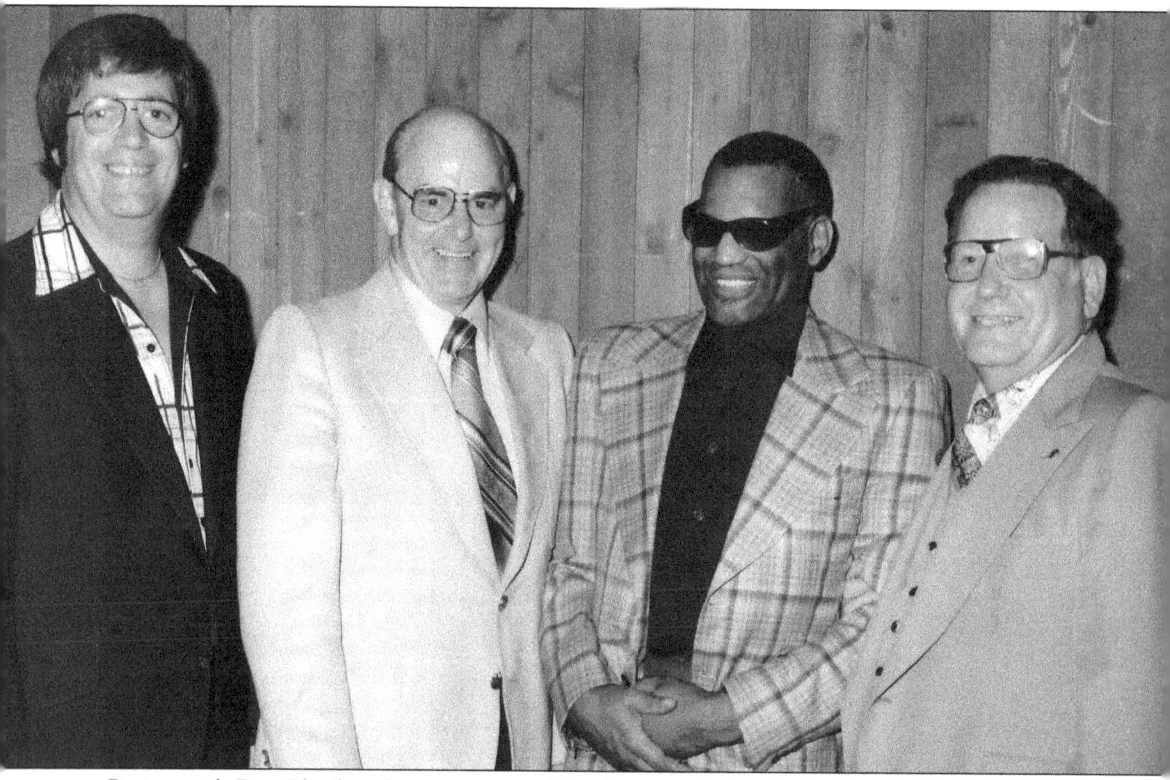

Posing with Ray Charles, the co-owners of the Ocean Shores Inn and the Golden Gull—Dick Morris (left), a grocer who operated the Dick's IGA before retiring after 30 years, and Kyle Smith (center), part owner of the Royal Pacific, the Tyee, and Surfside 12—and Buz Edquist, a Sequim grocer, purchased the inn for $400,000. The remaining two partners later bought out Edquist. Smith was owner of Smith Western Company in Tacoma. The two owners kept the lineup of famous entertainers in place for years, until they sold the inn in 1995. (Kyle Smith, Smith Western Company.)

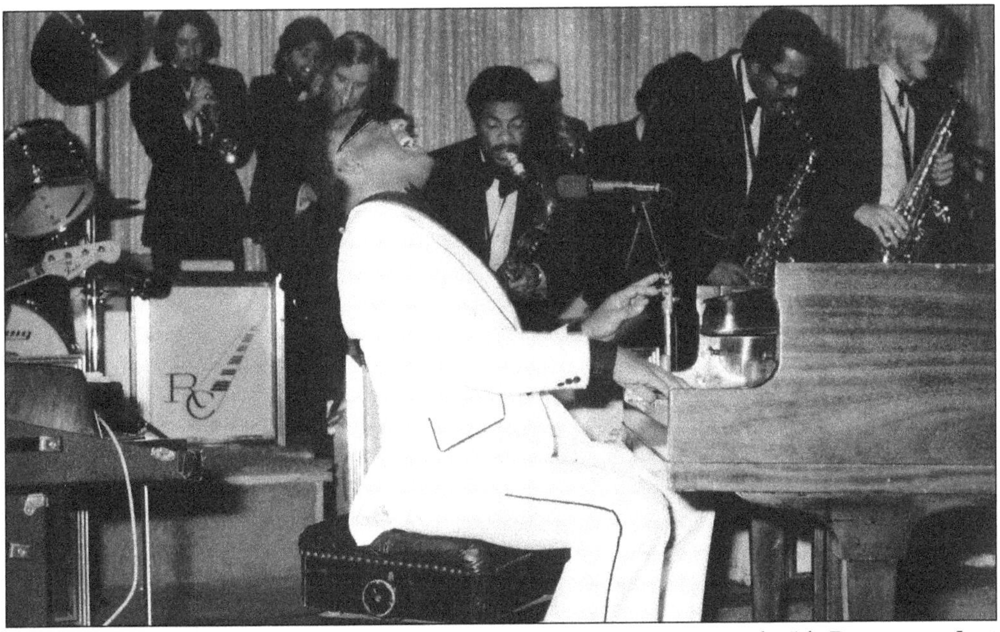

While Hollywood stars and singers such as Ray Charles, Diane Warwick, 5th Dimension, José Feliciano, and the Jerry Quarry heavyweight boxing fight were a big draw, the longest run of any entertainer was Belante, better known as Mr. Hypnosis, who kept returning to amaze and delight his fans until the last year of the inn. To enjoy the entertainment, the Horizon Room served a Chateaubriand dinner for two for $23 with a $5 dessert of cherries jubilee. In later years, Coquille St. Jacques scallops were a mere $10.95. (Kyle Smith, Smith Western Company.)

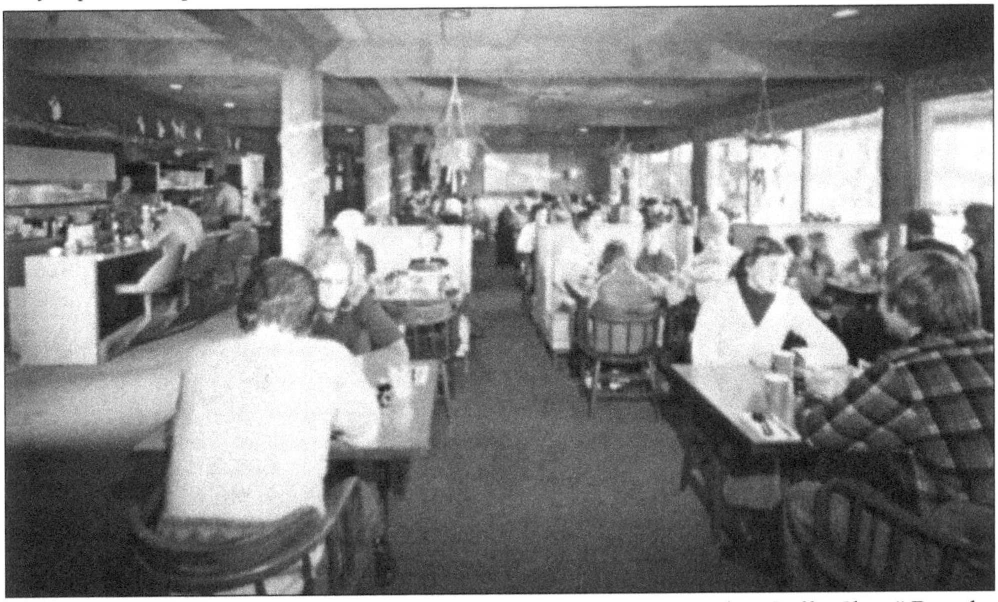

The heart of Ocean Shores was the Chantrelle Grill, better known as the "Coffee Shop." Decades of townsfolk made a daily trip to have Barbara Morris's excellent soup and jawbone about the local politicians, city street, who sold what lots, and the latest local scandal. While the grill was under the ownership of AVCO, you could buy a steak and egg breakfast for $3.75 or razor clams and scrambled eggs for $2, along with other regular menu items. (CHSGWC.)

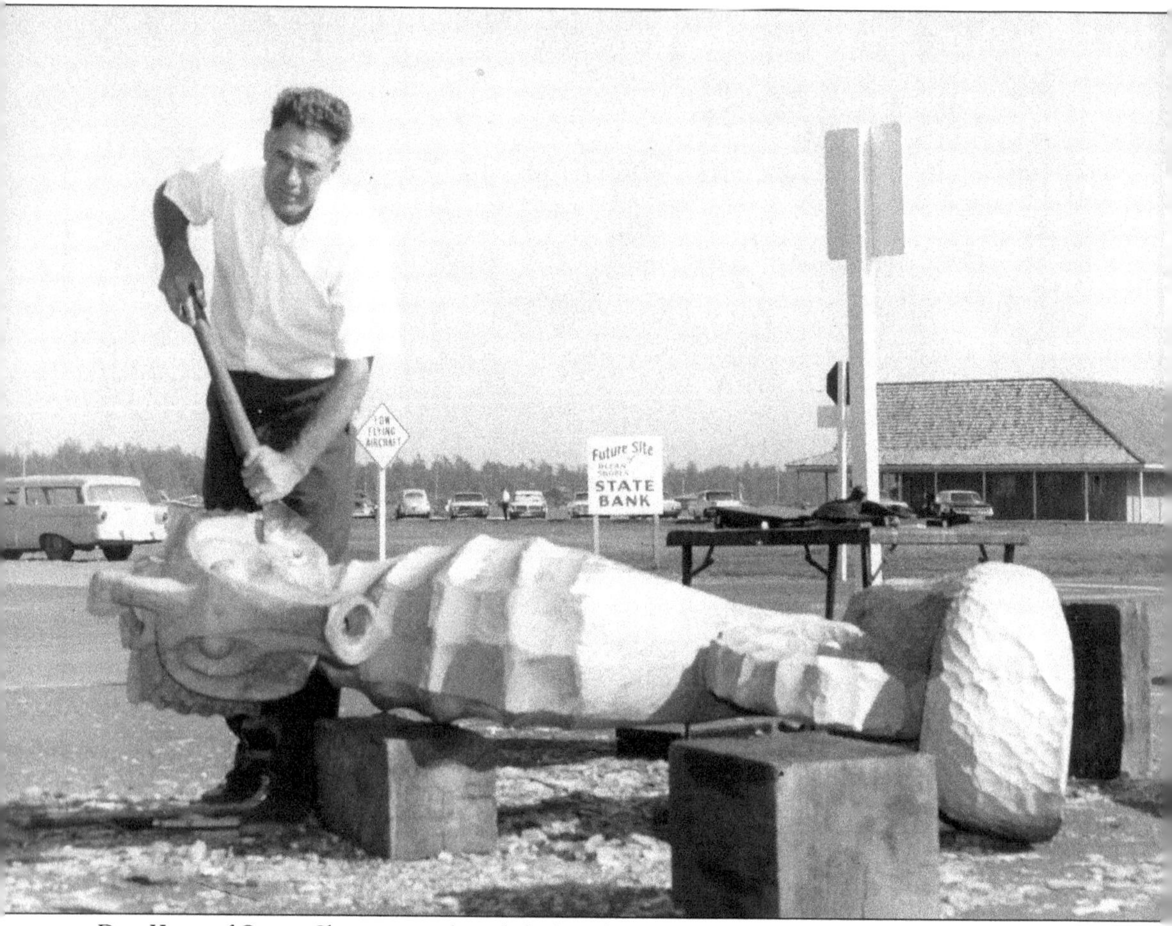

Don Keyes of Ocean Shores contributed the hand-carved, cedar sea horses that first stood in the median of Chance la Mer Boulevard and Ocean Shores Avenue before being placed in front of the Ocean Shores Inn. Generations of families had their photographs taken with the sea horses, one of which resides in front of the Ocean Shores Interpretive Center. The backward tail of the city's symbol was often commented upon by marine biologists, but the design was a deliberate use of the "S" in Ocean Shores by Bob Godden, a Seattle artist. Keyes contributed a number of carvings throughout the city and was chosen to replace the prow for the *Golden Hind* tall ship after the original was lost at sea. In August 1967, someone stole one of the sea horses. Radio station KGHO, Aberdeen, stepped in and publicized the misdeed, and the culprit eventually turned in the 200-pound sculpture. (CHSGWC.)

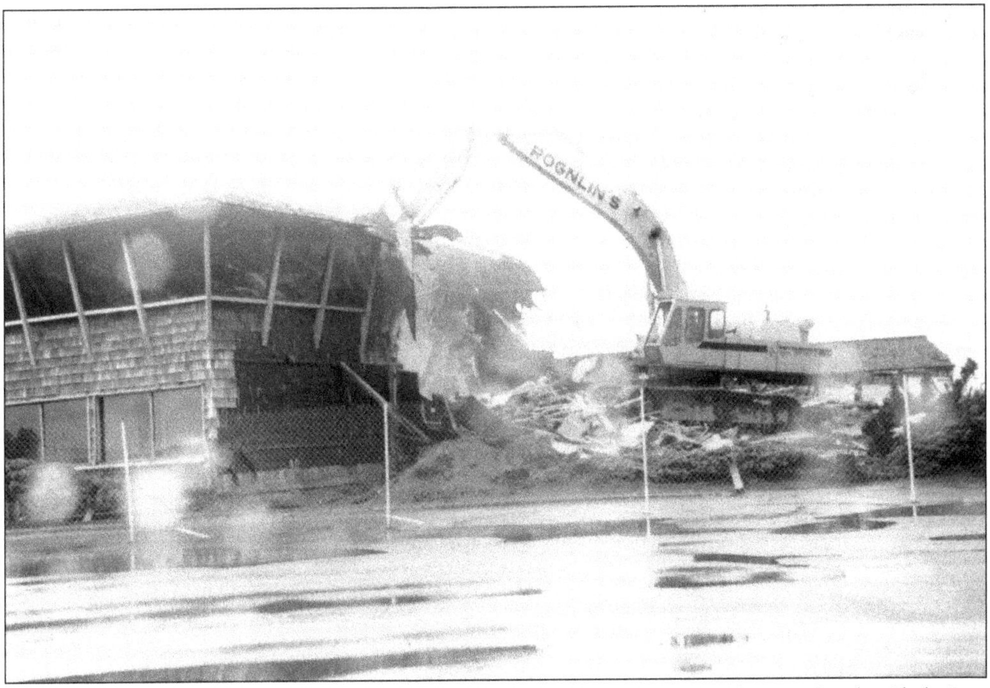

It was a sad day when the Ocean Shores Inn bit the dust in 1994 to make way for the Shilo Inn Suites Hotel. A grand evening goodbye celebration hosted by Dick Morris and Kyle Smith drew nostalgic folks from around the United States to give the old girl a send off into the ether world. Hundreds showed up for the auction to purchase pieces of the inn. (CHSGWC.)

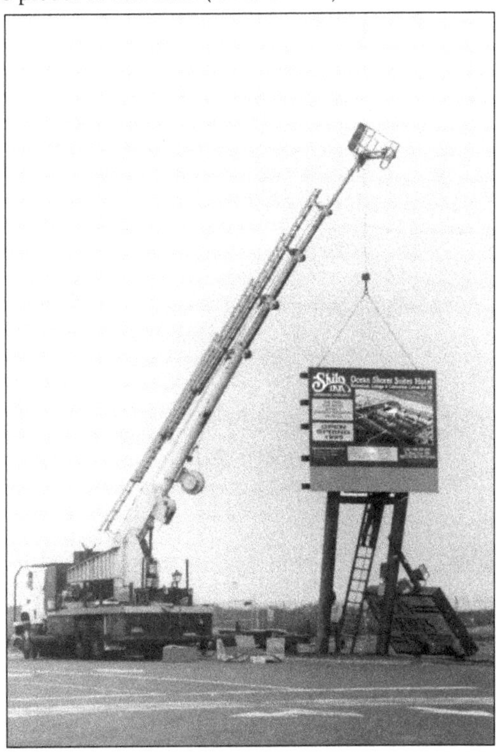

A crane removed the 1960s Ocean Shores signage (leaning against the sign base) and lifted the Shilo Suites Hotel and Convention Center sign in place for the 1995 opening. (CHSGWC.)

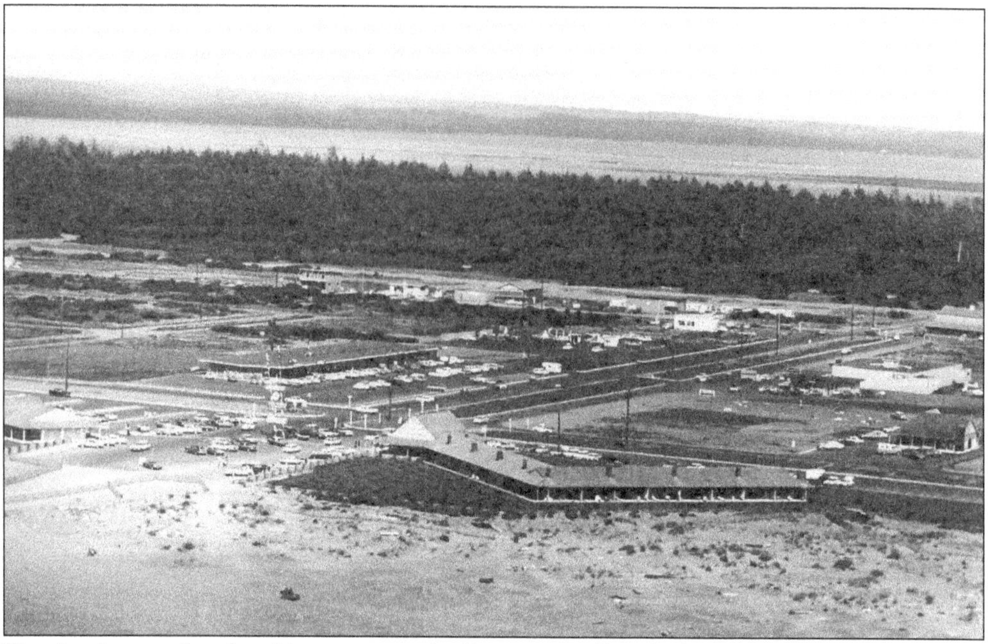

The first historic hotel and business was the Executive Villa, which served as sales headquarters and conference rooms. Colorful dividers provided sunbathers with wind protection at the Executive Villa, where they could cool off by strolling across the lawn and dipping their toes into the Pacific Ocean. The sprawling Executive Villa was quite a change from a travel trailer parked on the sand to sell lots sight unseen and, in many cases, straight off a map without platted lots. The newly constructed shopping area and the sparse building indicate this photograph was taken about 1962. (AMH.)

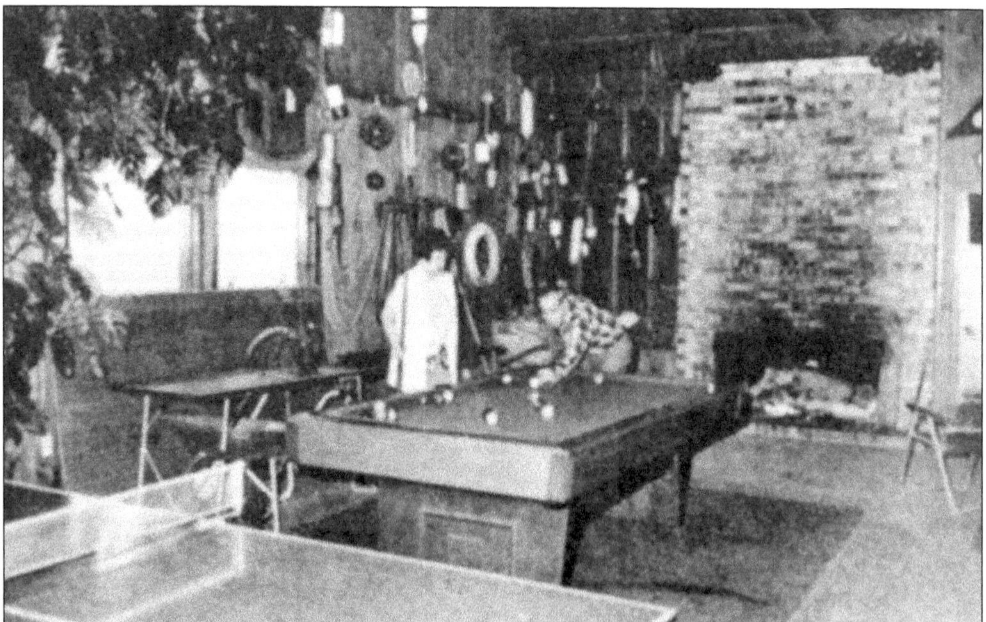

Vagabond House Motel, with its wall decorations of beach-combed items and the pool table, ping pong table, and other wet-weather games, was a family favorite. (CHSGWC.)

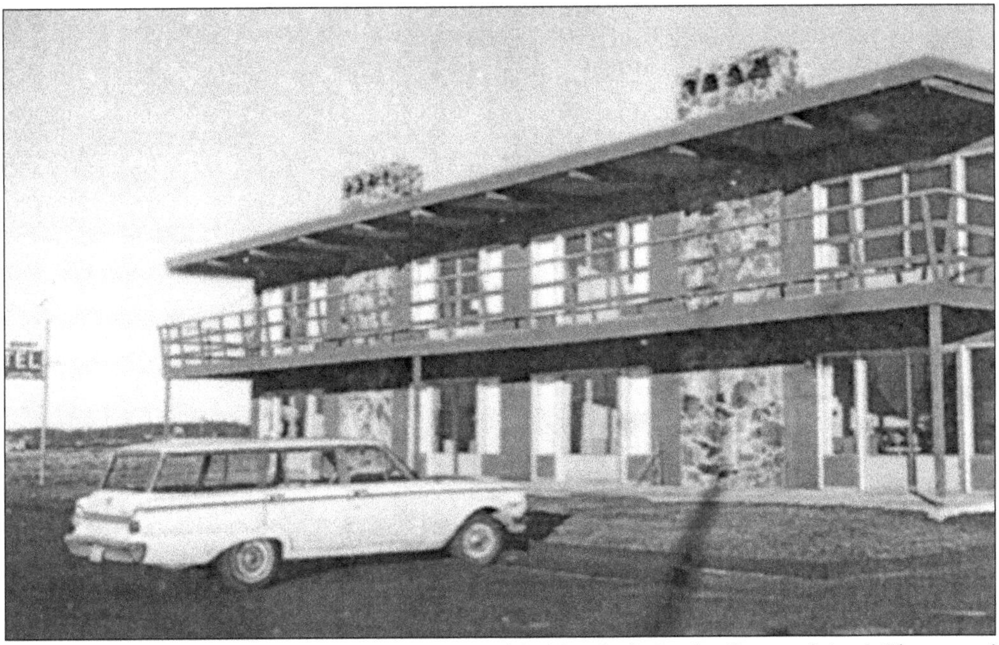

Many families have fond memories of staying at Ralph Aberthal's Gitche Gumme Motel. The second condominium hotel to be built in the city was sold exclusively by Don Gaddis, John McCarthy, and John Carter with condo units priced from $5,950. The first portion opened in June 1963. Aberthal fit right into the characters who made early Ocean Shores so interesting. Who could forget his grand notion of bringing in donkeys for his guests to ride and pet—the same donkeys whose braying kept nearby motel customers awake all over "Motel Row." Following Aberthal's death, his daughter and son-in-law, Nancy and Dirk Swearingen, managed the motel. (CHSGWC.)

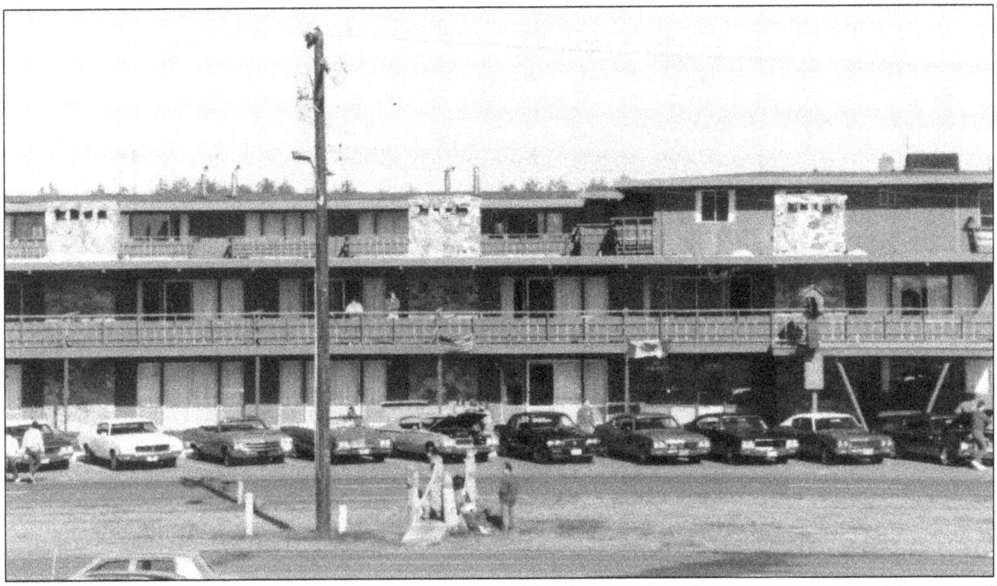

Canadians and the "Flying Farmers" were enamored by the Gitche when it was managed for several decades by Don and Shirley Wise. The footbridge over the swampy median in the forefront of the photograph was launched with a bottle of champagne in a tongue-in-cheek celebration by friends declaring it the "Don Wise Bridge." It was later replaced during city street upgrade. (CHSGWC.)

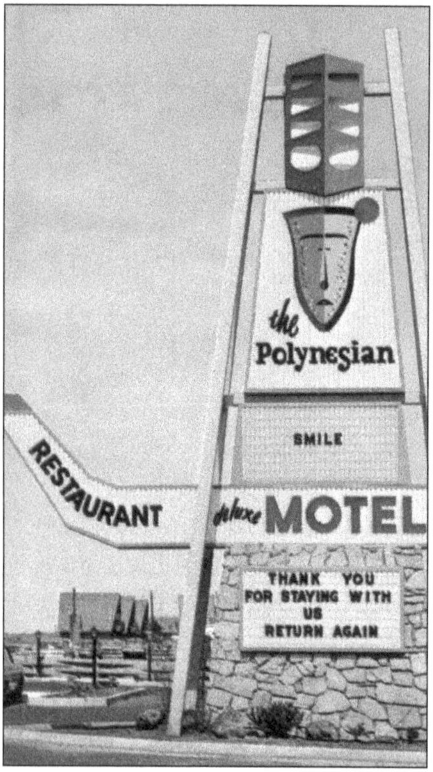

The Polynesian, affectionately known as the "Poly," was associated with many stars, including guest John Wayne during the filming of the movie McQ. The Batjack-Warner Brothers film crew was so popular that the local folks threw a barbeque for them at the Division 4 Park in 1973. Later, a worker, Kurt Cobain, earned enough to fund a band called Nirvana known for grunge rock music. (CHSGWC.)

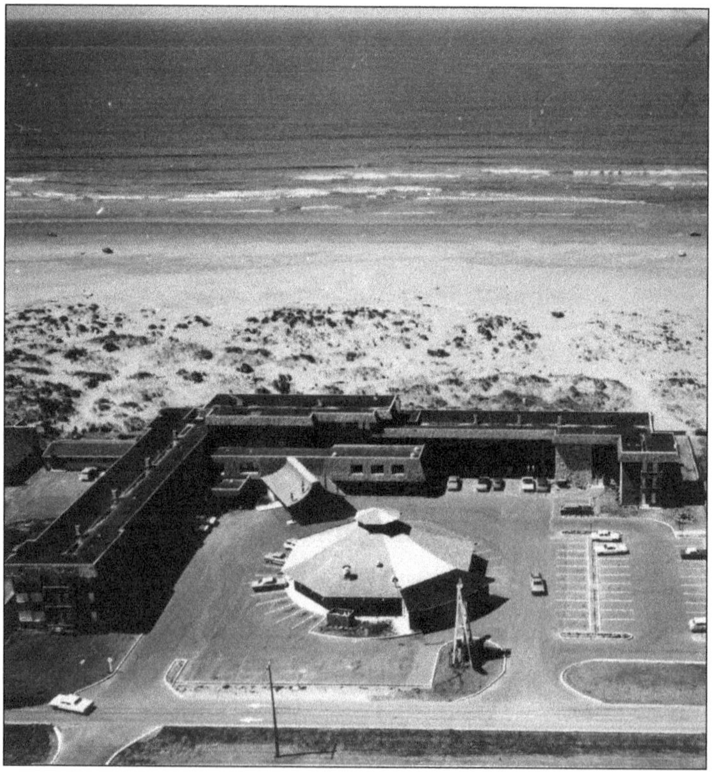

Construction of the Polynesian-themed condo-motel and restaurant was eagerly awaited by new owners such as Dr. and Mrs. Bob Benzak of Seattle who recall excitedly scaling ladders to peak through window gaps to check out the construction progress of their second-story unit. The 70 deluxe condo-apartments were a new innovation for supporting a tourism facility. The Poly, with its banquet room that seated 260 and a conference room that held 1,000, served meals from Mr. "J.'s" Restaurant. (CHSGWC.)

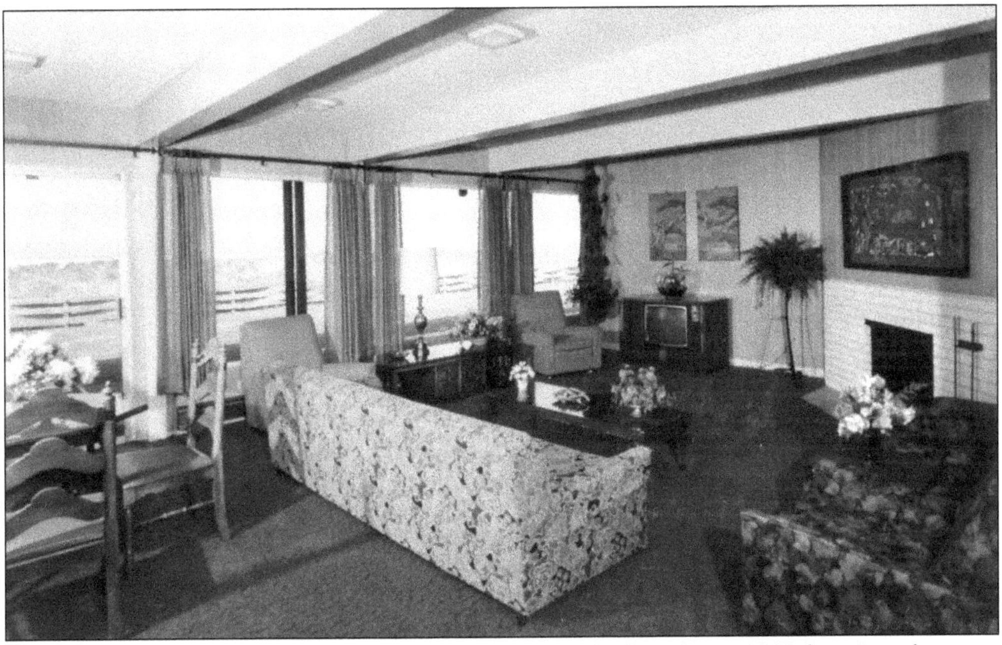

Canterbury was quite the place with the interior furnished in classic 1960 faux-Scandinavian designed furniture and the golden colors of the era. Outside, the building has maintained its timeless architecture. From September to May winter rates were in place with rooms priced at $15 (summer $18.50) and one-bedroom units rented for $24 (summer $34). Of course these units had their own fully-equipped kitchen and fireplaces. An extra person was $3.00, with children under 12 paying $1.50 each day. (Ken Elgin, Canterbury Motel; Kyle Smith.)

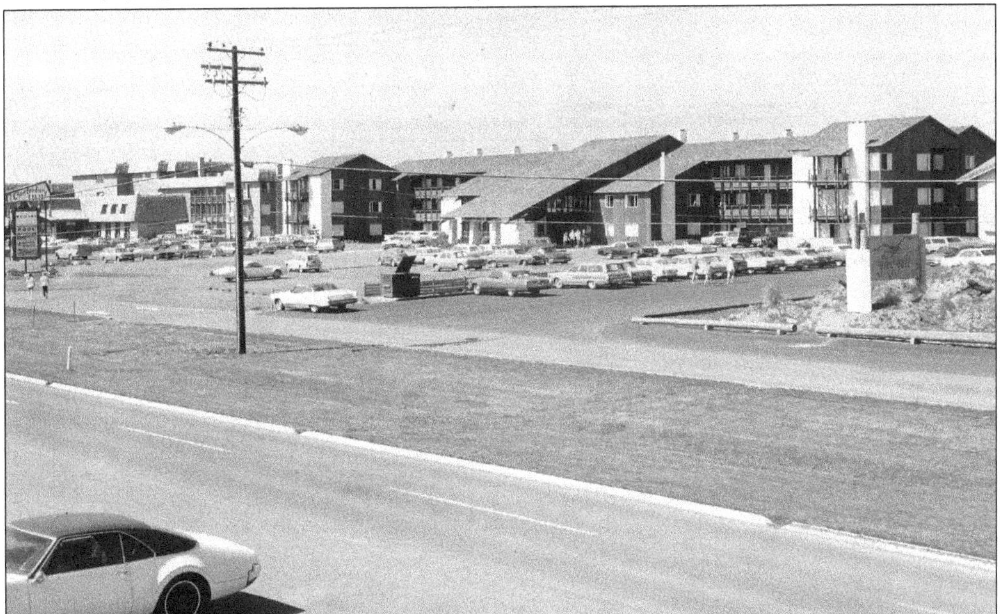

Canterbury opened with $380,000 in presales of the condo units that sold for $9,500–$27,000. A longtime manager, Marty Cunningham, and his wife were involved throughout the community. (Ken Elgin, Canterbury Motel; Kyle Smith.)

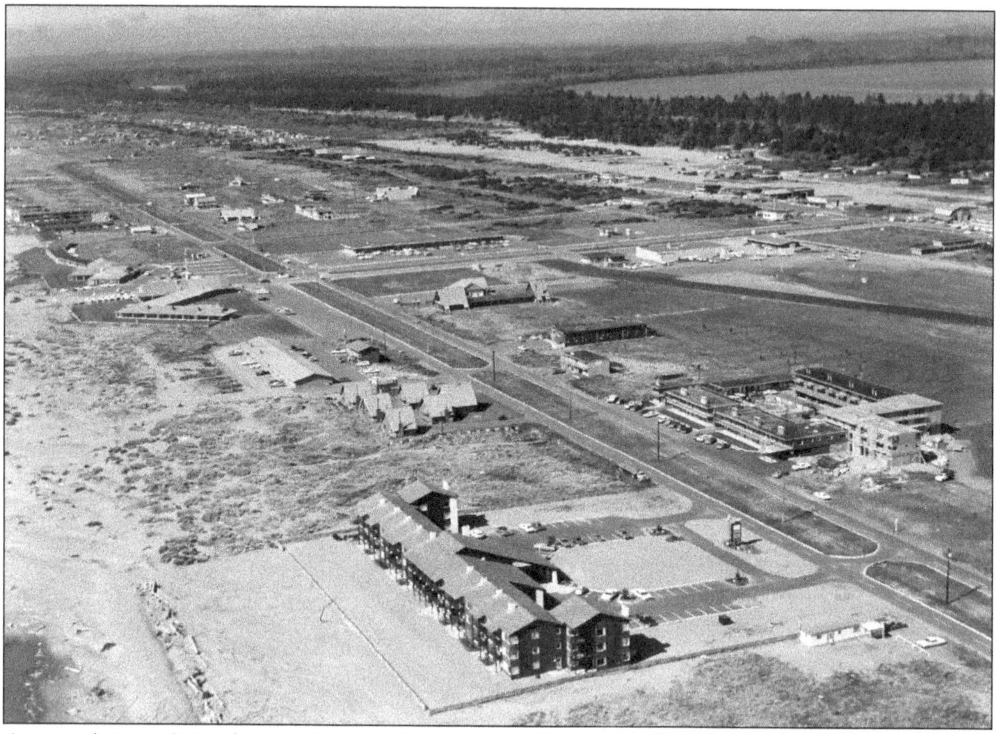

An aerial view of Motel Row taken north in April 1967 includes, form left to right, the Canterbury, Gitche Gumee, Beachcomber, and Executive Villa. (Ken Elgin, Canterbury Motel.)

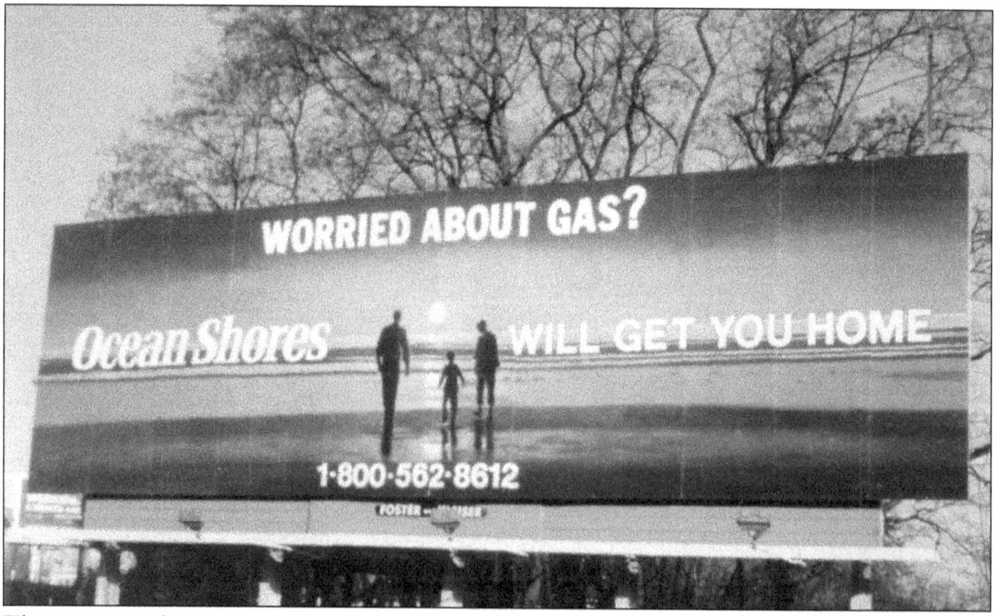

The gas crisis during 1973 was just another challenge for the motel and business owners who competed with ski resorts for winter revenue. Ford Wilgus, Jerry Kehoe, and Tim McClelland were instrumental in raising funds for I-5 billboards offering families gas money to come stay in town. (Ken Elgin, Canterbury Motel.)

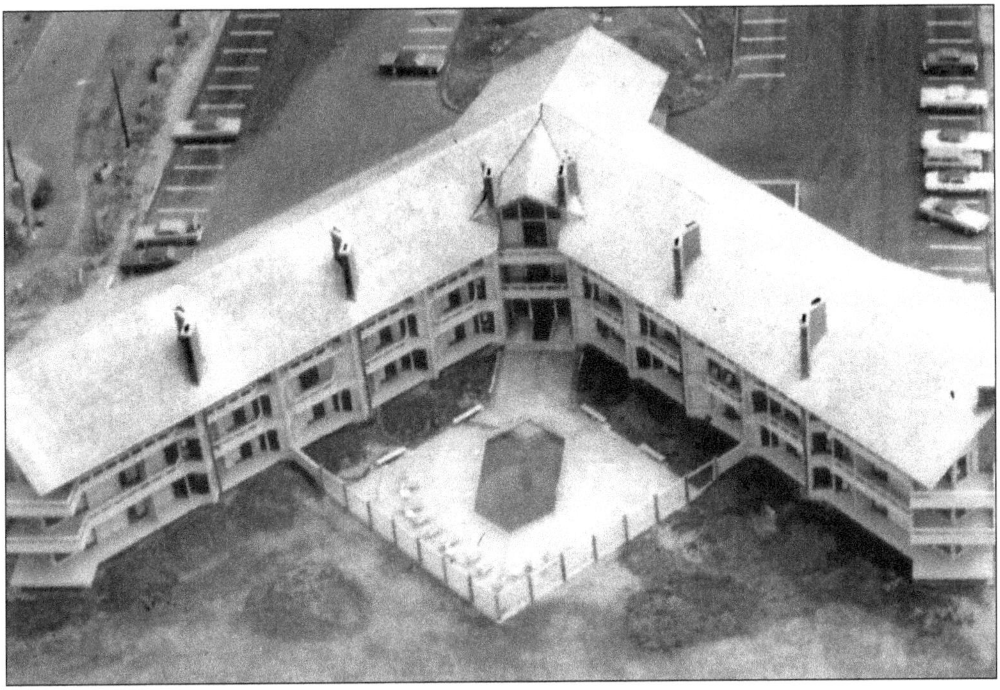

The flying-wing design of the Gray Gull, which opened in 1969, was unique among city motels. (CHSGWC.)

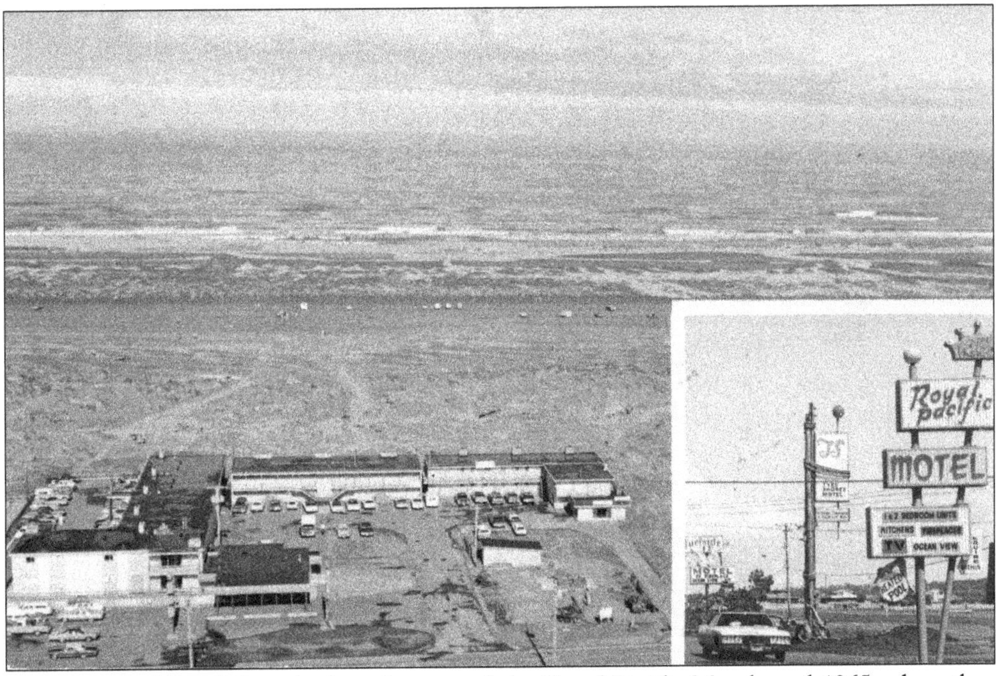

Katherine and Ben Mucci built and operated the Royal Pacific Motel until 1965, when they purchased the Tyee Motel with John and Mary Vukovich; the two families also added the Surfside 12 to the complex. (Smith Western Company.)

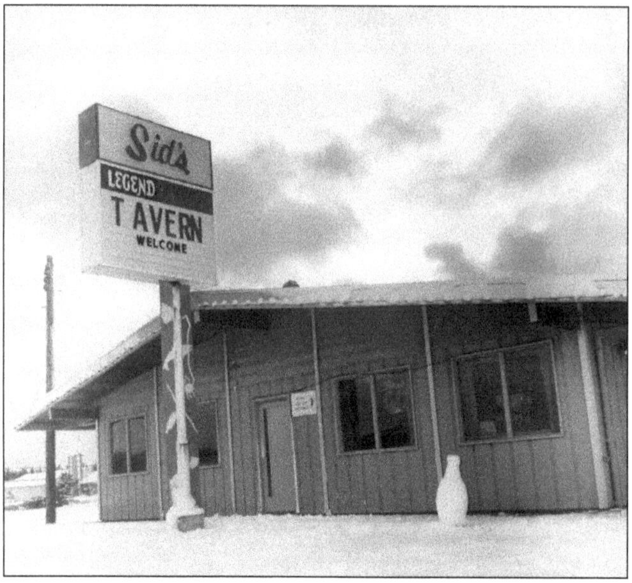

Among the classic businesses of the era was Sid's Legend Inn, finished in 1967. It was built by Ray Perrin. Among its famous, or infamous, exploits was sponsoring the wet T-shirt contest during the raucous annual February Fog Festival. It was later owned by Bill Ratliff, better known as "Clovis." Later the Legend was owned by Karen and Larry Thevik. It may be the only tavern in Grays Harbor where regular Sunday mass was held. Father Dominic conducted services prior to the construction of a parish church at Hogan's Corner. (CHSGWC.)

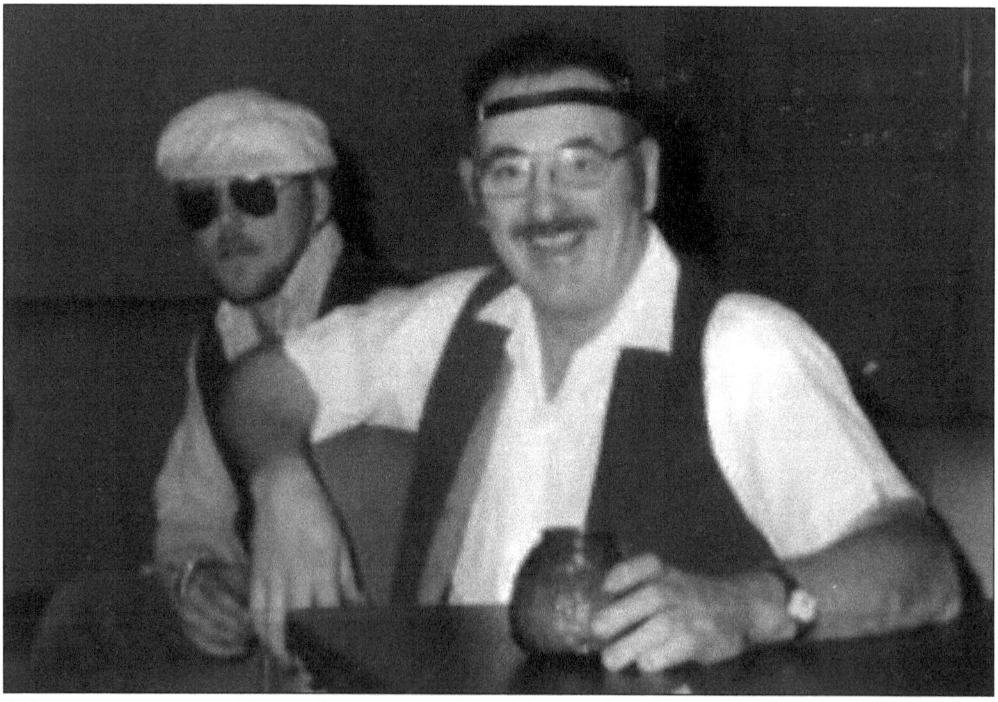

A born entrepreneur, Clovis, shown at the Legend, owned and operated the Pedicab Rickshaw Service that cost 75¢ a person to ride around the downtown area. For service to Oyehut, Illahee, or the golf course, three people could ride for $2, but there was no way they would take you to the North Beach Drive-In Theater at Hogan's Corner. Clovis owned a number of businesses, assisted by his daughter, Karen Quinn, who became owner and manager of Clovis Rentals and Glass Shop following his death. (Karen Quinn.)

Four

Bay to Bar to Ocean

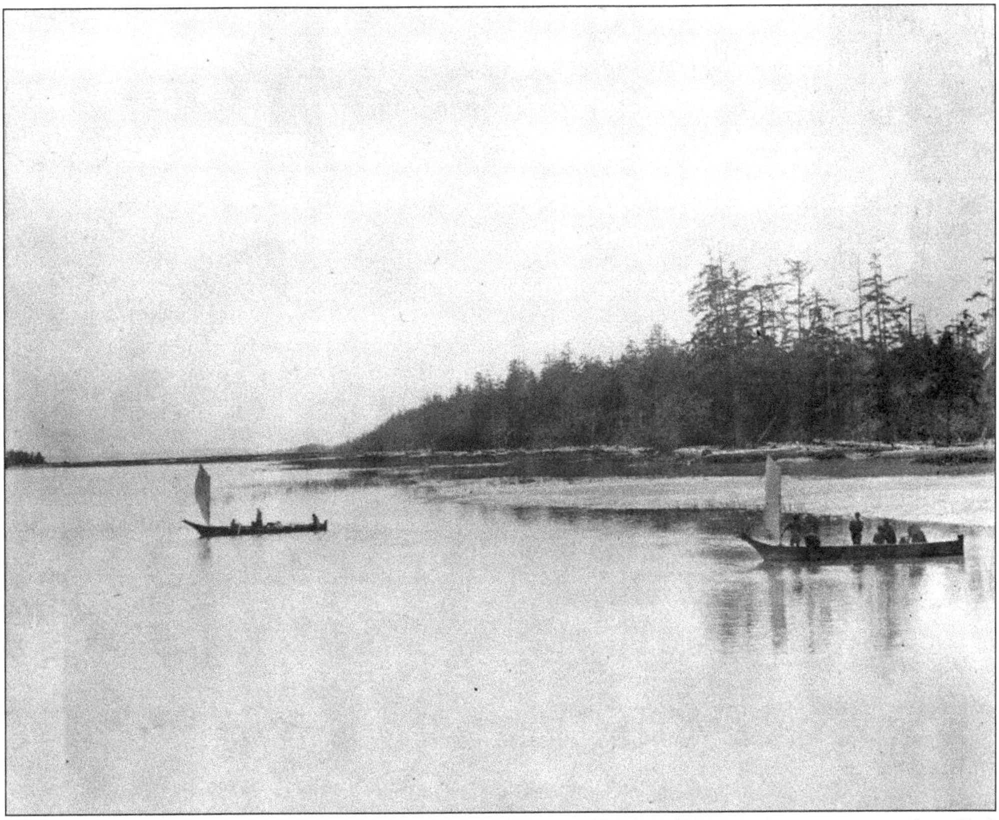

Ocean Shores peninsula has a longtime maritime history. The local Native American people called those who appeared by ship *hoquats* (boat people). The local Native Americans', particularly the Quinaults', great adaptability soon placed wind-driven sails on the sea and some river dugouts. Did the idea first come from the Chinese junks caught in the Japan Current to land on their shores? That is possible, as many local coastal dialects contained Chinese words such as *hyak* (fleet of foot), which is emblazoned today on the high school sports uniforms. (CHSGWC.)

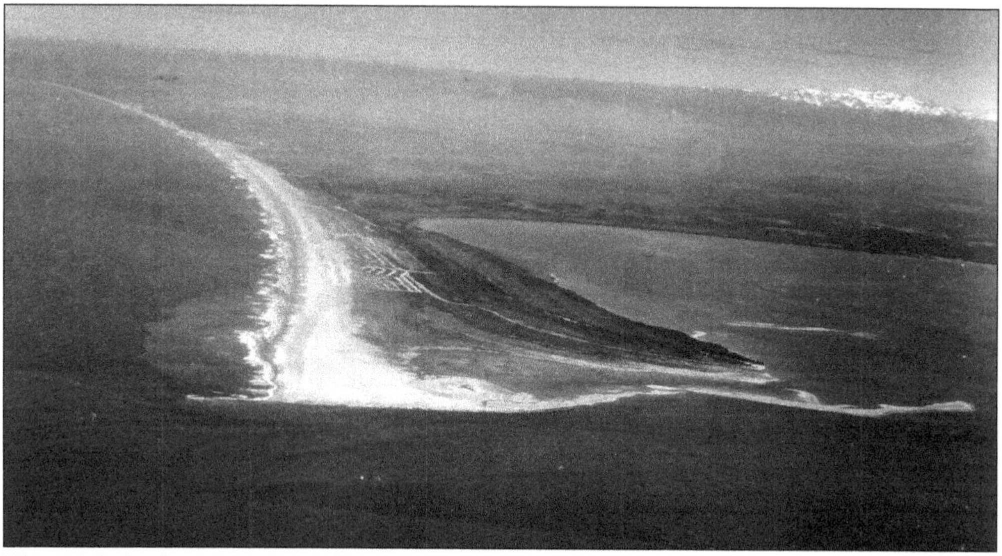

This 1968 bird's-eye view of the marina shows the basin that replaced the remainder of Armstrong Bay. (CHSGWC.)

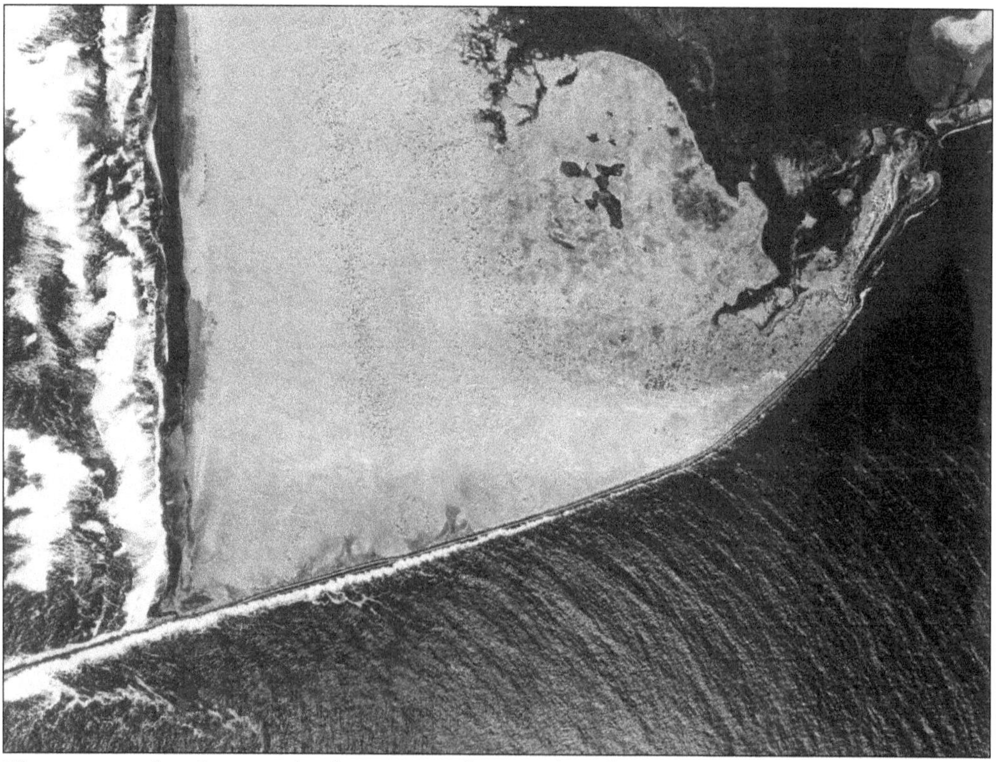

The major southend marina development set the stage for selling prime ocean—and Grays Harbor Bar—view lots built on these two portions of land, as seen in these 1952 Army Corp of Engineers ortho photographs. This of the North Jetty was only barren sand that was often over-washed and unstable land, which the original developers planned to use as a "Sea Park." It was platted and developed when Wendell West Development Company and the Bank of California acquired the property. (CHSGWC.)

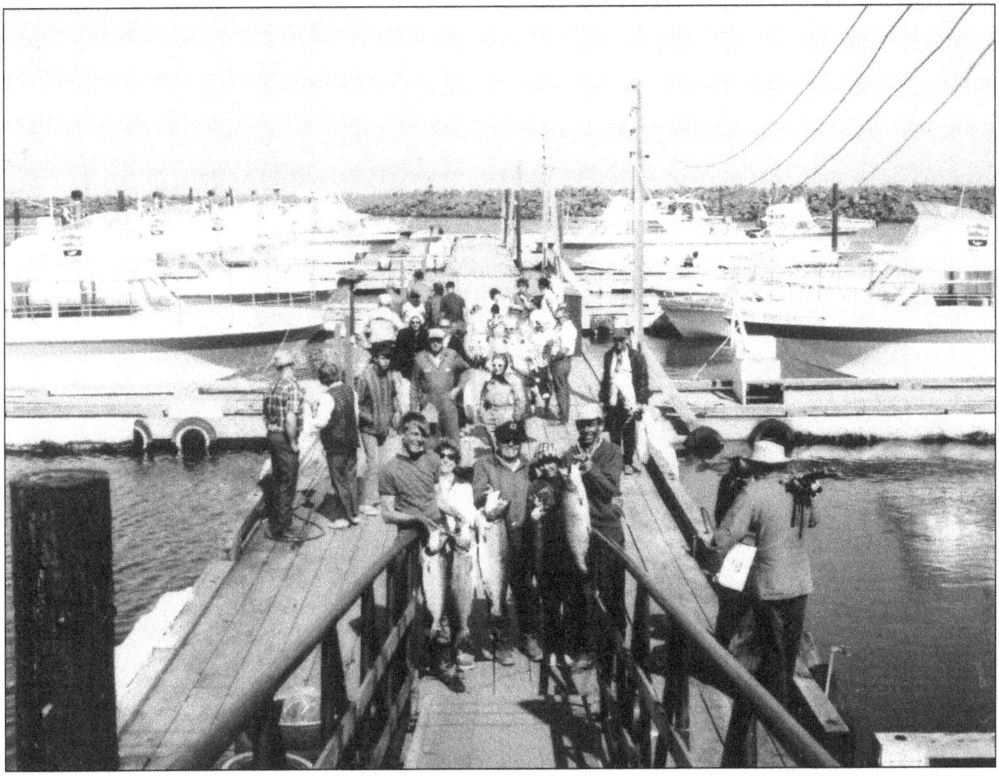

Happy fishermen are shown coming home in 1969 with their day's catch from the marina charter fleet that was available seven days a week. The Silver King 49-unit motel and the Marina View Restaurant were owned by Bob Rogers. Silver King Charters' custom-built, 38-foot fiberglass boats were the fastest on the coast with a speed of 20 knots. In 1965, Ocean Shores and the South Beach were the hottest fishing section of Washington's coastal waters. Its allowable catch was estimated at 49,900 chinook (king) salmon by the State Department of Fisheries, 88 percent more than the next in line, Sekui-Pillar Point, with 26,400. Commercial fishermen were not as happy in 1979 when they blockaded the Ocean Shores, Westport, and Illwaco marinas to protest the numerous commercial fishing closures mandated by the state. (CHSGWC.)

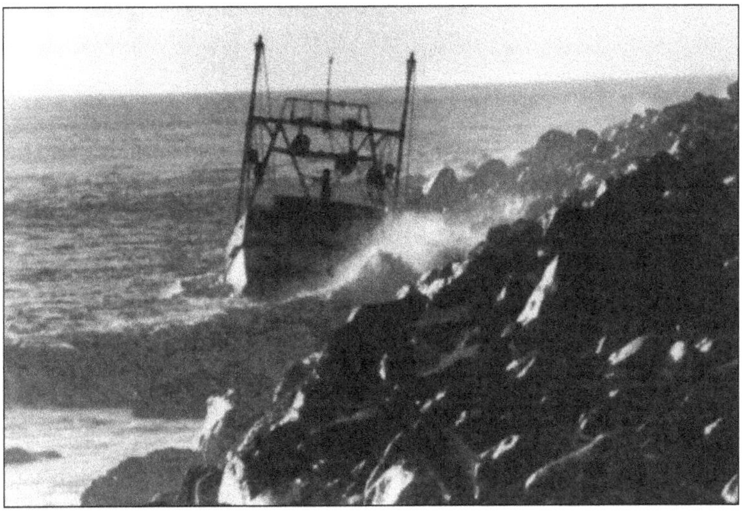

The Grays Harbor Bar is considered the second-worst bar on the West Coast, with the Columbia River Bar deemed the worst. Local fishermen, although wary, end up ashore on the North Jetty, a fate not unlike that of the FV *Tiffany* in June 1983. (CHSGWC.)

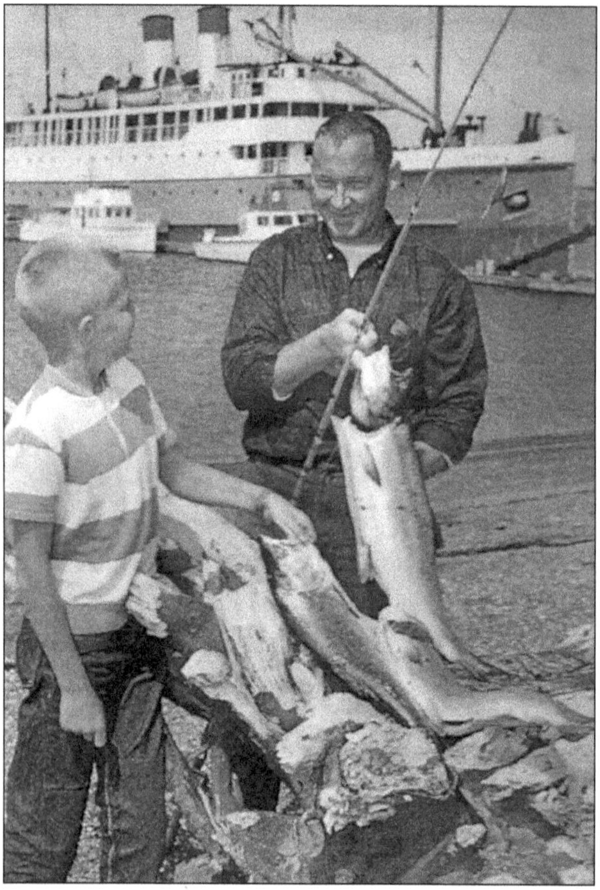

This father and son duo was pretty happy with their day's catch from the SS *Catala* fleet, which served as a test market for the marina complex. (Thorn Ward.)

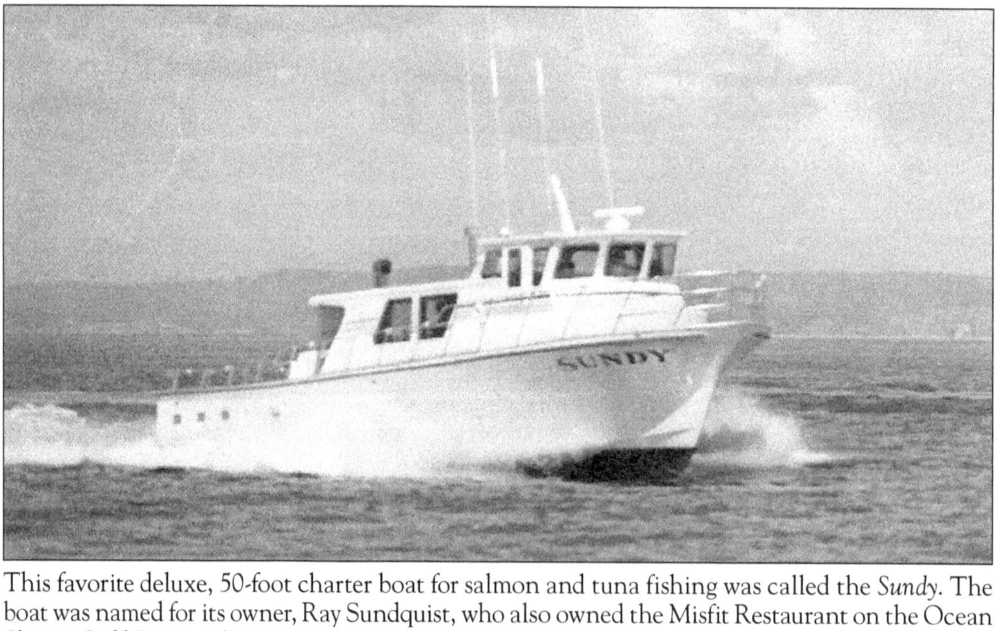

This favorite deluxe, 50-foot charter boat for salmon and tuna fishing was called the *Sundy*. The boat was named for its owner, Ray Sundquist, who also owned the Misfit Restaurant on the Ocean Shores Golf Course. (James Degarimore; CHSGWC.)

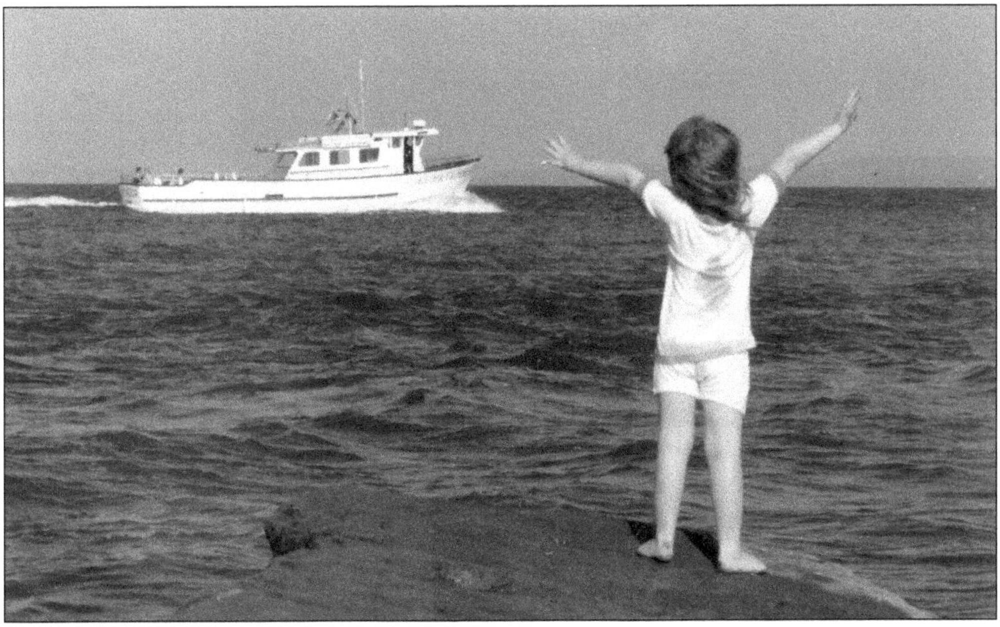

Visitors like Kelsey Woodwick loved to bid bon voyage to the *El Matador*, the longest running of the seasonal foot-passenger ferries, which was photographed in 1981. The 2-mile ferry ride eliminated the 56-mile drive around the east end of the harbor. (CHSGWC.)

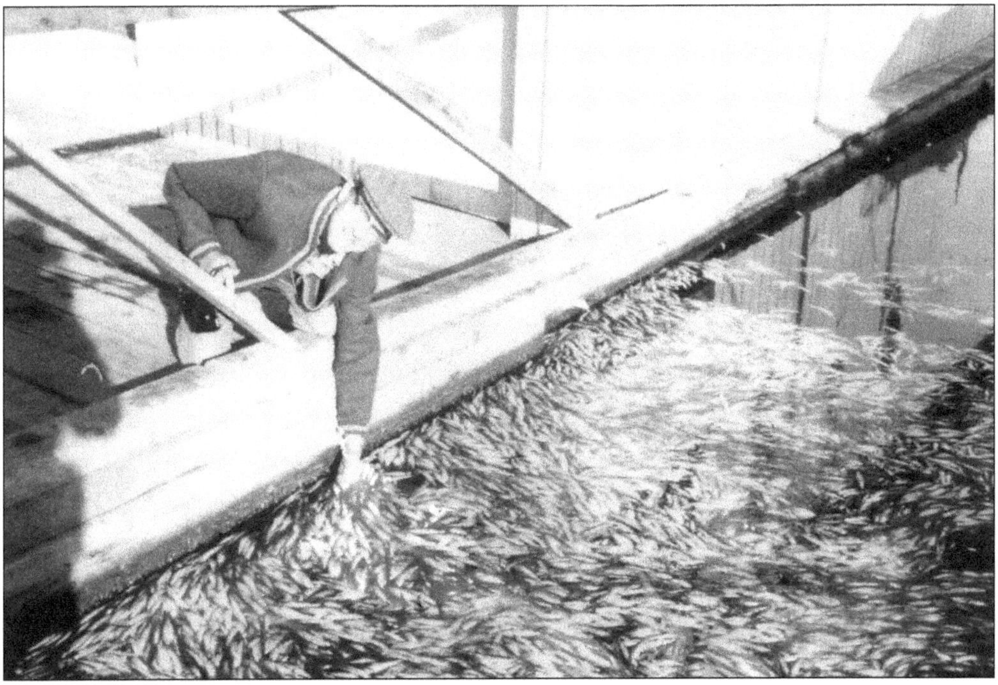

Milo Schneider, police commissioner, dips anchovies out of the marina boat lift, amused that the entire town was slippery with the fish that rained from the sky on January 10, 1972. Schneider, as a Lion's Club member, provided many carved, historical signs such as the history of the city and the history of the SS *Catala*. The lift could move boats up to 50 tons from the freshwater canals to the saltwater of the North Bay of Grays Harbor. (Ocean Shores Police Department.)

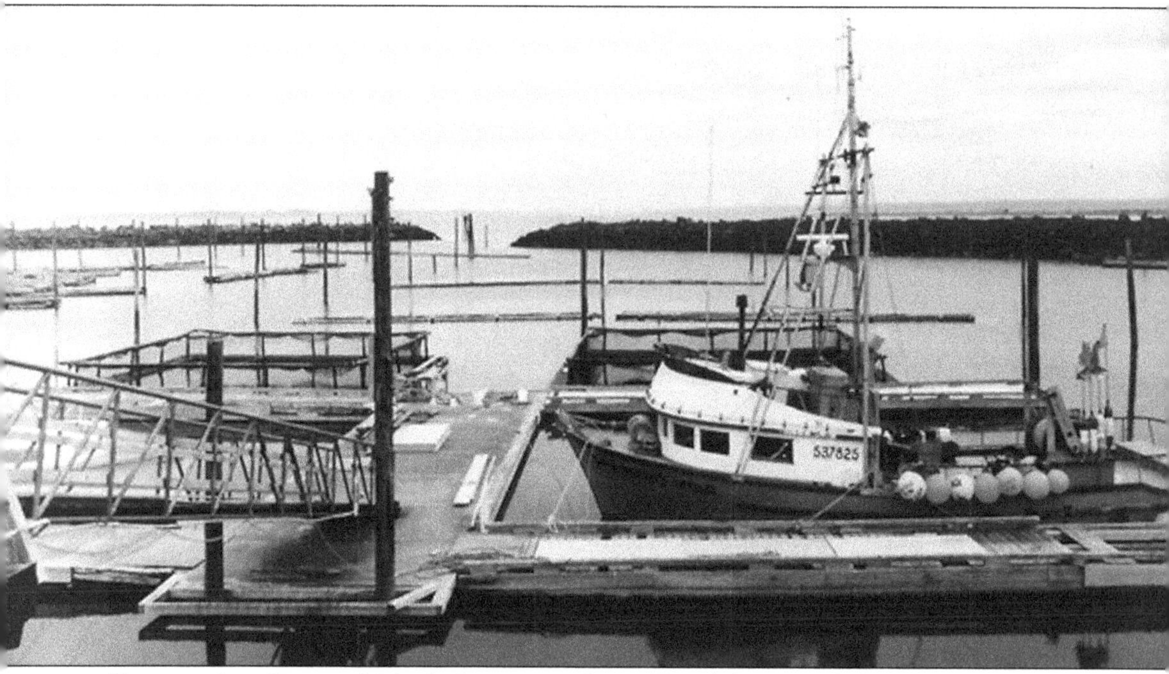

For more than 30 years, *Midnight Star* captain Larry Thevik has provided customers with freshly caught fish, crab, and tuna straight off the decks at the marina mooring. Thevik purchased the vessel from Gary Ruston, who also operated out of the marina. (CHSGWC.)

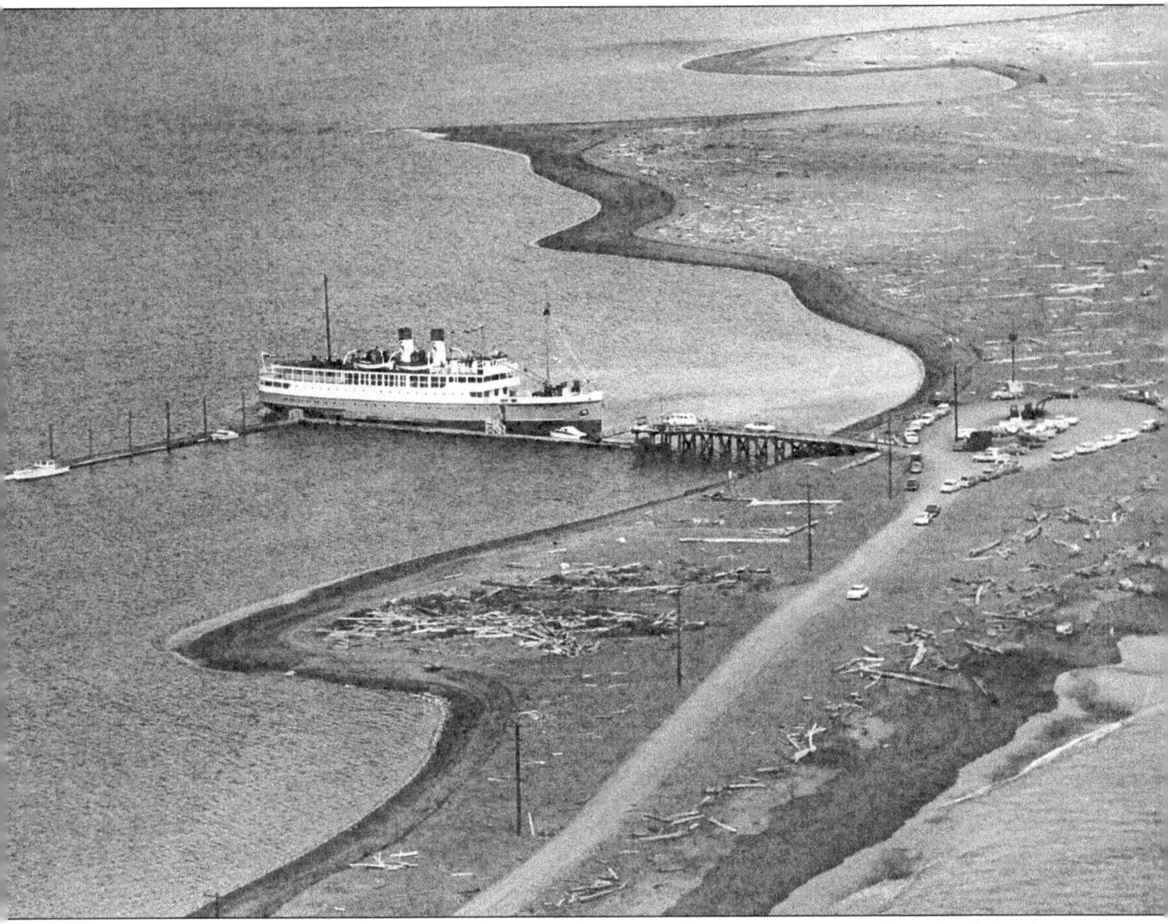

Purchased by the Ocean Shores Development Company from a Vancouver, British Columbia, corporation, the SS *Catala* was rescued from her fate as a fish barge. Over $1 million was spent restoring the ship before it was used as a "botel" and sales office in Seattle during the 1972 Seattle World's Fair. Following the fair, it was sold to a California couple to become a nightspot at Long Beach. After the venture failed, the corporation towed the vessel back to Ocean Shores in 1974 where it was anchored off Seagull (Protection) Island and used as a botel and charter fishing headquarters, complete with a sewer treatment plant in a former engine room. It served as a test market for a marina. The *Catala* was first managed by Alice Werner and Ken Kehrlie. Later a causeway was built to cross the old Oyehut Channel during high tide from the mainland to the fishing fleet, lounge, dining room, and overnight accommodations. (AMH.)

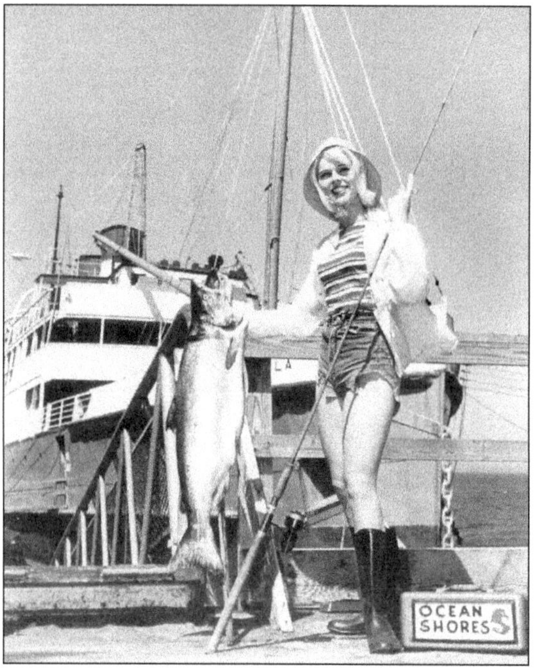

Lovely Marilyn Hubler of Aberdeen was photographed by Del Mulkey to lure customers to the *Catala*'s fleet of charter boats. She remembers being called out of classes to shiver in the cold and wet because Mulkey thought the light was right. (AMH.)

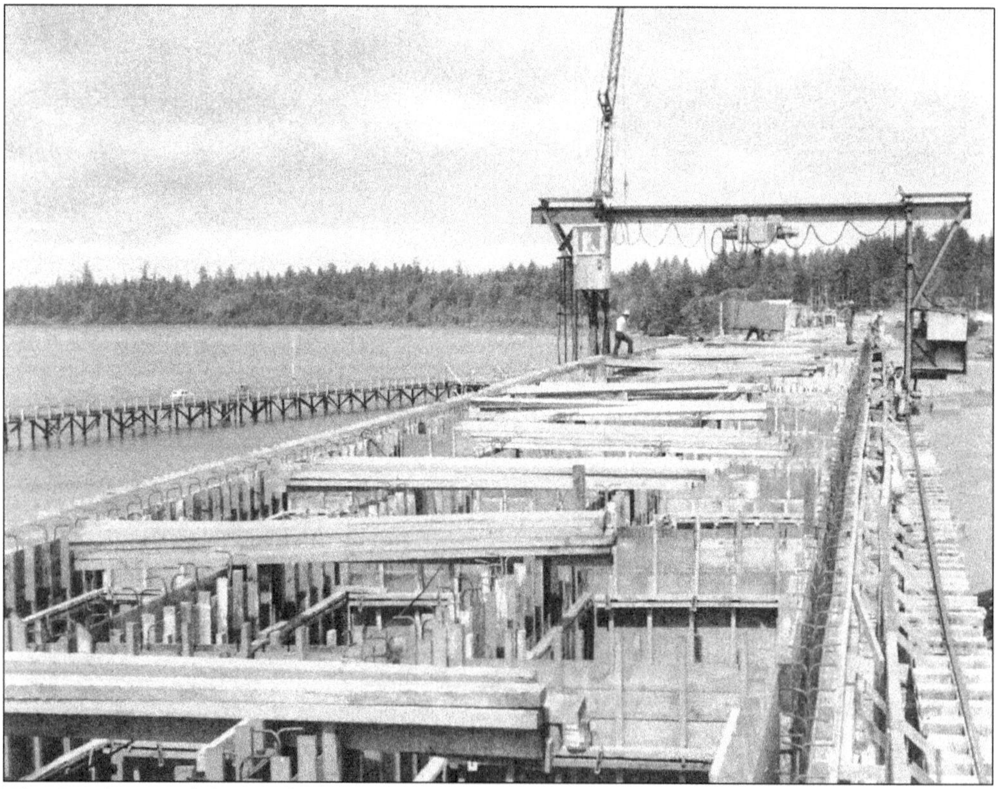

The *Catala* proved the need for a complete marina with construction beginning in 1974. Dock construction was a major project that included building a .25-mile boardwalk. The enclosed waters covered 7 acres, holding 150 berths. (AMH.)

Five

Classic Celebrations

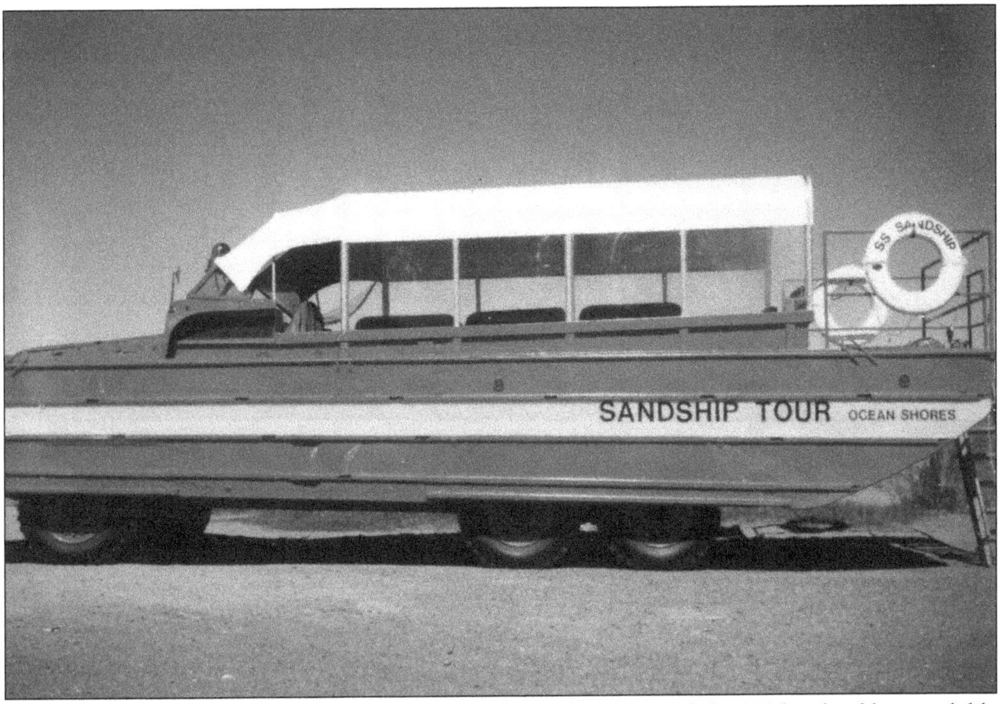

Newspapers, with their tourism special editions, have always touted the 101 kinds of fun available within the city. Perhaps one of the fondest fun-time occupations was riding "The Duck." Don Heath purchased the World War II amphibian to provide colorfully narrated tours of the city's land and water. Named the SS *Sandship*, it became affectionately known as "The Duck." Built in 1942 for land invasion, the 21-passenger, six-wheel-drive vehicle's 16-gauge steel hulk made quite a splash when it entered the Pacific Ocean surf. (Don Health family.)

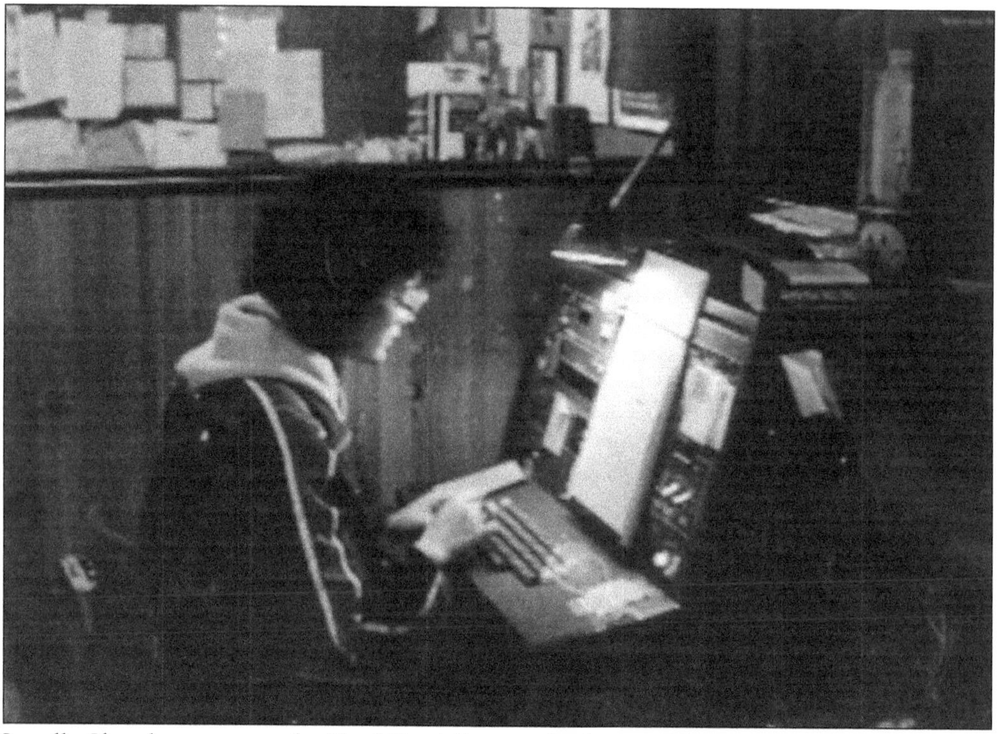

Lynelle Church sets type at the *North Beach Beacon,* the first weekly newspaper that followed the new lowercase style of the day. Published by David Gauger, a Raymond, Washington, newspaperman, the *Beacon* published huge annual tourism tabloids bragging about the area's recreational offerings. It ceased to exist after several changes of ownership. (CHSGWC.)

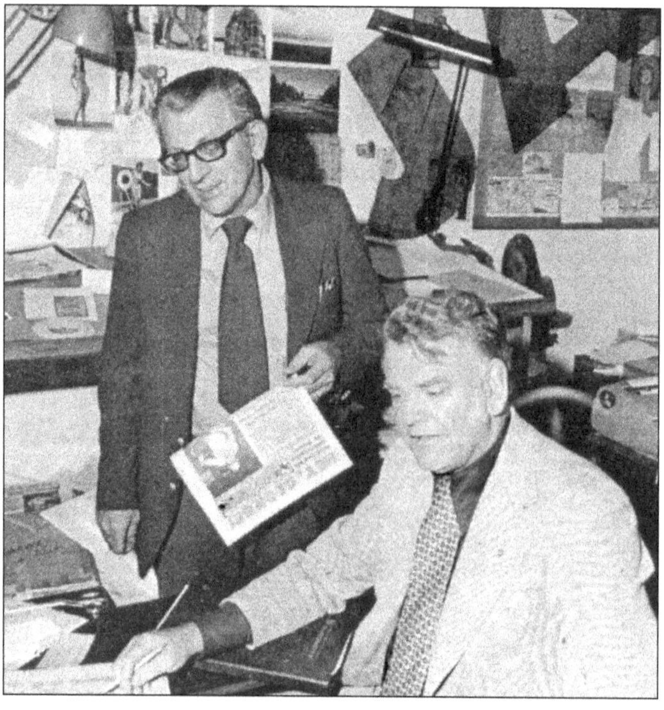

Bob and Thorn Ward operated the development company's newsletter, the monthly *Observer.* It was augmented by a variety of house organs, such as the *Sand Doings*, the Galilean *Chapel Chat*, and others. The *Observer* was purchased by Robert Focht, owner of Robert Focht Advertising Company and former advertising director for the Aberdeen *Daily World* newspaper, and Ernie Linnekohl, co-owner and manager of radio station KGHO. The two later owned the *Elma Chronicle*. (CHSGWC.)

Robert Focht began publishing the *North Coast News* with Gene Woodwick as editor in 1985. He is shown here with young John Parnell in the office located on Point Brown Avenue. (CHSGWC.)

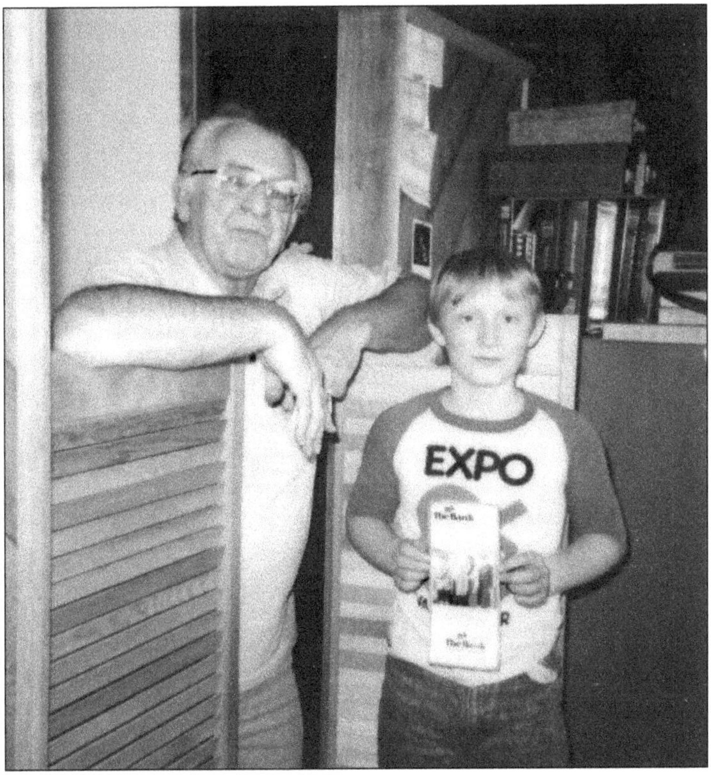

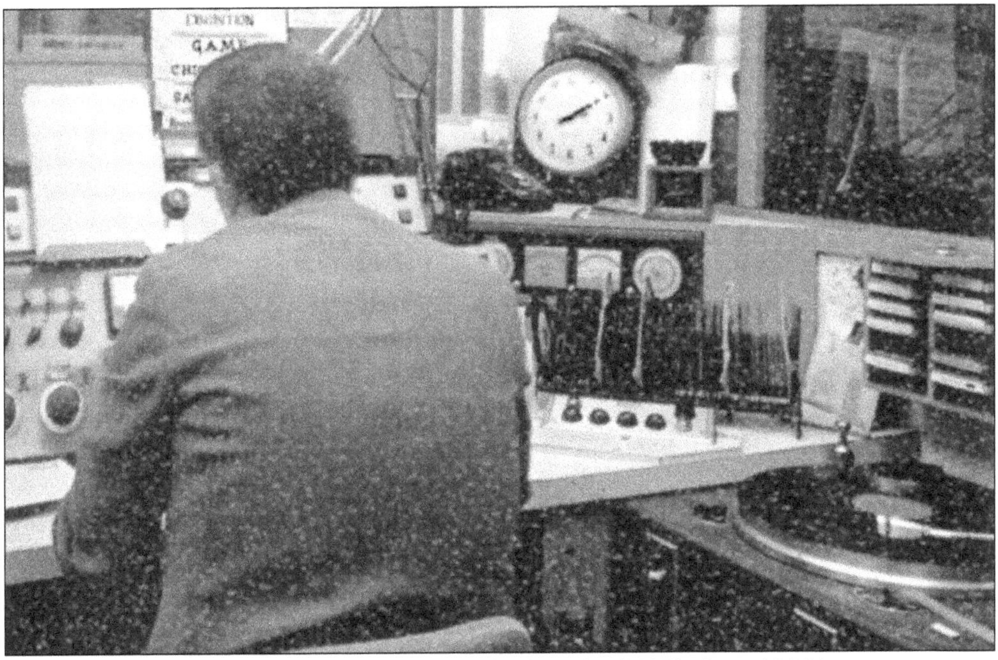

DJ Dale Gunderson was the main man for KDUX-FM radio (104.7) whose 48,000-watt station was located on the southeast grounds of the Community Club. One of its most popular programs was Paul Harvey. Terry McMonglee was sales manager. The present-day, volunteer-operated station KOSW 91.3 went on line in July 2004. (CHSGWC.)

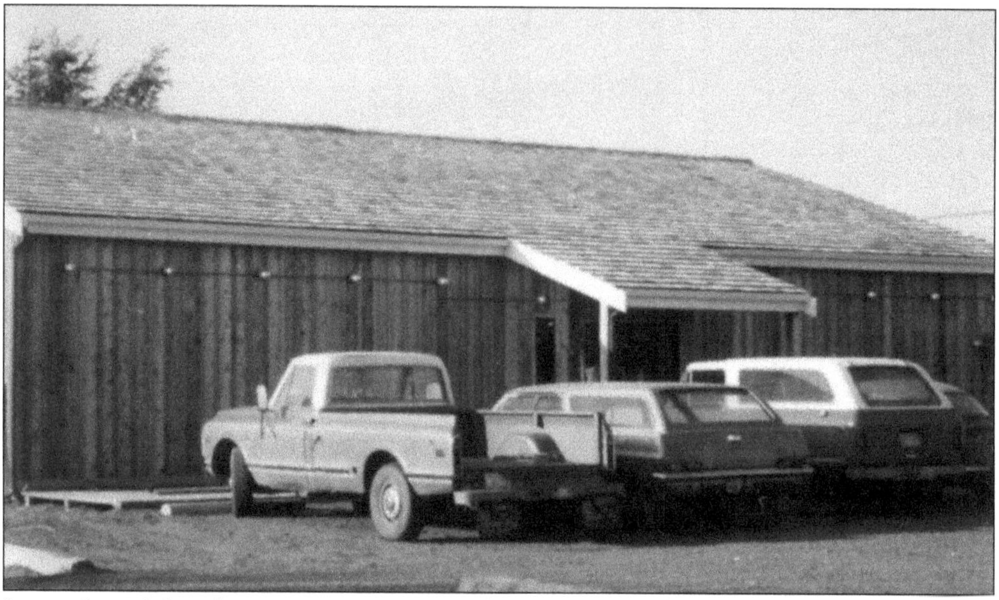

In another of their business expansions, Ruth and Tim McClelland replaced a tin building adjoining their Homeport Restaurant with a cedar structure that housed both Marjuli's Gallery and the city's first community-operated Channel 13 NBC (North Beach Community) television station, run entirely by volunteers. (Tim and Ruth McClelland.)

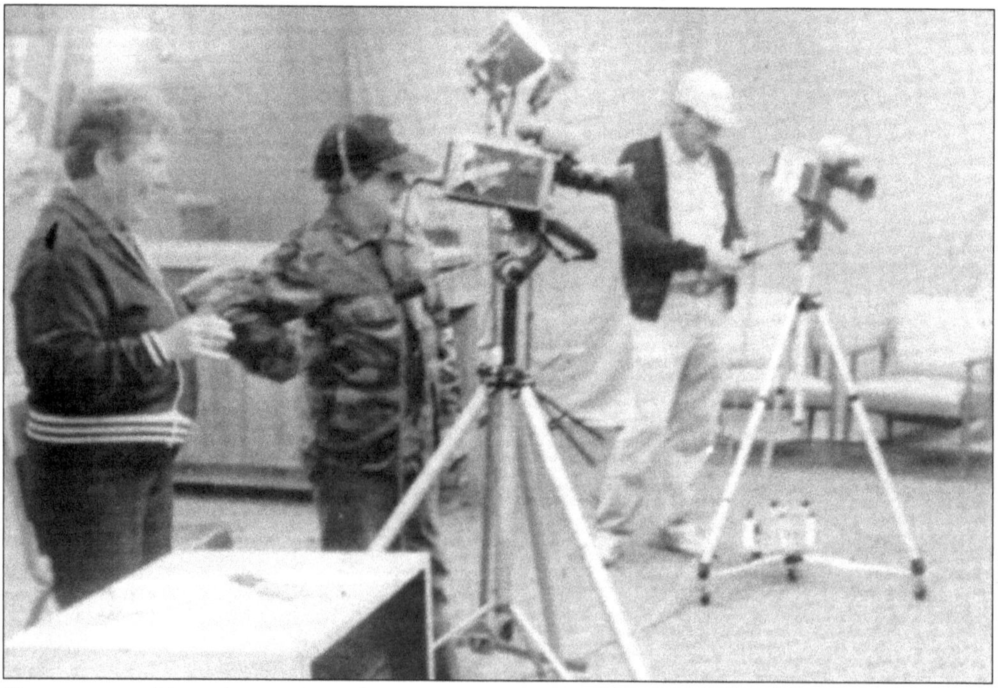

Cameras were big and sometimes the cameramen were small, especially when Sean Woodwick, age 12, and Georgejean Lucas (left) filmed weekly shows for NBC-TV. Charles "Lucky" Luck and his wife, Virginia, operated the station for 10 years. All of the local motels had the station tuned in to provide fun-time information and news of the town when guests checked into their rooms. (CHSGWC.)

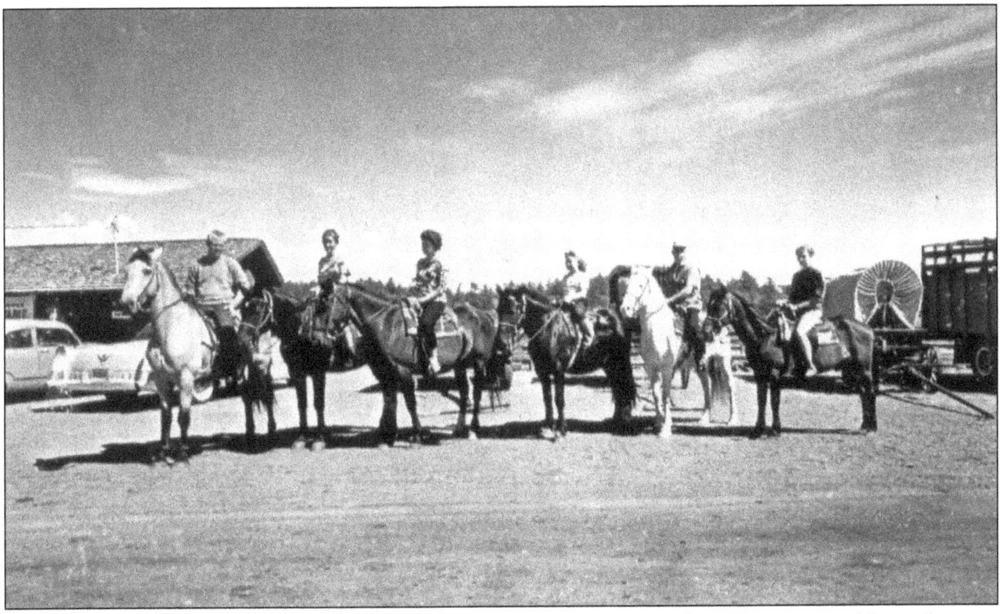

Horse barns once graced the area now home to the IGA supermarket. Tourists could rent horses, take a wagon ride, eat barbecue, and enjoy hayrides. Division 12 had been platted as a horse heaven for horse fanciers with riding trails, corrals, and riding areas protected from vehicular traffic and where adjacent homeowners could build their own corrals and stables. (CHSGWC.)

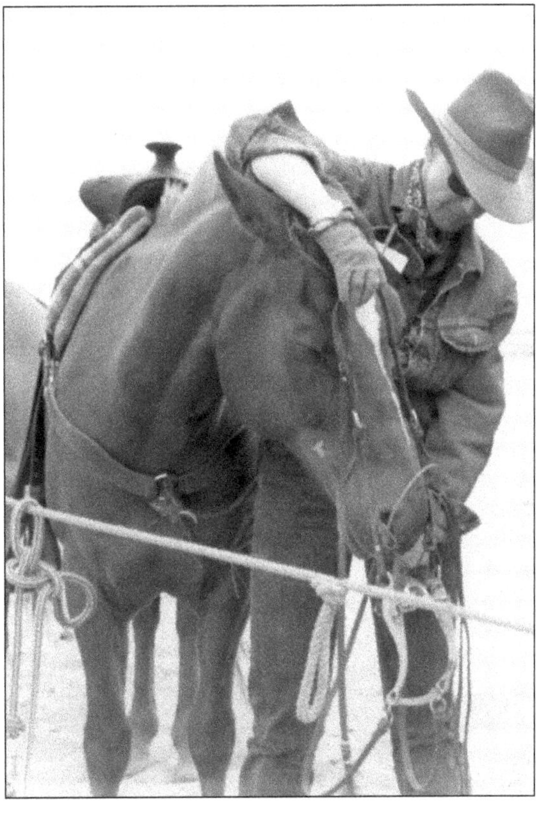

Horse rides remained a major tourist attraction as the town grew. Once the horse barn was torn down to make way for progress, beach cowboys trucked in horses for the tourists. Cowboys such as this one were great romantic fodder for teenage girls to regale their chums about after the return home. (CHSGWC.)

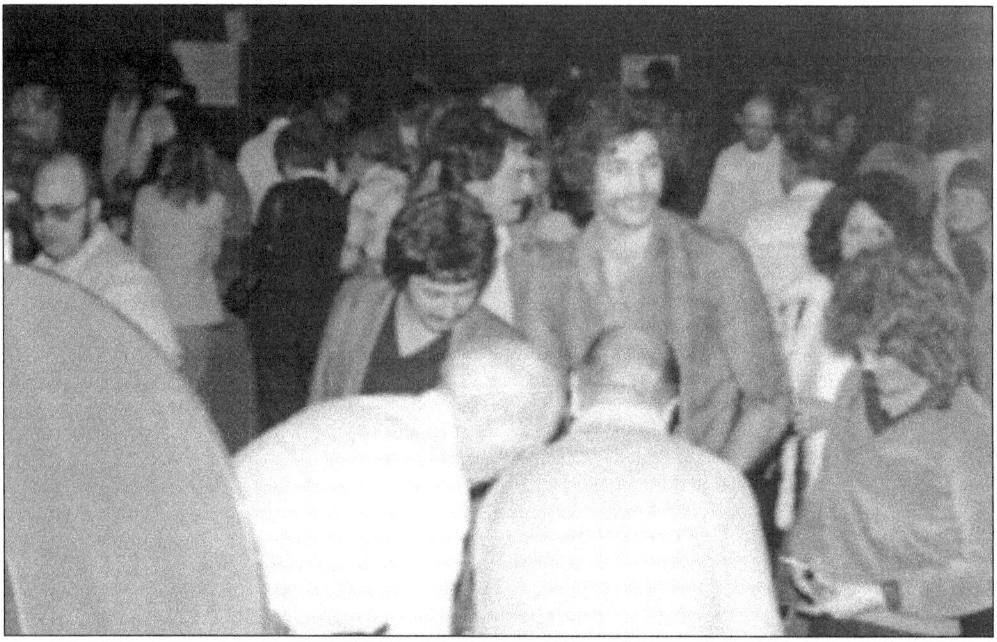

Gambling was an interest of the business community almost since the inception of the development, with former state attorney general Don Eastvold as one of its champions. Later, when Mike Valdez was president of the chamber of commerce, the issue was again a favorable topic. From the mid-1970s to 1990s, gambling was available nearly every winter weekend with the games rented to volunteers from nonprofit groups by the fire department to augment their own budget. The tables were always crowded with those anxious to go home with more money in their pocket than what they had brought to town. (CHSGWC.)

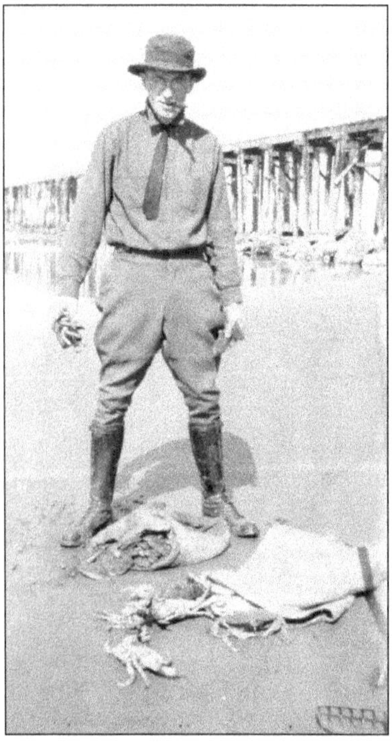

This 1915 snapshot of Buzz Rankin from Portland, Oregon, indicates that crabbing at the North Jetty rail line was a tourist attraction. Today crabbing off the marina groin takes the modern crabber fairly close to Rankin's favored spot. (CHSGWC.)

An Aqua Dart, though popular, never made it to the mass market. (CHSGWC.)

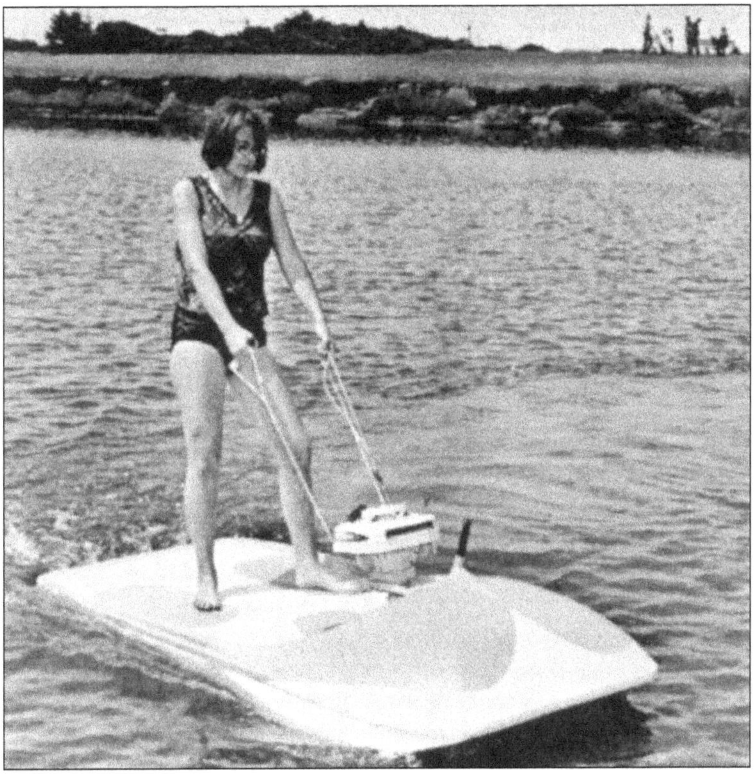

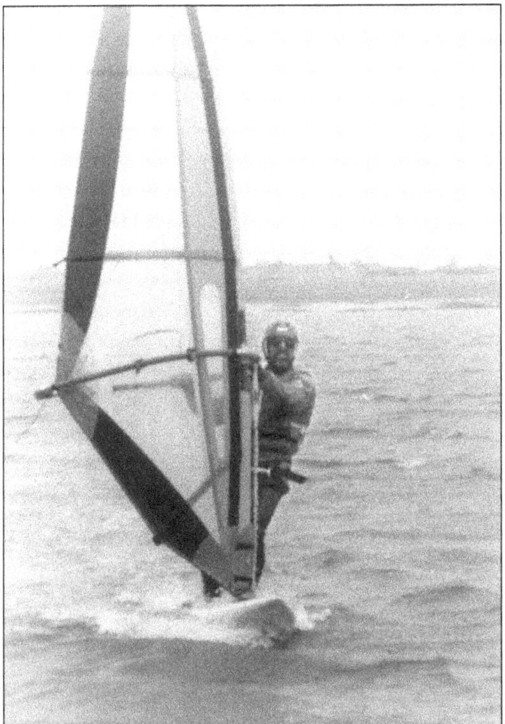

In 1993, sailboarding became a popular sport. Surfing is done on the harbor side of Damon Point. (CHSGWC.)

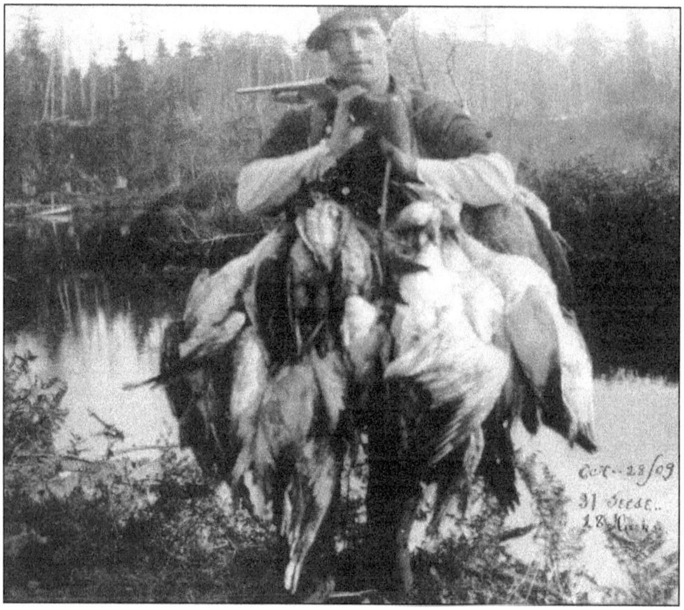

Today the bird lovers hunt with their cameras; however, the town does have two bird-hunting areas within the city limits, one by the airport and one within the Oyehut Game Refuge. During the turn of the 20th century, Cliff Summerlin snapped this fellow hunter loaded down with one day's take of geese and ducks. In 1961, overzealous or nearsighted duck hunters shot holes in several aluminum boats on Duck Lake, nearly giving heart attacks to their occupants. (PM.)

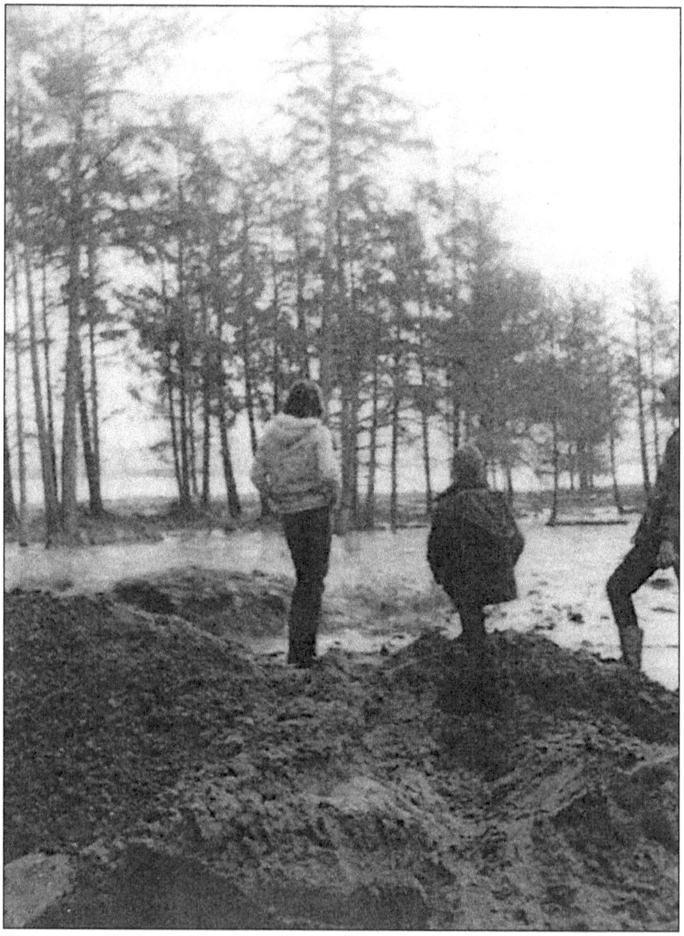

Ralph Minard's grandchildren, Patty Seaman (left), Bill Seaman (center), and Barb Seaman Lyda inspect the land-clearing project for the southend's new clubhouse and swimming pool facility. The development company's sales pitch included covenants for pocket parks and community club facilities for a variety of recreational opportunities. (MFP.)

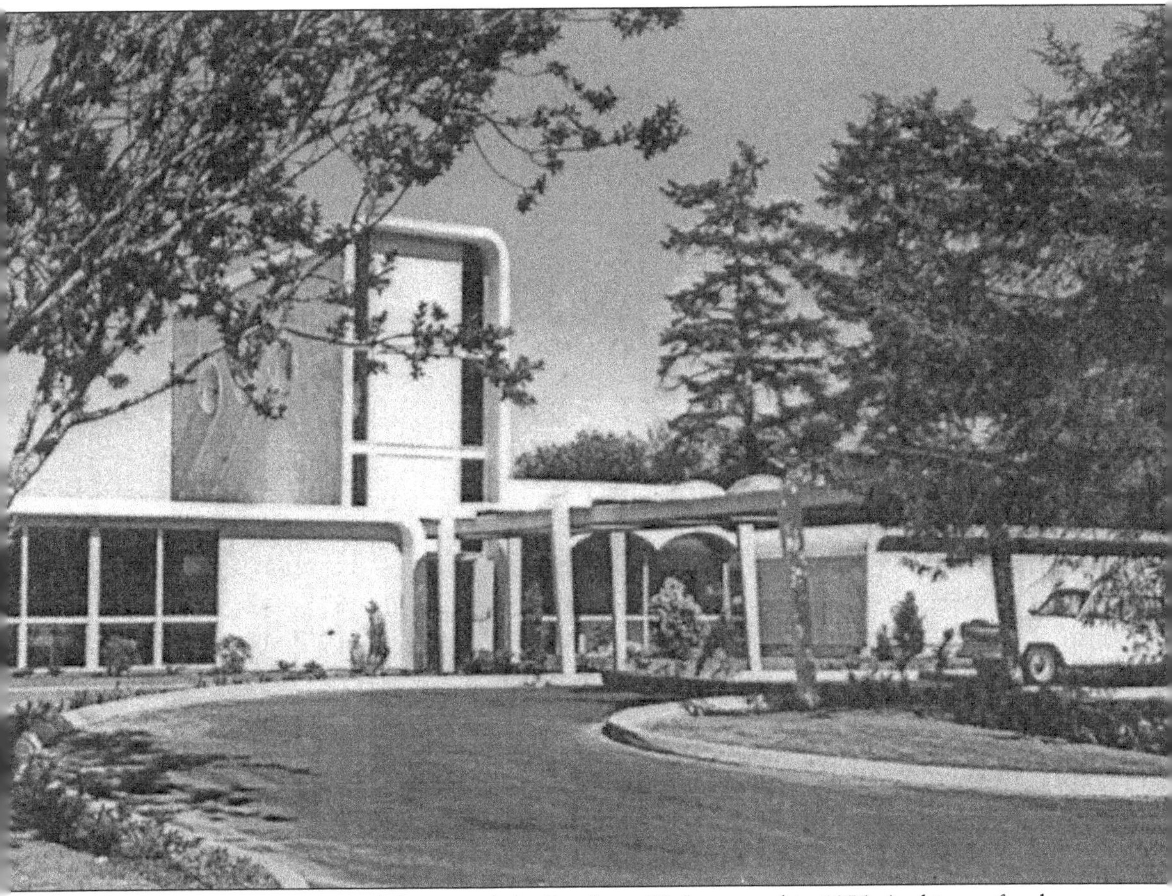

The division 15 community club, termed the Bayshore Club, opened in 1975. Architects for the unique building were C. W. Doty and C. E. Bertraun. The two-story tower and the distinctive round windows were removed in subsequent remodeling. The development boasted some type of recreational facility in nearly every division. (CHSGWC.)

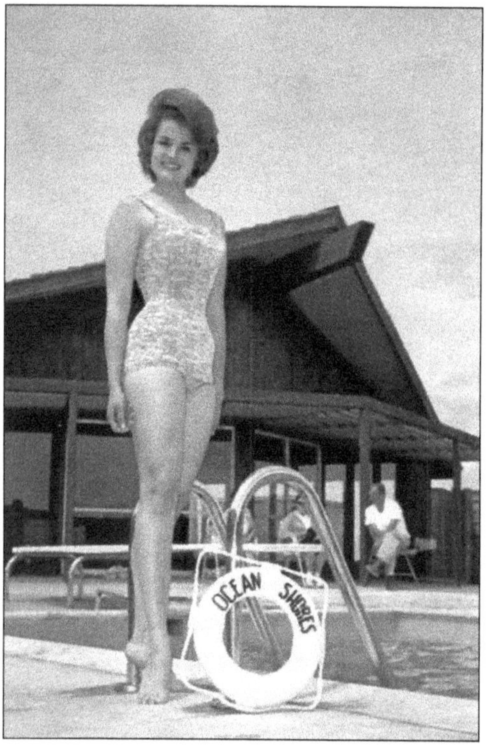

Another famous cheesecake shot by photographer Del Mulkey is of the lovely Geraldine Jerijuno poolside at the division 2 recreation center, the first community club facility and park built by developers. (CHSGWC.)

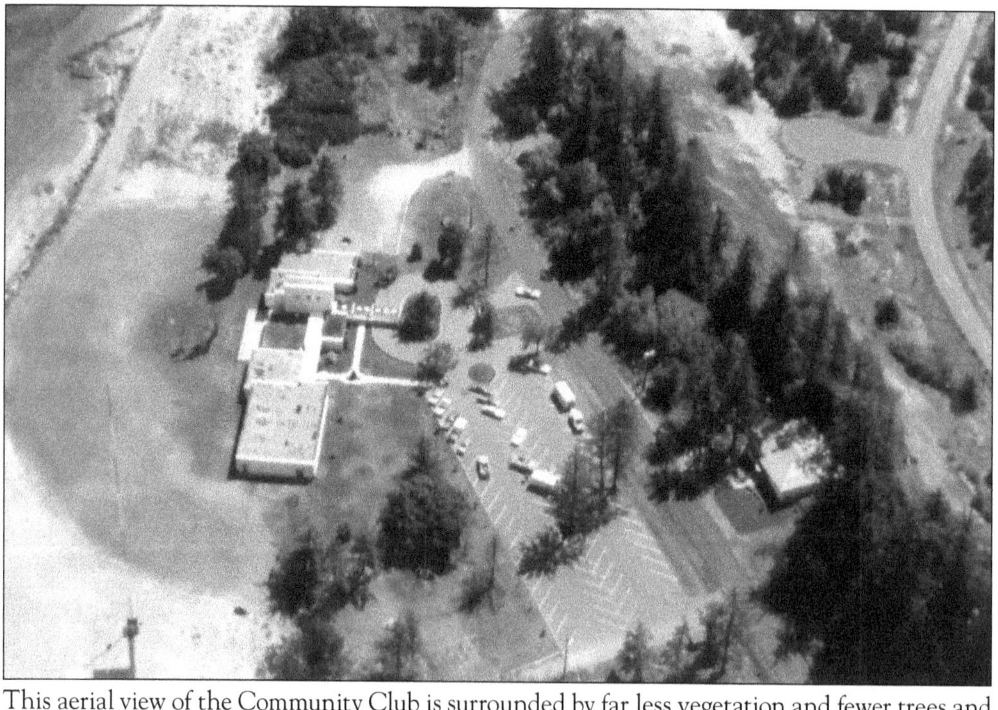

This aerial view of the Community Club is surrounded by far less vegetation and fewer trees and homes than in present days; however, the Bert Duncan home can be seen across from the parking lot. In 1972, the club deeded the beach frontage along the entire west side of the peninsula to the city along with the tide gate and Parcel 2 for a second fire station location. (CHSGWC.)

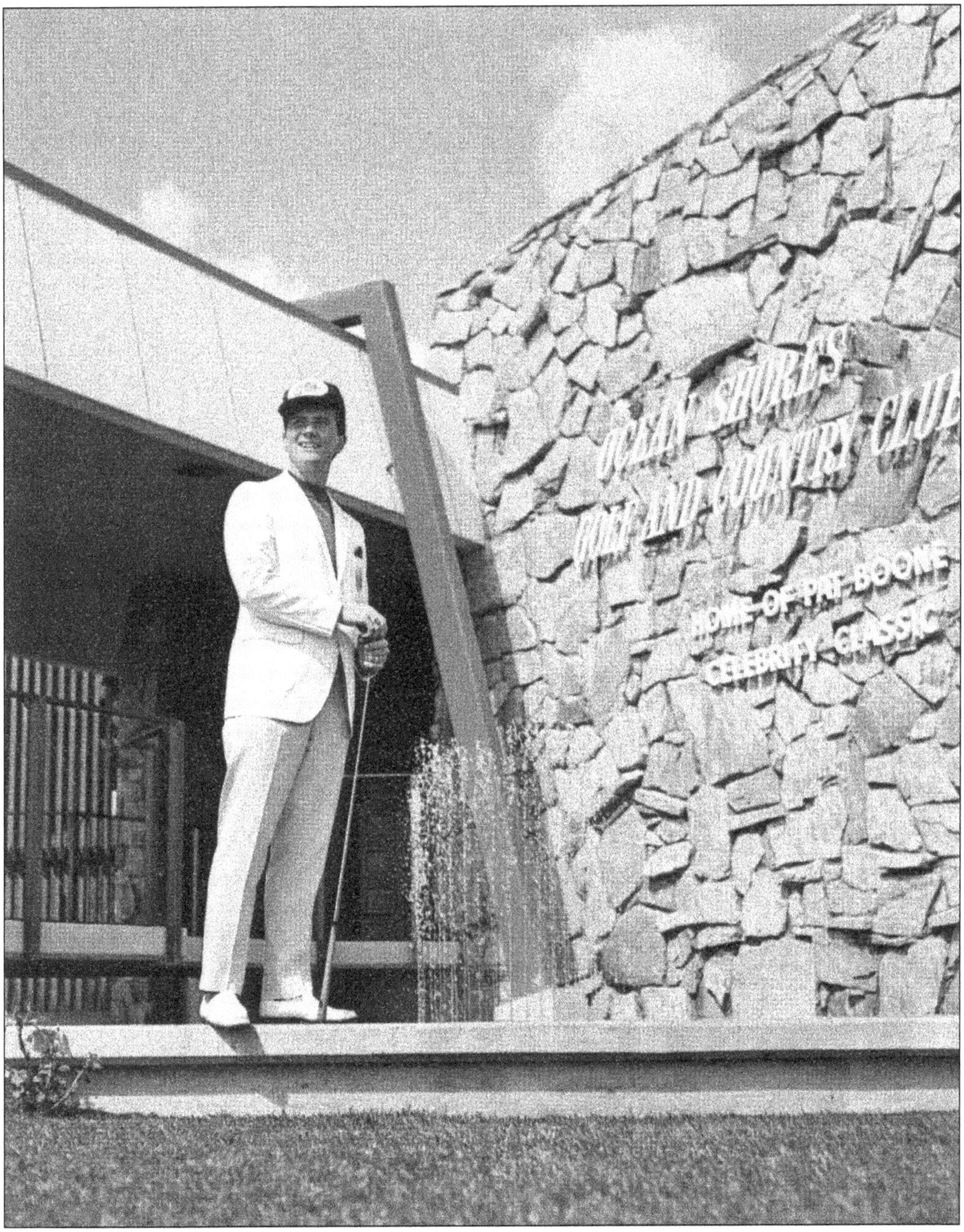

Classic celebrations have been at the heart of community life since the club's inception, but the most remembered was the Pat Boone PGA Golf Classic. Boone, singer star for Dot Records and host of the Golf Classics, posed in front of the $300,000 clubhouse built by Washington Development Company, who also built the city gates. The clubhouse, with its rock-clad exterior boasting eight fountains and decks surrounding two sides, had a view of the course. The first golf tournament in 1968 pushed construction down to the wire with the carpeting still being installed during registration. In November 1974, the city voted to issue $575,000 in bonds to purchase the Ocean Shores Golf Course with its airport facilities. (CHSGWC.)

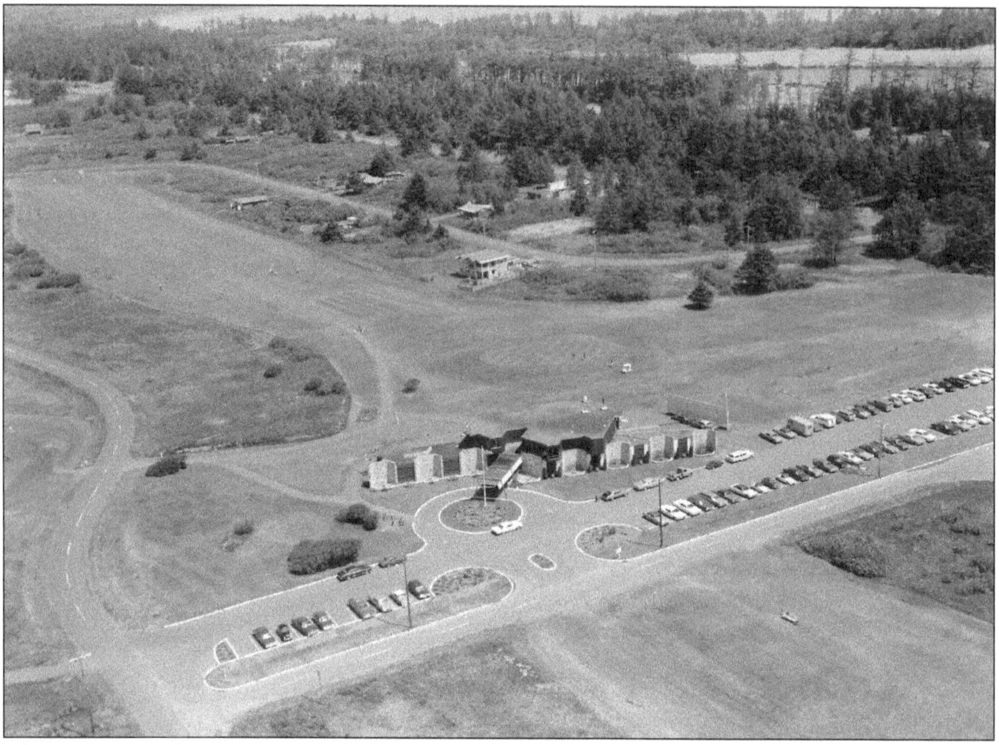

The original six-hole golf course that opened in 1962 was eventually expanded to a PGA-rated, 18-hole course with a portion of the course placed near the downtown airport. By 1969, it was the only 18-hole course on the West Coast of Washington State. (CHSGWC.)

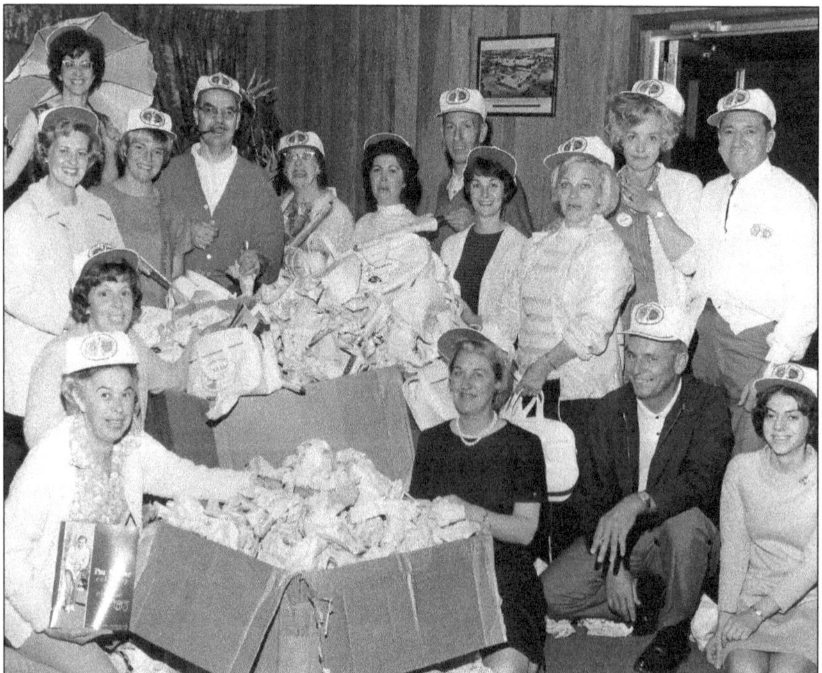

In 1967, this work crew showed off some of the "goodie bags" to illustrate a small portion of the effort required to bring the first Pat Boone Golf Classic to Ocean Shores. (CHSGWC.)

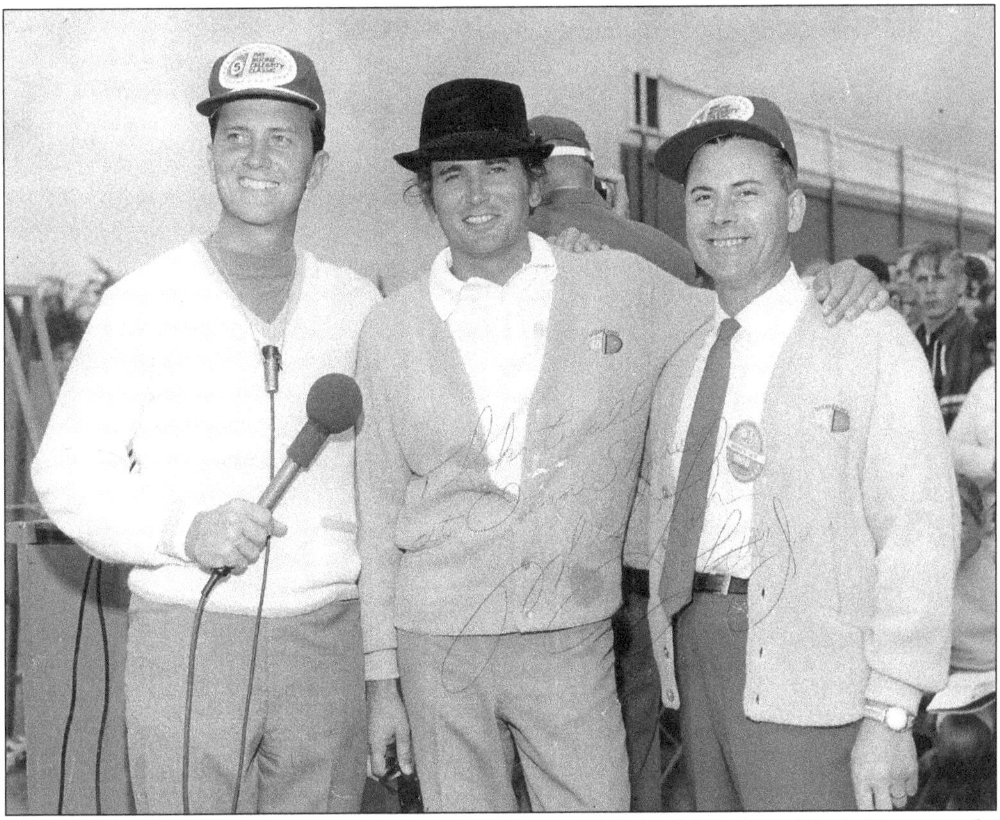

Posing for the camera are, from left to right, Pat Boone, Michael Landon of *Little House on the Prairie*, and an unidentified Gold Classic official. (CHSGWC.)

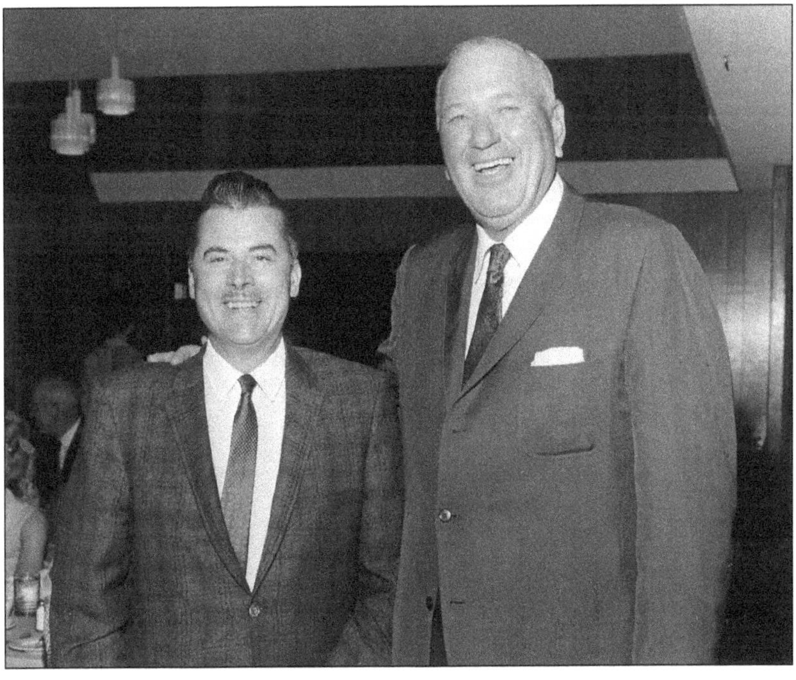

Moksha Smith (left), senior Partner in the Wendell-West Company, poses with Dizzy Dean at the 1969 Classic. (CHSGWC.)

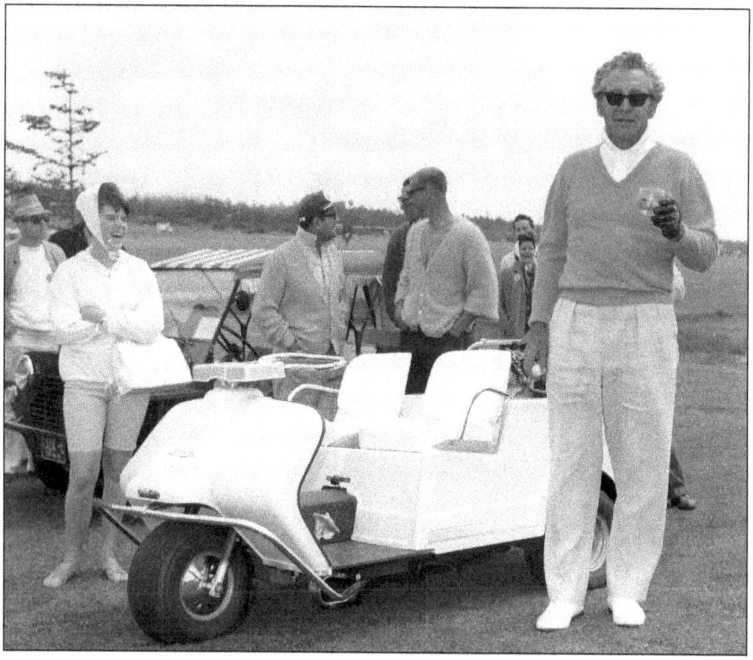

Forest Tucker (right) was the star of television's *F Troop*. (CHSGWC.)

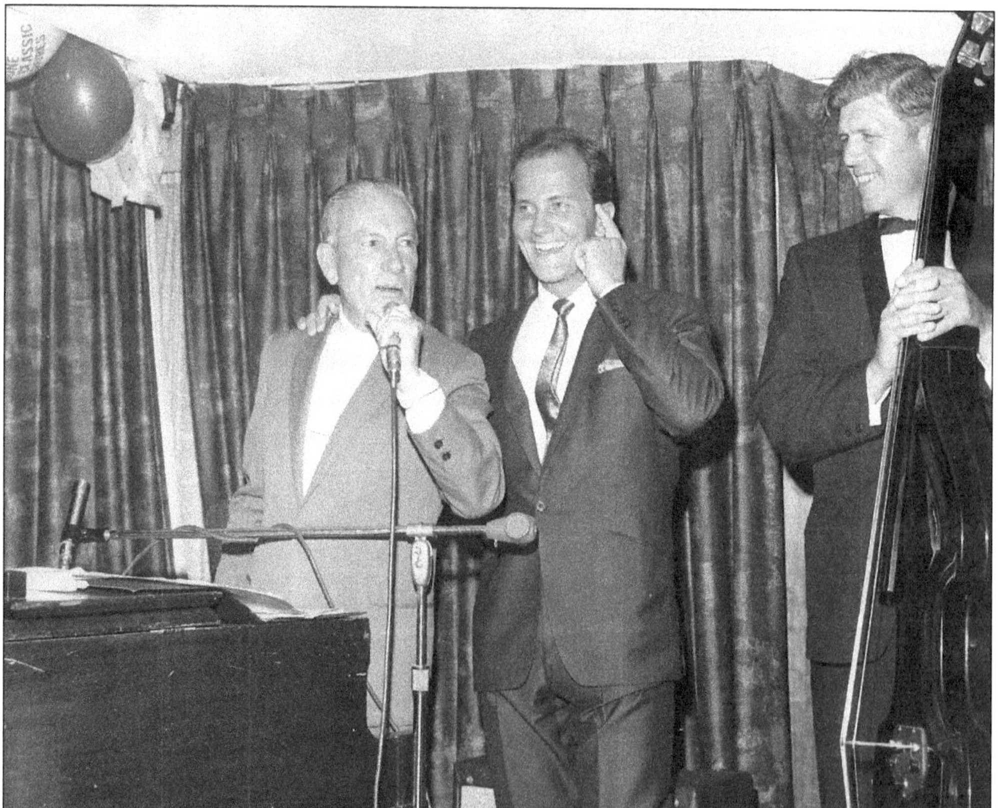

Hoagie Carmicheal (left) and Pat Boone, on stage at the Ocean Shores Inn, engage the crowd. (CHSGWC.)

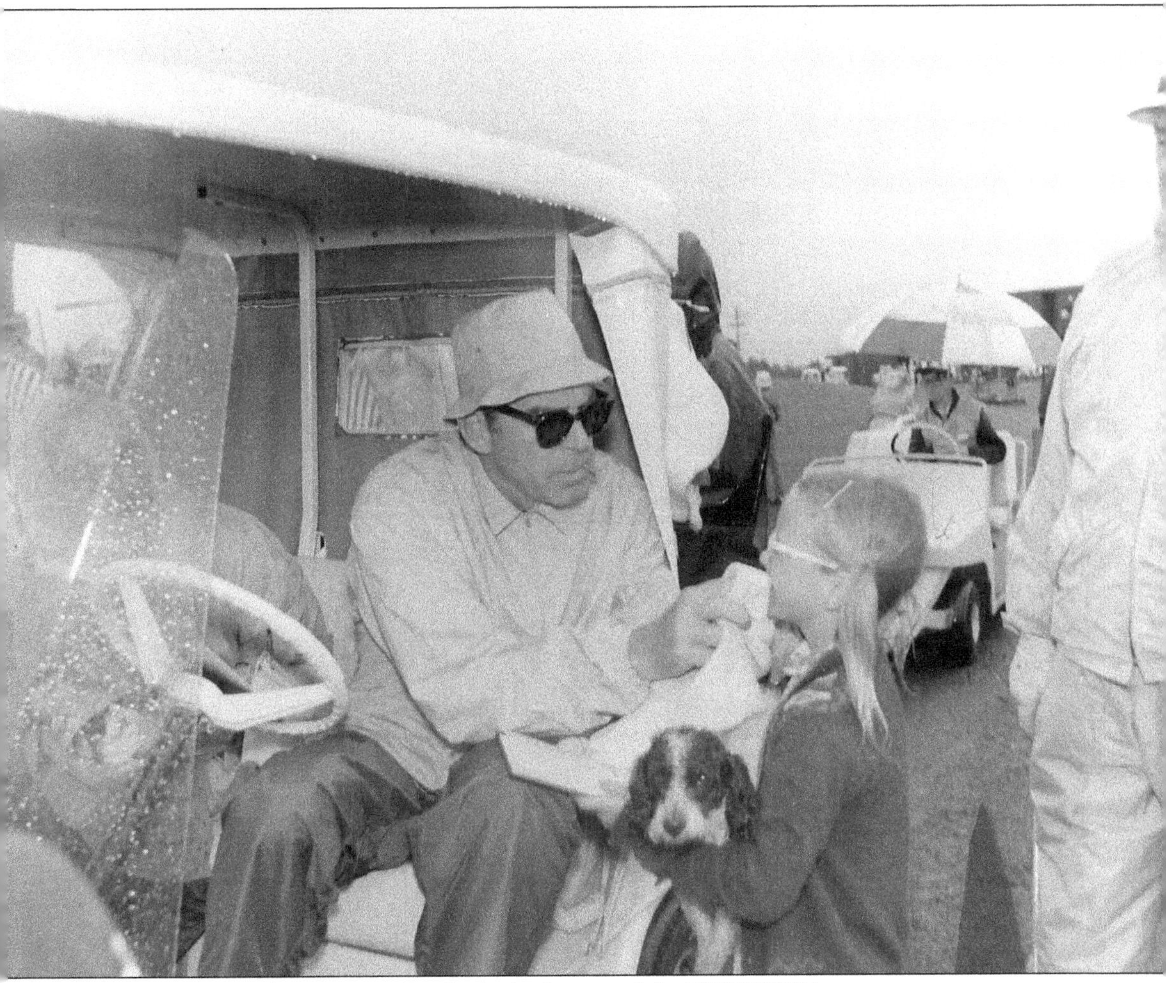

Fred McMurray takes time out for the little things in life. (CHSGWC.)

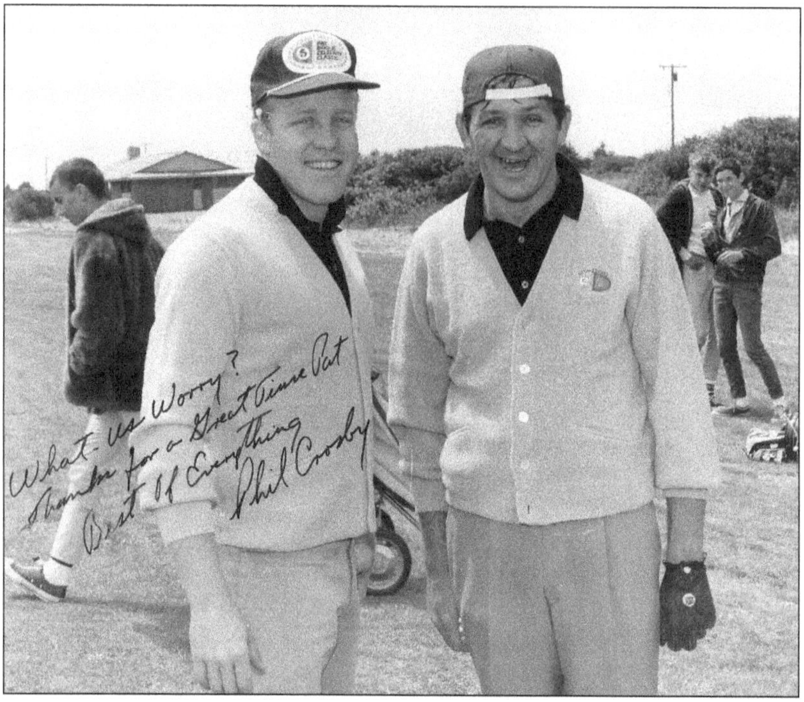

Phil Crosby (left) and George Lindsey (Goober Pyle of *The Andy Griffith Show*) truly enjoyed the golf and the crowds. (CHSGWC.)

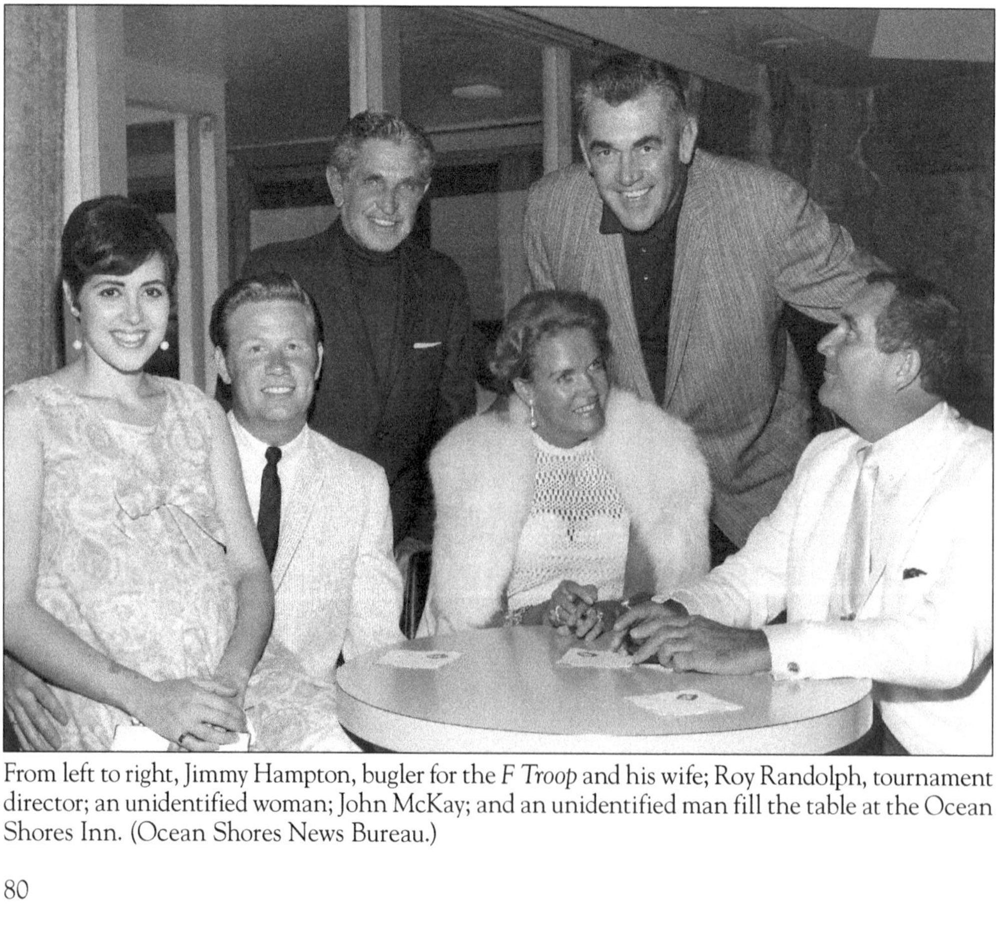

From left to right, Jimmy Hampton, bugler for the *F Troop* and his wife; Roy Randolph, tournament director; an unidentified woman; John McKay; and an unidentified man fill the table at the Ocean Shores Inn. (Ocean Shores News Bureau.)

Joe Namath (right) was eagerly sought after for photographs such as this one taken with unidentified people. (CHSGWC.)

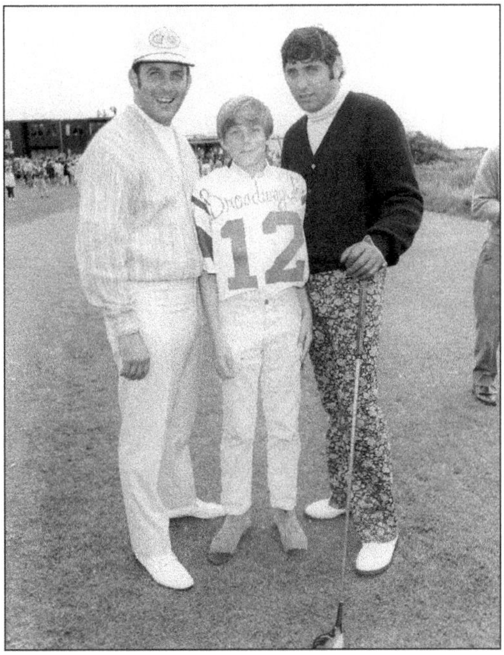

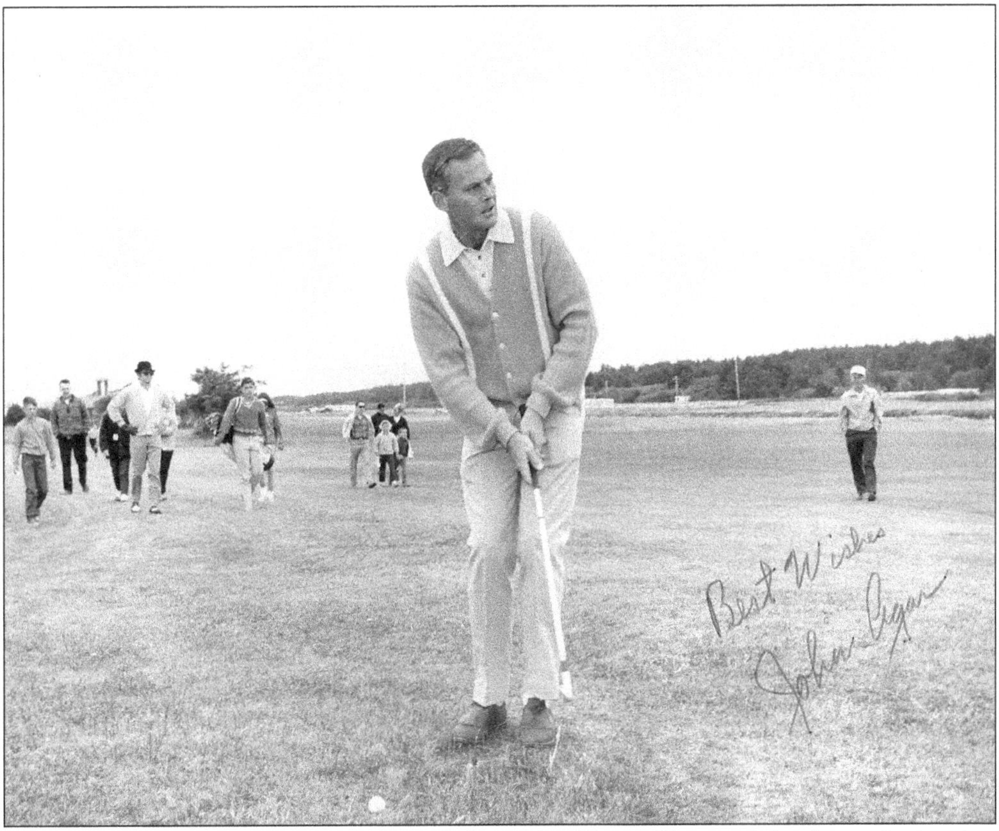

John Agar, the star of many westerns, including John Wayne films, and the former husband of Shirley Temple, spent a lot of time with the tournament folks. (CHSGWC.)

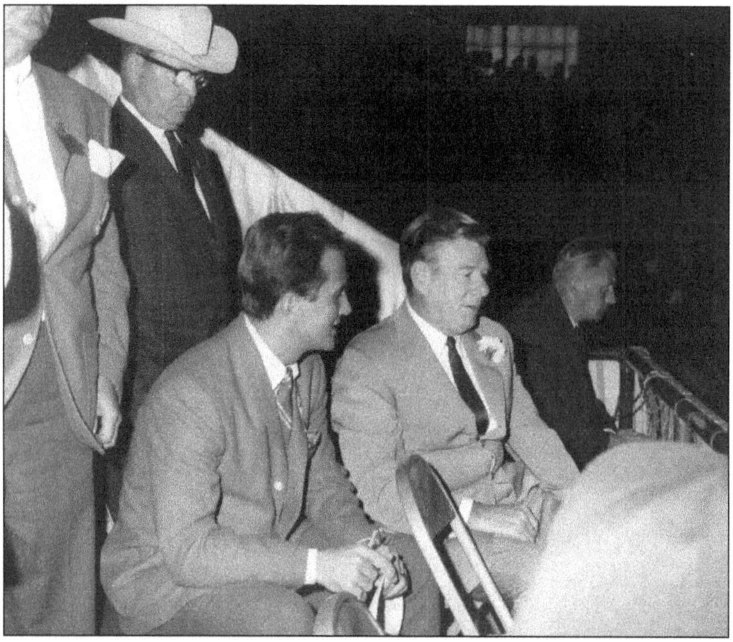

Pictured here are Pat Boone (left) and Arthur Godfrey. (CHSGWC.)

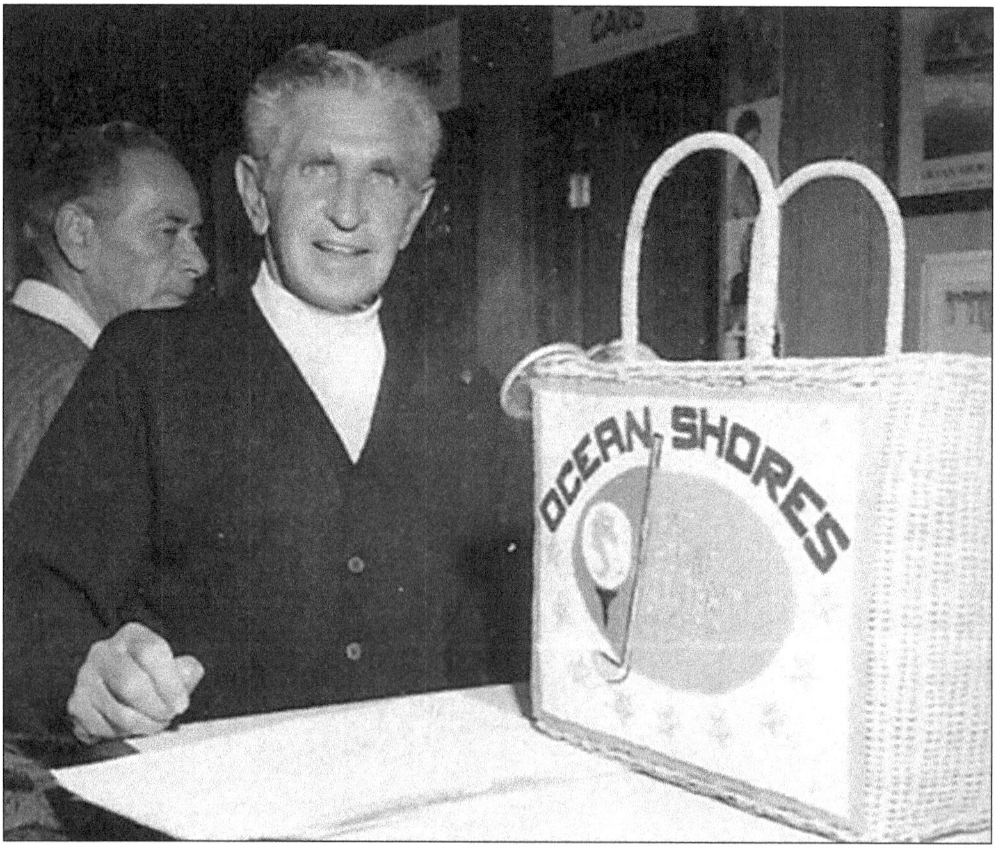

Bob Steele, a popular participant in the Classic Golf games, displays the seashore grass basket full of goodies given to the contestants. (CHSGWC.)

Bill Bixby and Shug Fisher were two of the hardworking event coordinators. (CHSGWC.)

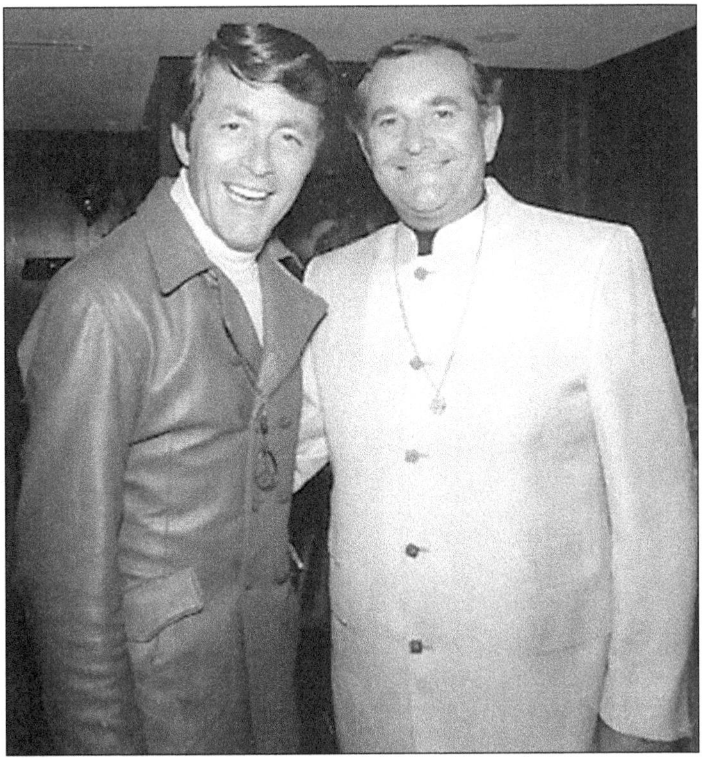

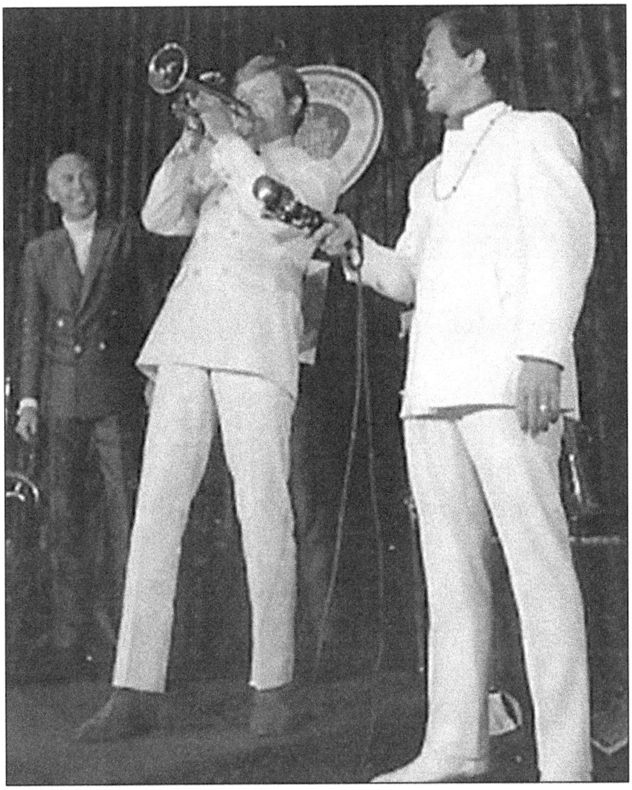

Jimmy Hampton of the *F Troop* plays the bugle for Pat Boone (CHSGWC.)

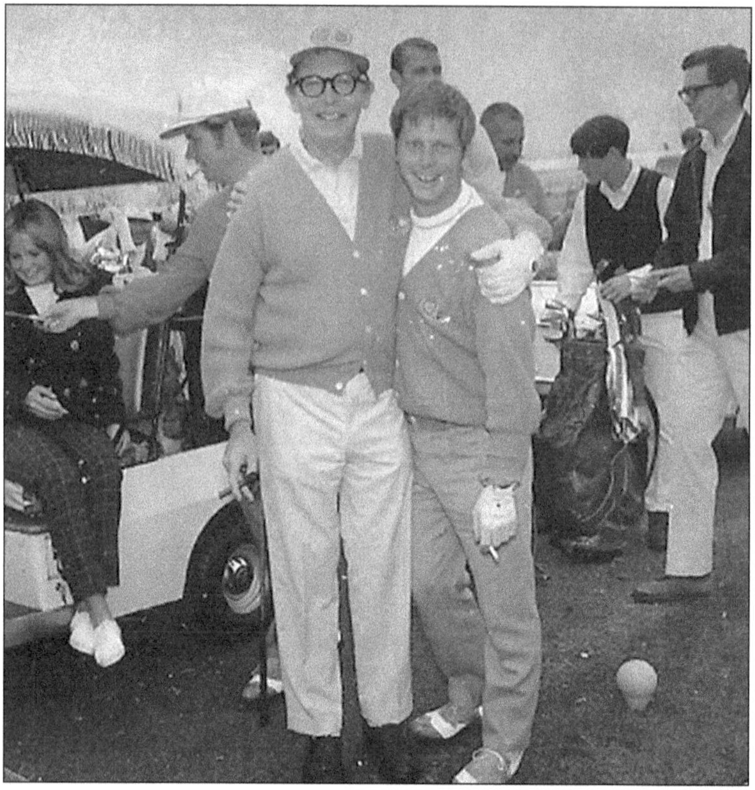

Milton Berle and Robert Morse (*Carol Burnett Show*) mugged for the camera. (CHSGWC.)

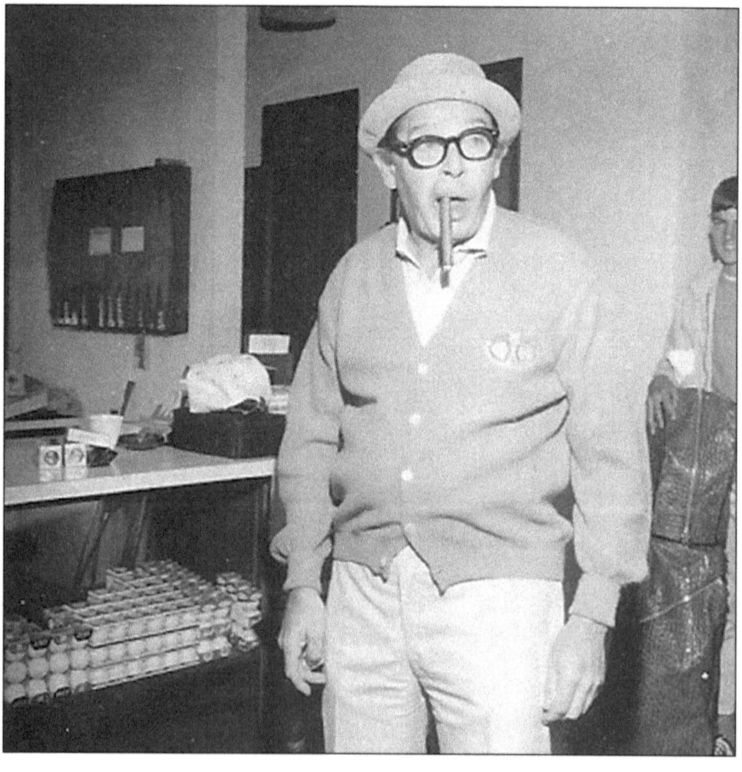

Milton "Uncle Milty" Berle took his golf seriously compared to his comedic television star persona. (CHSGWC.)

The Pat Boone family, shown here in 1978, was down to earth. The girls traveled with the folks, and mom Shirley Boone could be counted on to participate in events as emcee for fashion shows. (CHSGWC.)

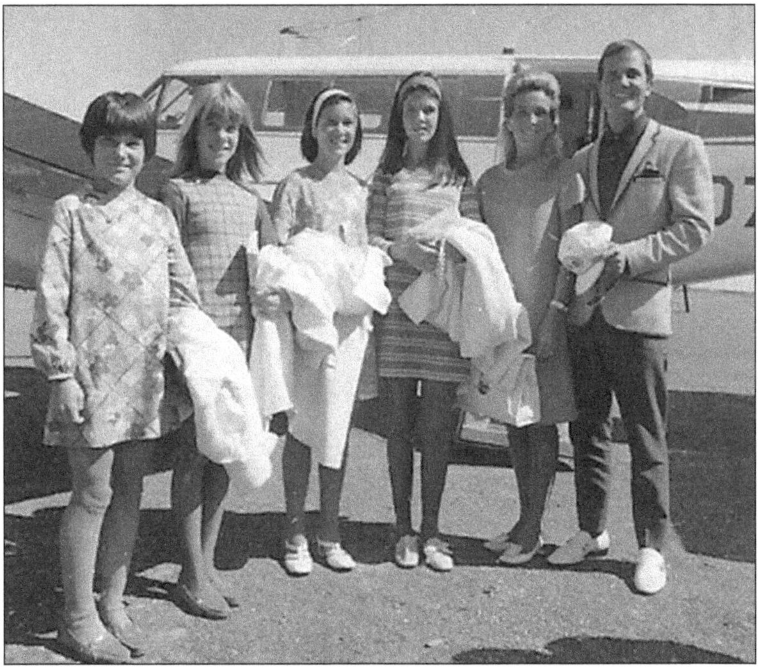

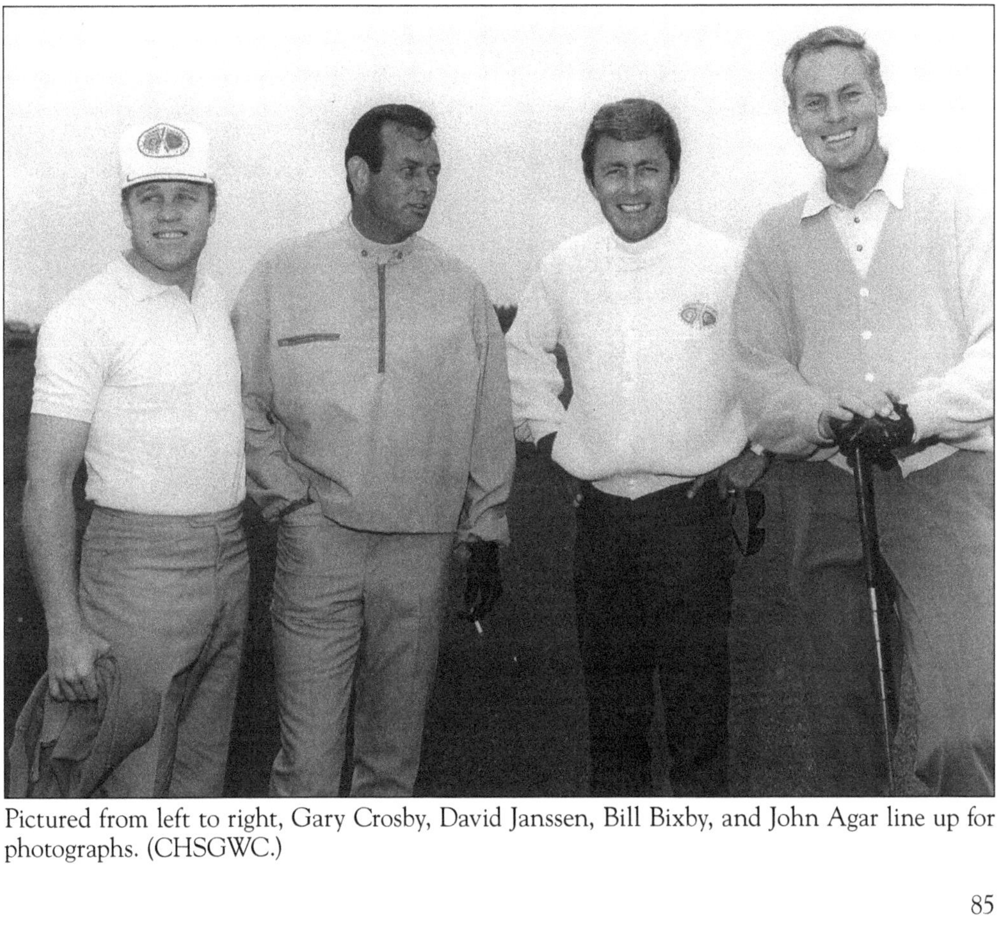

Pictured from left to right, Gary Crosby, David Janssen, Bill Bixby, and John Agar line up for photographs. (CHSGWC.)

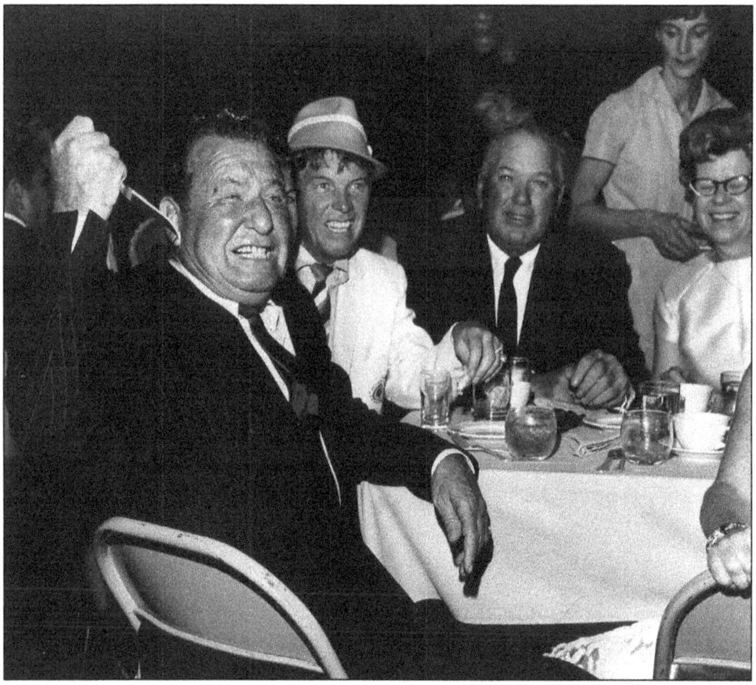

Phil Harris goes after the cameraman while, from left to right, Jack Ross, Dizzy Dean, and an unidentified woman enjoy the humor. (CHSGWC.)

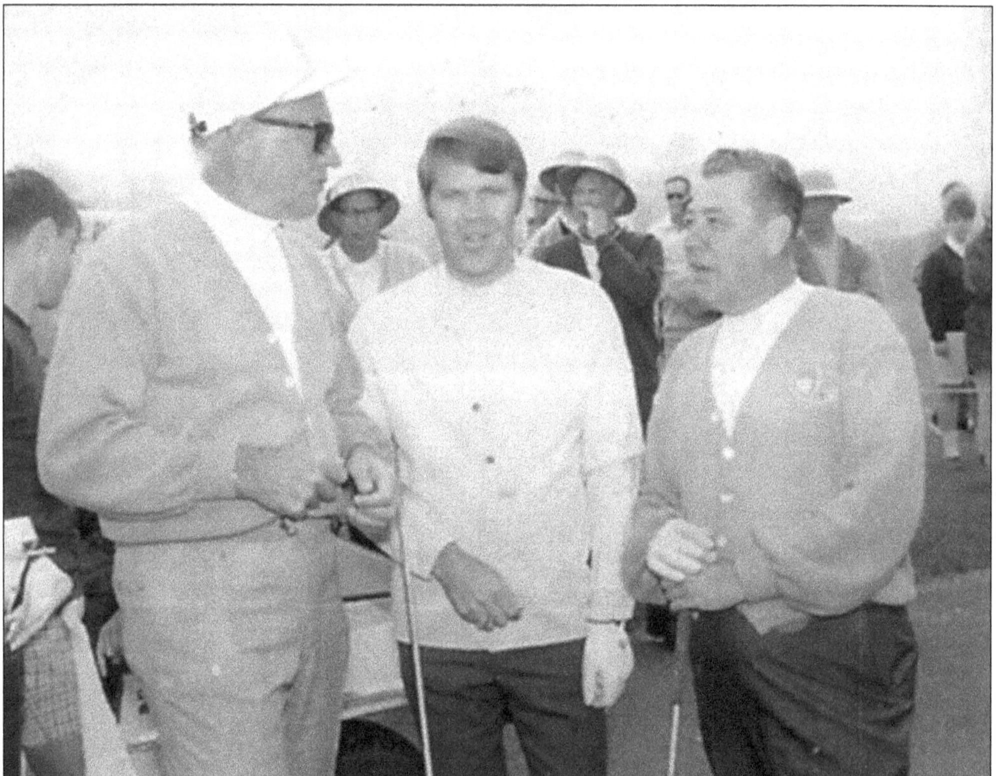

Bob Wilke (left), Glen Campbell (center), and Moksha Smith discuss how the day of golf is going. (CHSGWC.)

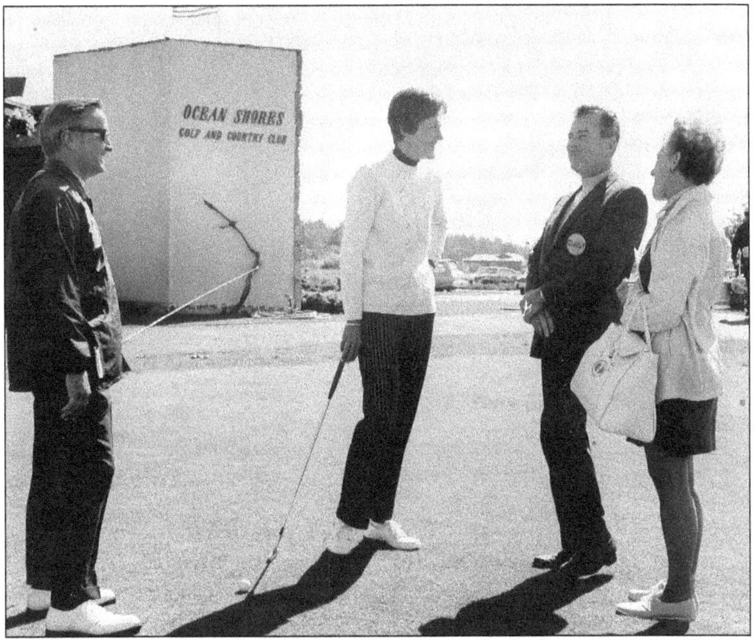

Kathy Whitworth, the 1968 Ladies Professional Golf Association's leading money winner with $48,379.50 (an all-time record), is pictured here with Mr. and Mrs. Moksha Smith. (CHSGWC.)

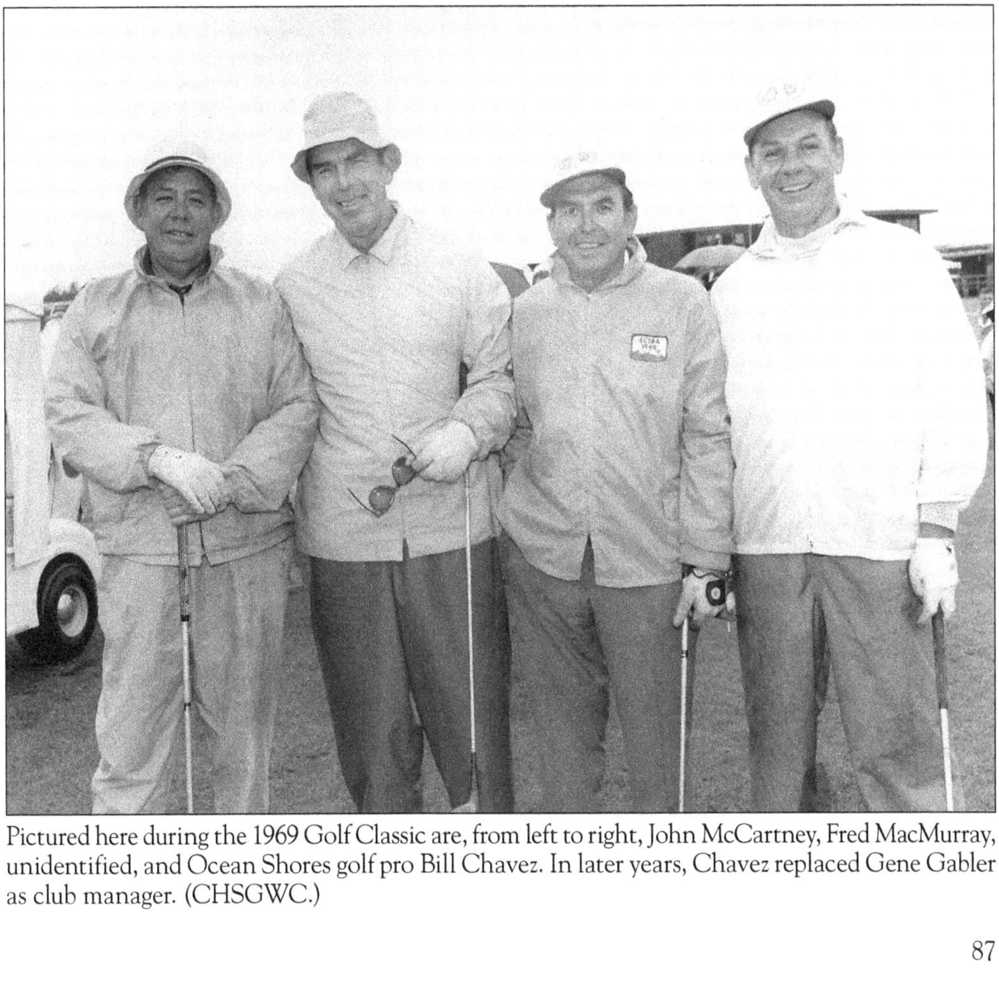

Pictured here during the 1969 Golf Classic are, from left to right, John McCartney, Fred MacMurray, unidentified, and Ocean Shores golf pro Bill Chavez. In later years, Chavez replaced Gene Gabler as club manager. (CHSGWC.)

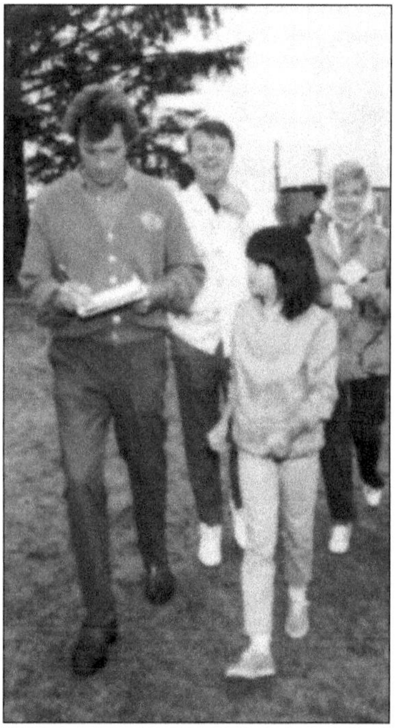

Clint Eastwood, *Rawhide* star, was the object of 1969 autograph seekers. (CHSGWC.)

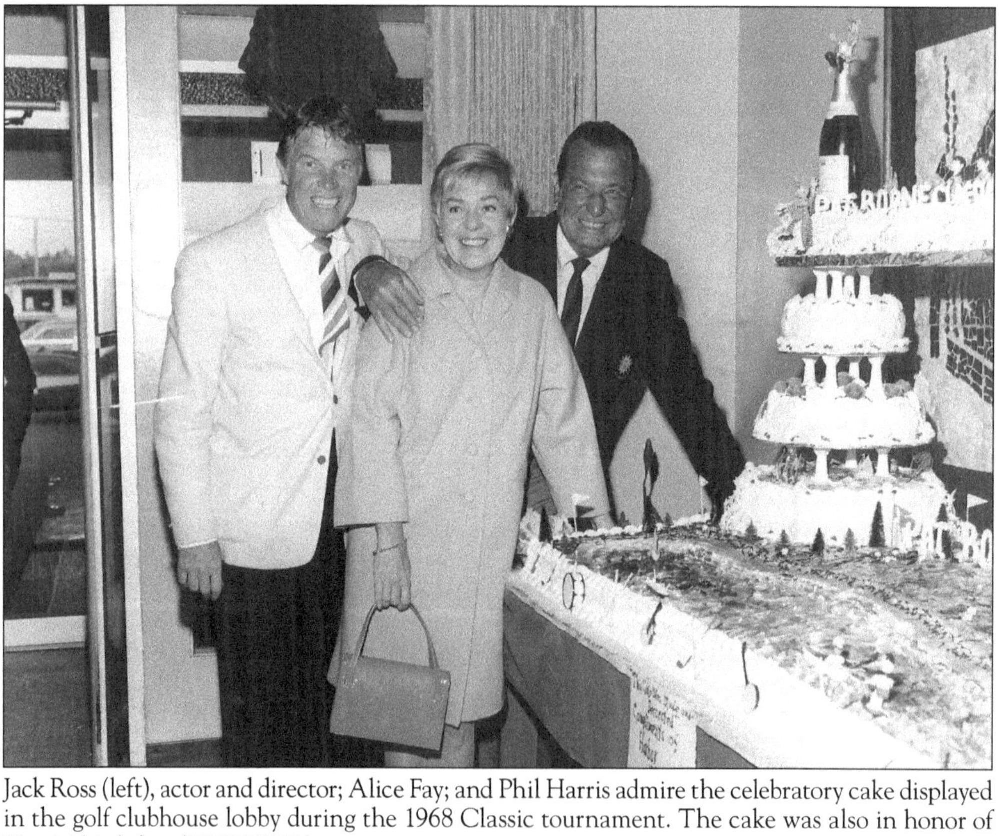

Jack Ross (left), actor and director; Alice Fay; and Phil Harris admire the celebratory cake displayed in the golf clubhouse lobby during the 1968 Classic tournament. The cake was also in honor of Harris' birthday. (CHSGWC.)

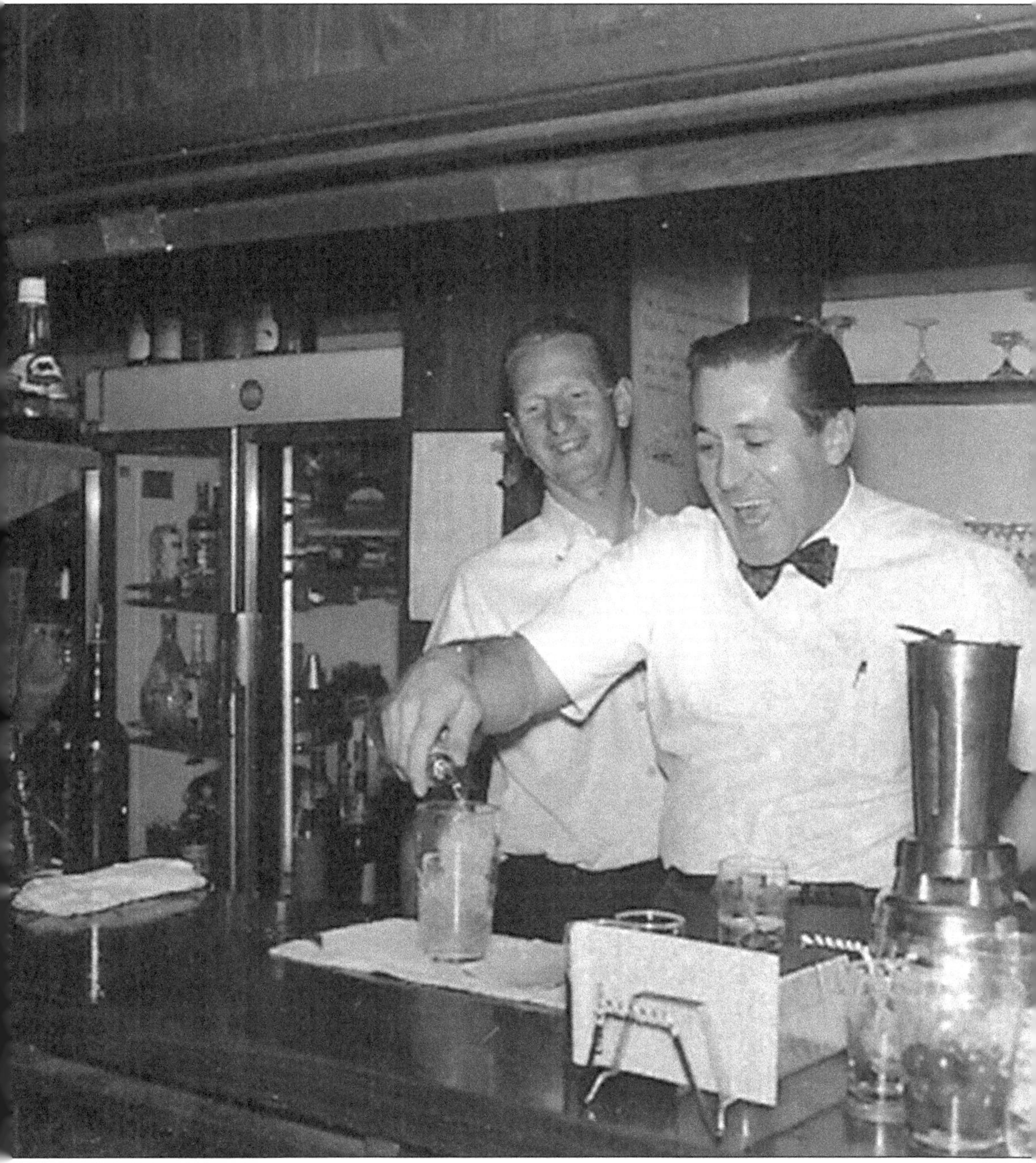

Bartenders Al Nyquist (foreground) and Ed Aho were experienced in handling crowds of starstruck folks as well as discretely handling a few of the stars who celebrated a little too much. (CHSGWC.)

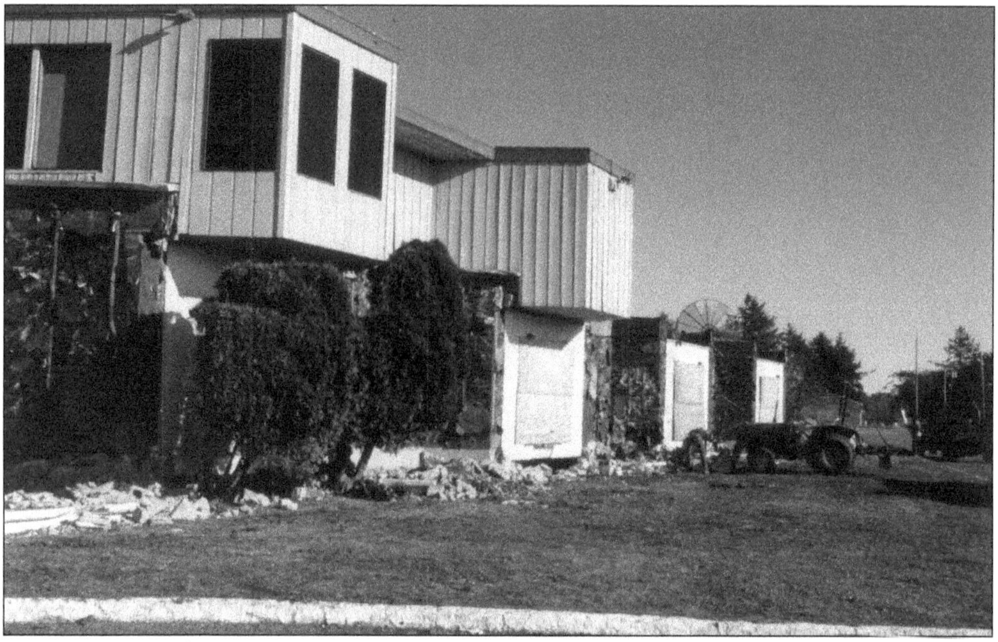

It was a sad day when the golf club building, with its coffee shop, pro shop, spacious bathrooms, and the Misfit Restaurant, was torn down to be replaced by a very mundane building housing the pro shop and course offices. The stone sign for the Ocean Shores Golf Course was salvaged from the old building's stone facing. (CHSGWC.)

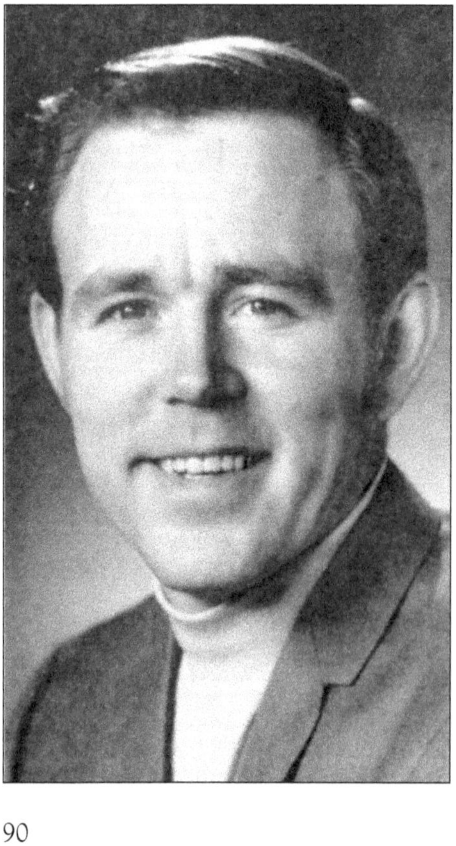

Golf pro Roy E. Eckersley was the host professional for the 1970 Wendell-West Invitational. Gary Baxter was assistant pro and Gary Hulet was shopman. Eckersley came to the Ocean Shores Golf Club on April 1, 1970. He teethed on a golf tee in Scotland, and at the age of nine played under Mick Bailey, the most highly regarded of Scottish teaching professionals. In America he served as a teaching assistant at Milwaukee's North Shore Country Club while attending Marquette University. Eckersley came to Ocean Shores after teaching for Inglewood Country Club for six years. He initiated women's and youth golf clubs. Eckersley has served as a pro on cruise ships and currently as an official for numerous Northwest golf tournaments to keep on top of his love of the rules of golf. (CHSGWC.)

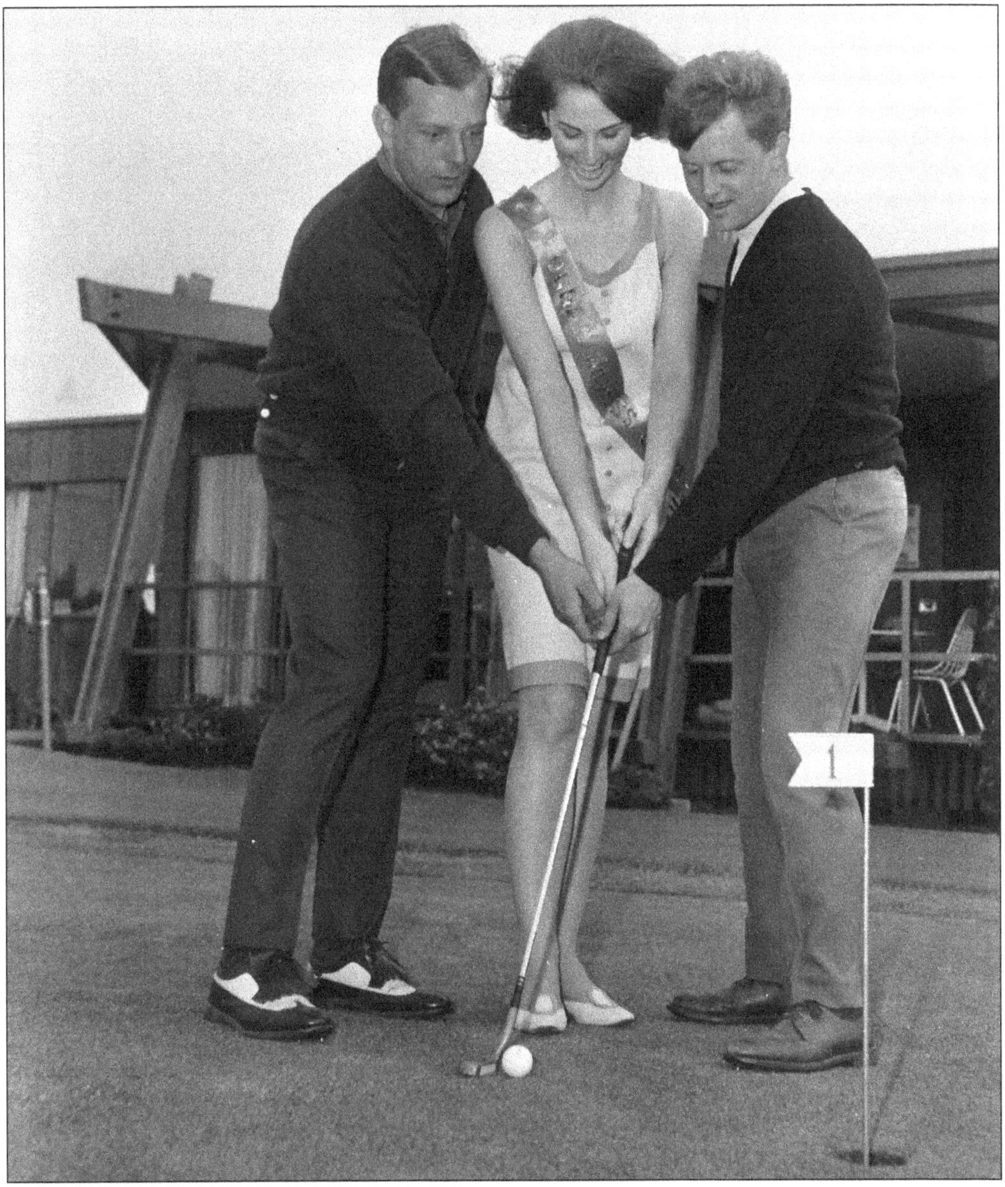

Two unidentified Sir Galahads assist Miss Ocean Shores, Shirley Keene, in getting ready for the Golf Classic tourney. (CHSGWC.)

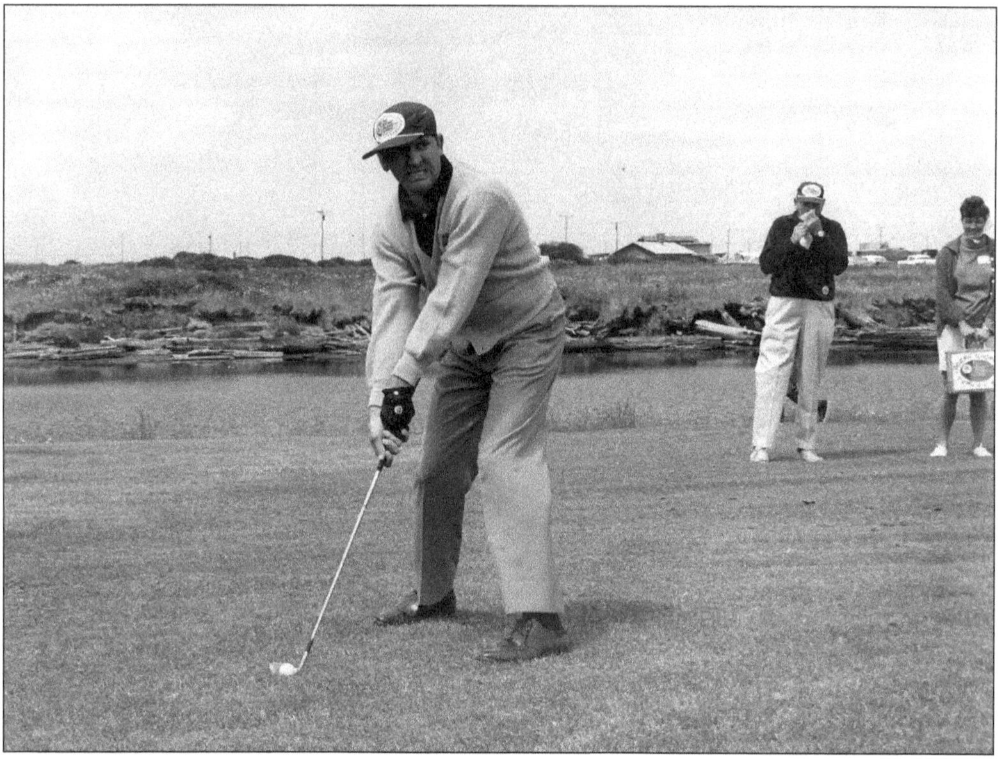

George Lindsey, Goober Pyle of *The Andy Griffith Show*, does not appear to like his shot. (CHSGWC.)

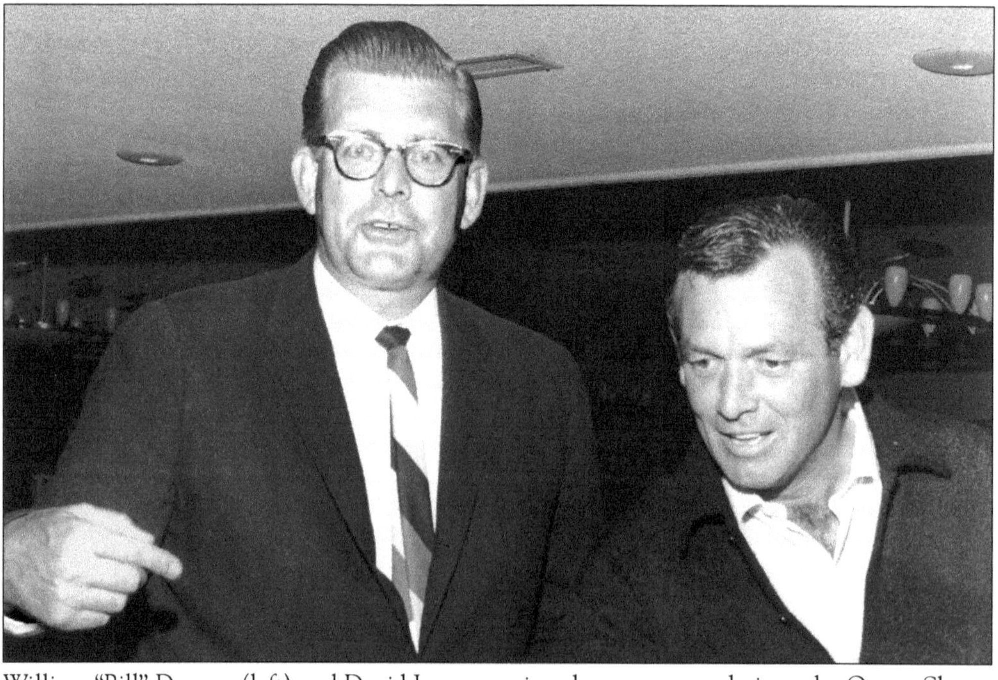

William "Bill" Devane (left) and David Janssen enjoyed some camaraderie at the Ocean Shores Golf Club's Misfit Restaurant. (CHSGWC.)

Leona LaBranch, better known to readers of Norah Berg's book *Lady on the Beach* as "Frenchy's wife," was an expert with a clam gun, as this photograph shows. (CHSGWC.)

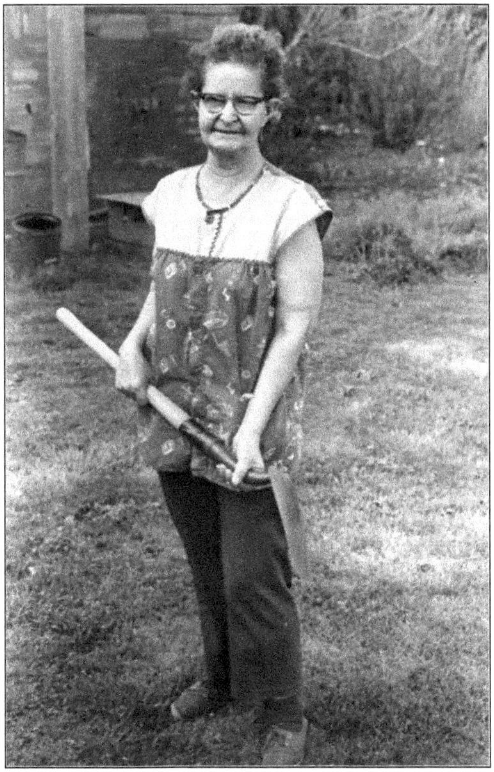

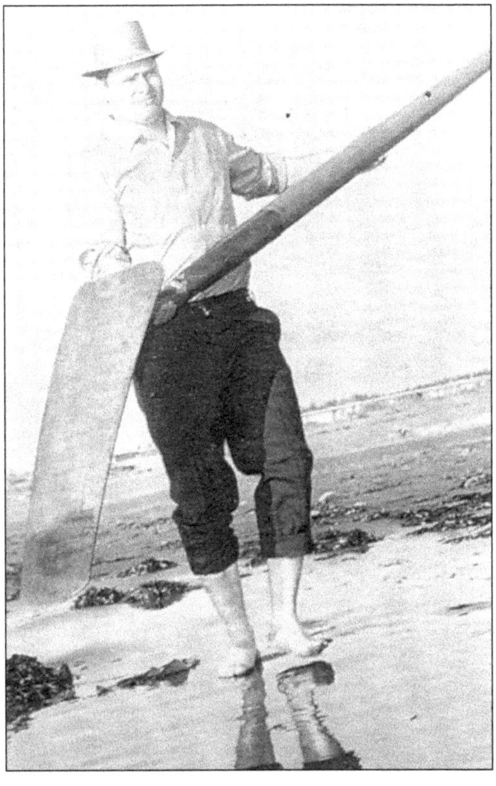

Ron Smith, a logger from Shelton, Washington, was the 1967 Clam Prix champion, receiving $500 and having his name engraved on the 12-foot clam gun. (CHSGWC.)

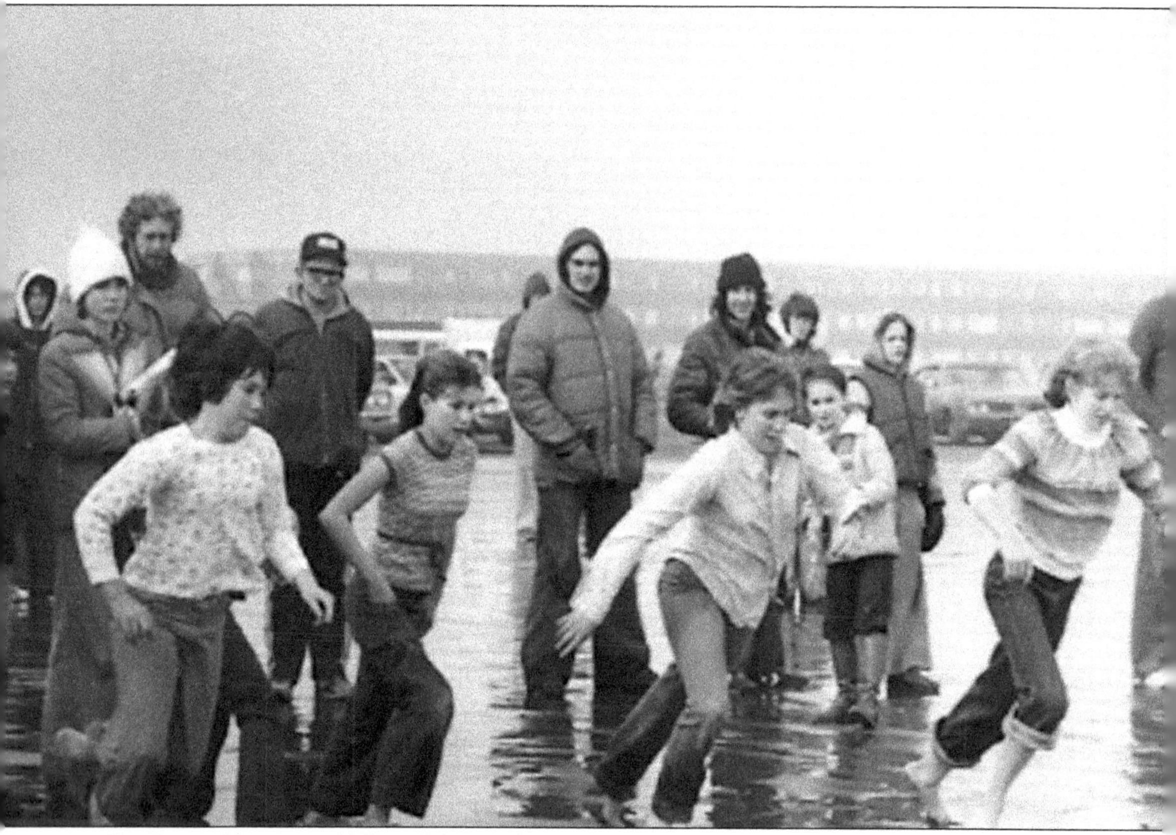

Fog Festival began in 1968 and featured a variety of activities, from the North American Mid-Winter Wading Championship races to a beer-keg toss, Clam Prix, Hobi Cat and dune buggy races, kick-the can, and the infamous wet T-shirt contest. The weather did not always cooperate for the festival, and in 1968, it was cancelled for four days when it was jinxed by sunshine. The Fog Festival drew the crowds to the beach to augment the tourism shoulder season. But it became too much of a good thing, with unruly crowds and overworked city, county, and state police officers unable to maintain crowd control. The city closed it down in the early 1980s. (Thorn Ward.)

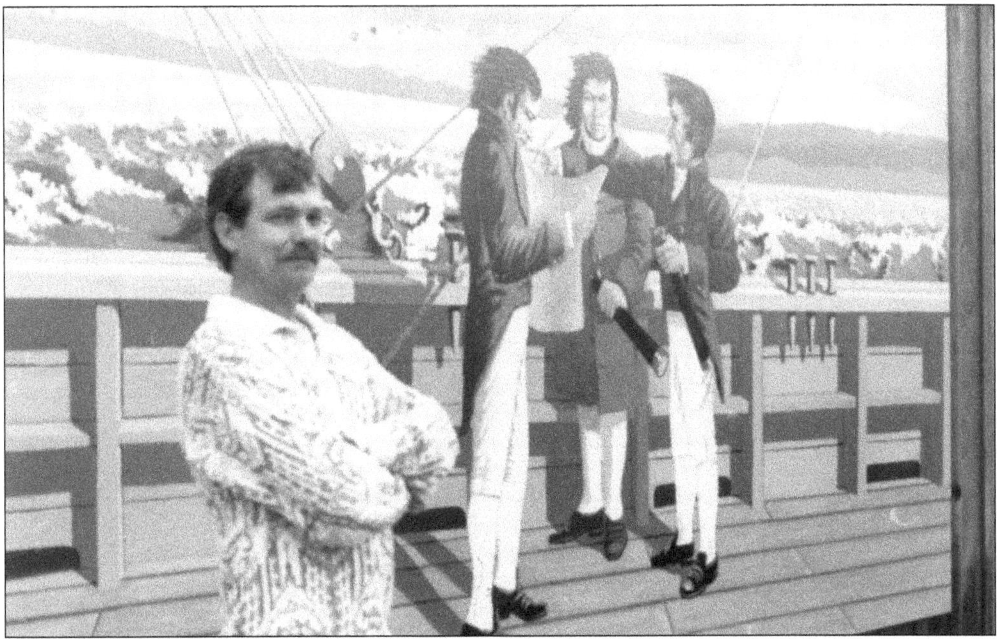

Dennis Hermey painted two of the Washington Centennial Celebration murals in downtown Ocean Shores. The one of Marjuli Gallery honored Capt. Robert Gray while the second, also located on the property of Marge McBride, showed Damon's Landing. (CHSGWC.)

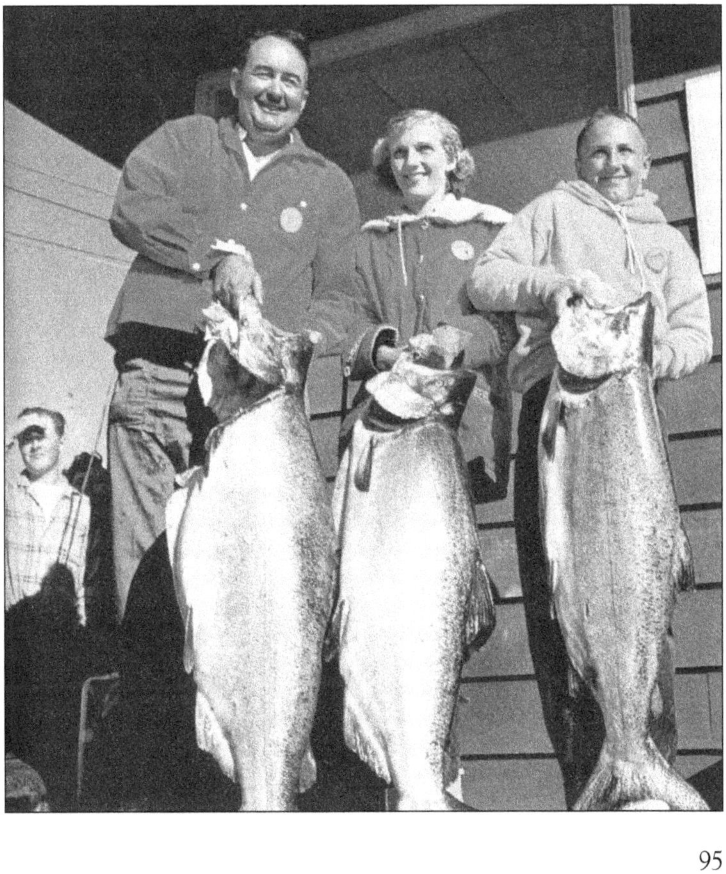

This was one happy family during the May 1970 boat show at the marina. While not as celebrity-centered as the golf tournaments, the boat show did feature Lt. Gov. John Cherbourg; Pat Boone; Len Sampson, Seattle radio and television personality; Miss Washington Susan Hyde; Miss Oregon Cynthia Lynn Harrison; and Miss Universe Laura Rae Smith. (CHSGWC.)

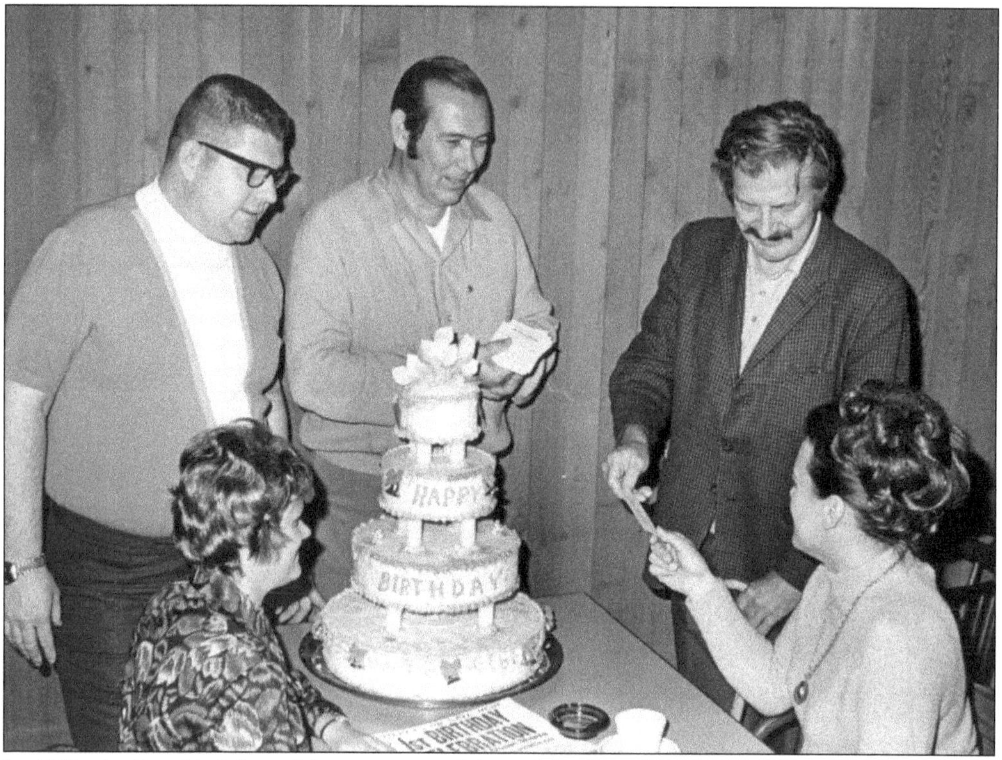

In 1971, the first birthday of the city was celebrated by, from left to right, Joan and Bill Marks, Lee Mayes, Bun Lewis, and an unidentified woman. (CHSGWC.)

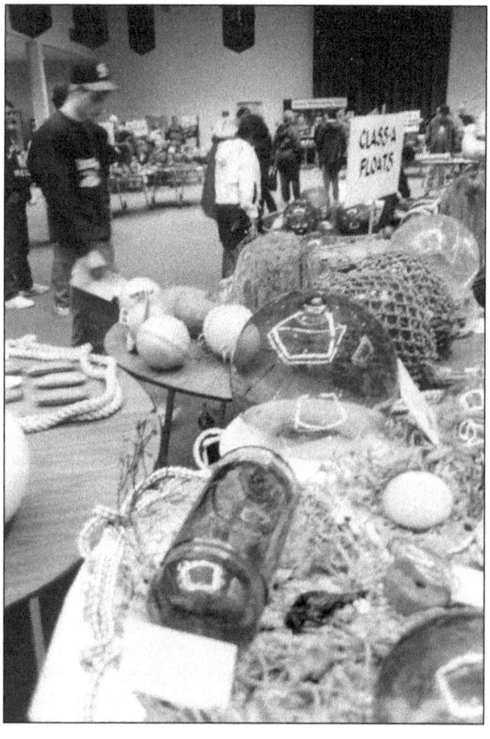

Drawing people from Alaska and the Pacific Rim, the Beachcomber's Fun Fair is a grown-ups' show 'n' tell time, a place to display glass fishing floats, flotsam and jetsam, bottles, shipwreck pieces, and whatever is found on the beach. The annual March show, open to all ages, was first organized by Carol Davis, Erma Bedilion, Gene Woodwick, and Al Rammer. (CHSGWC.)

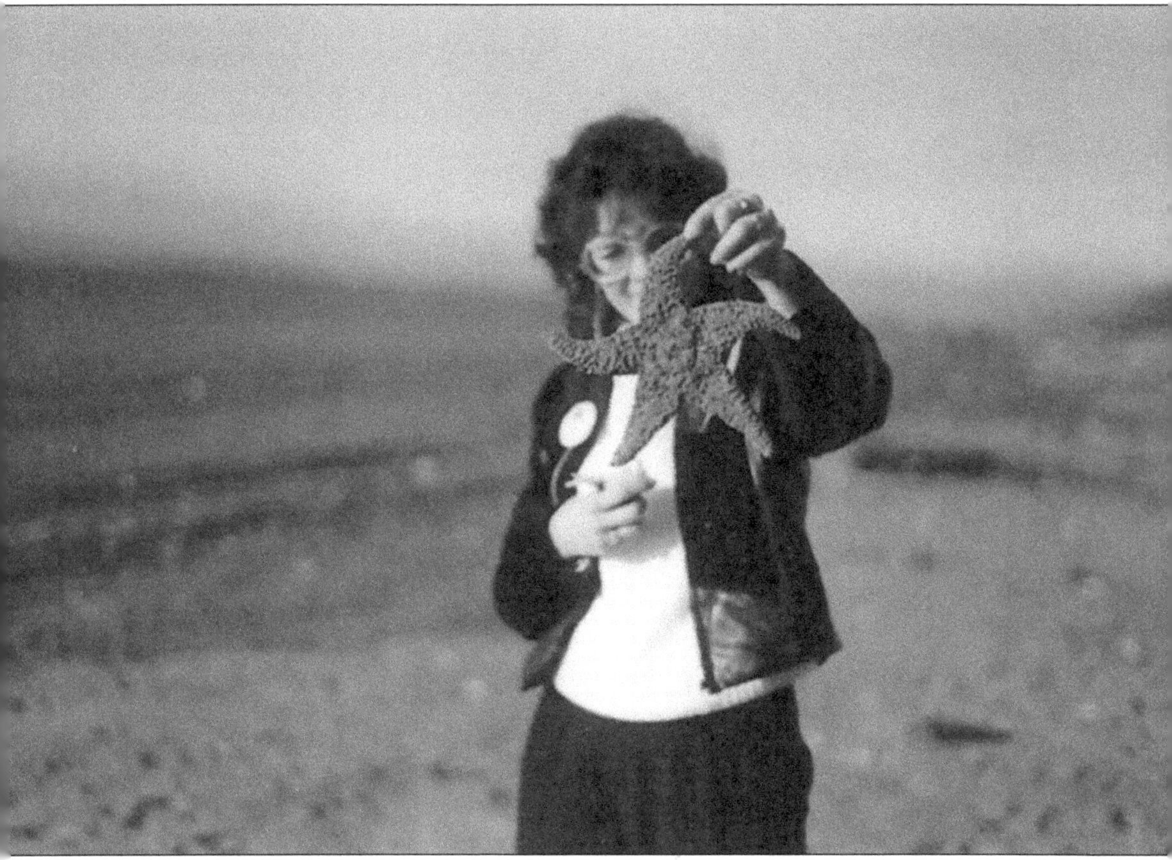

More than anything, folks like Lynelle Church just loved exploring the beach for flotsam, jetsam, and beach life. (CHSGWC.)

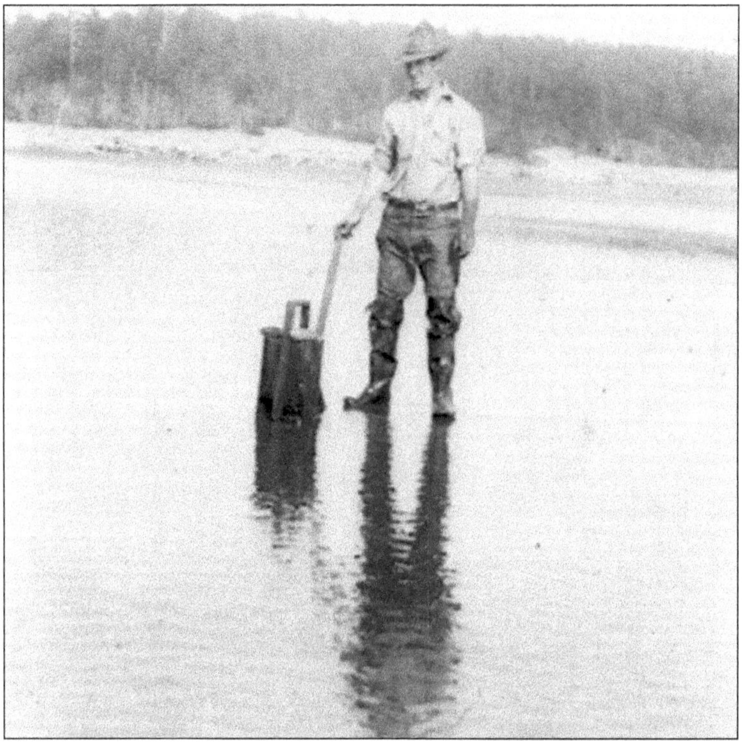

The timeless food gathering and recreational activity, digging razor clams, still draws thousands of folks to the Ocean Shores beaches for season openings. In 1925, Andy Williamson showed off his digging prowess, which was equaled by his brothers, Leon and Fred. Note the equipment of the kerosene can and a homemade clam gun. Diggers modified by shortening the handle and narrowing the blade for clam guns. (CHSGWC.)

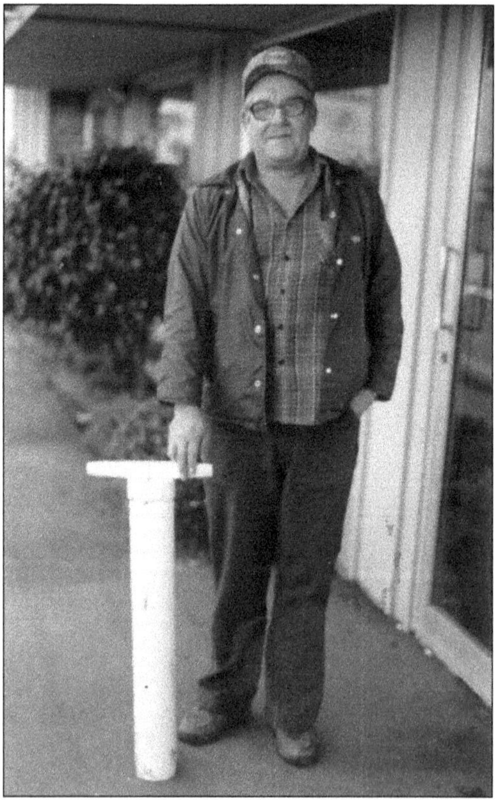

In 1988, George Vanderel invented his own PVC pipe clam gun to aid in digging clams for handicapped folks. He produced numerous guns for friends and neighbors. (CHSGWC.)

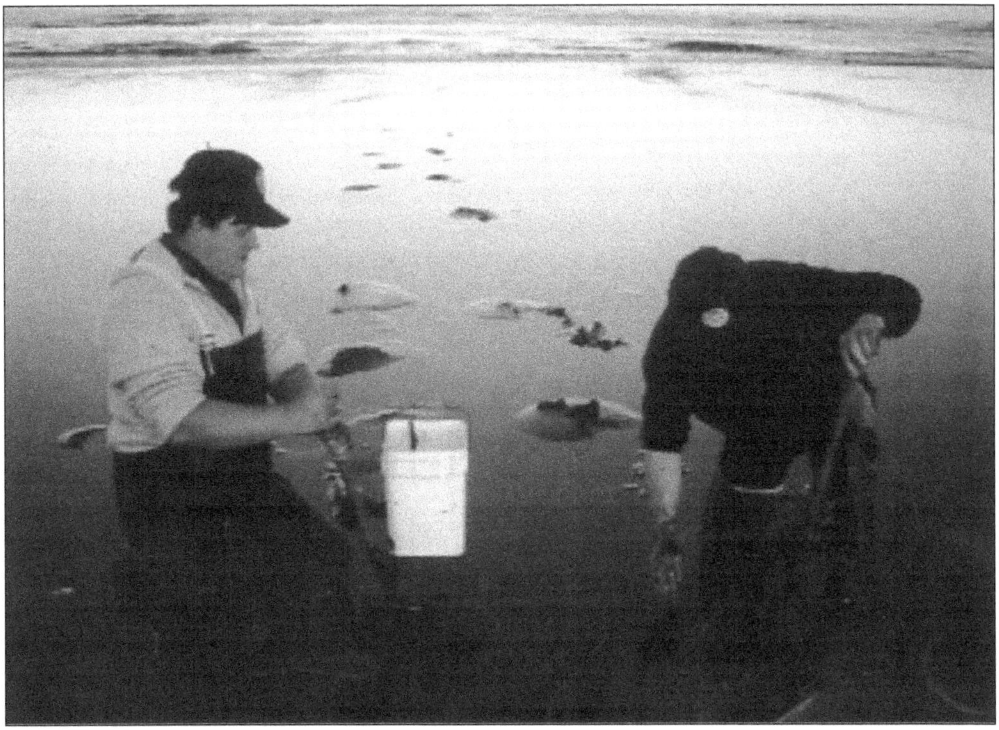

Washington Department of Fish and Wildlife (WDFW) biologists conduct annual test digs on the Ocean Shores beaches, such as this 1981 venture. (CHSGWC.)

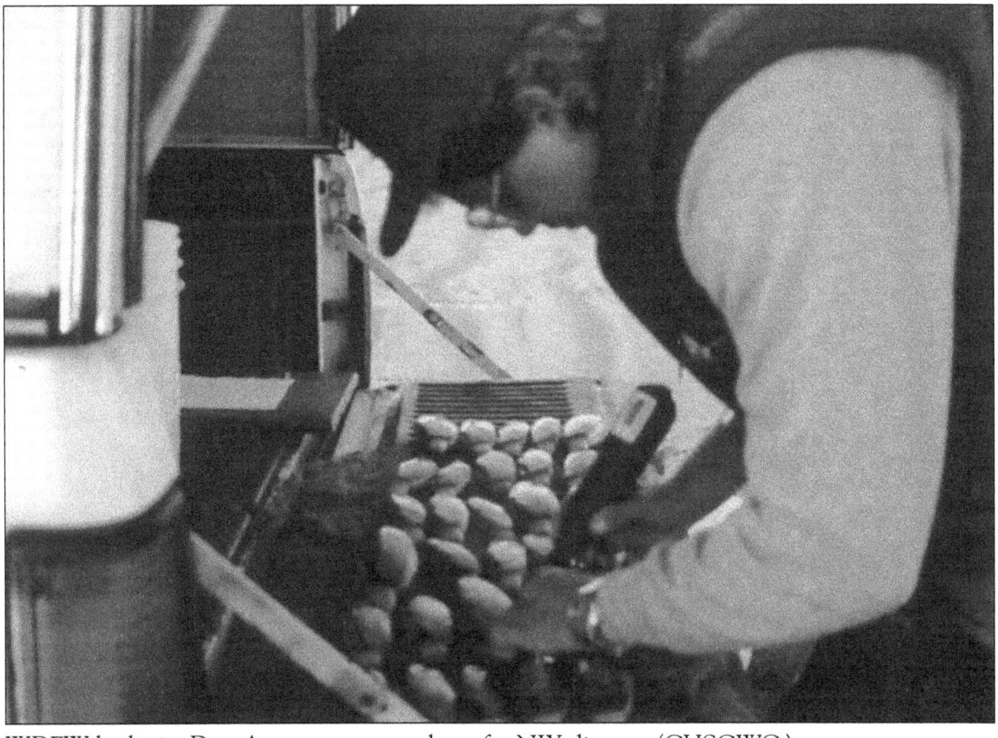

WDFW biologist Dan Ayers tests razor clams for NIX disease. (CHSGWC.)

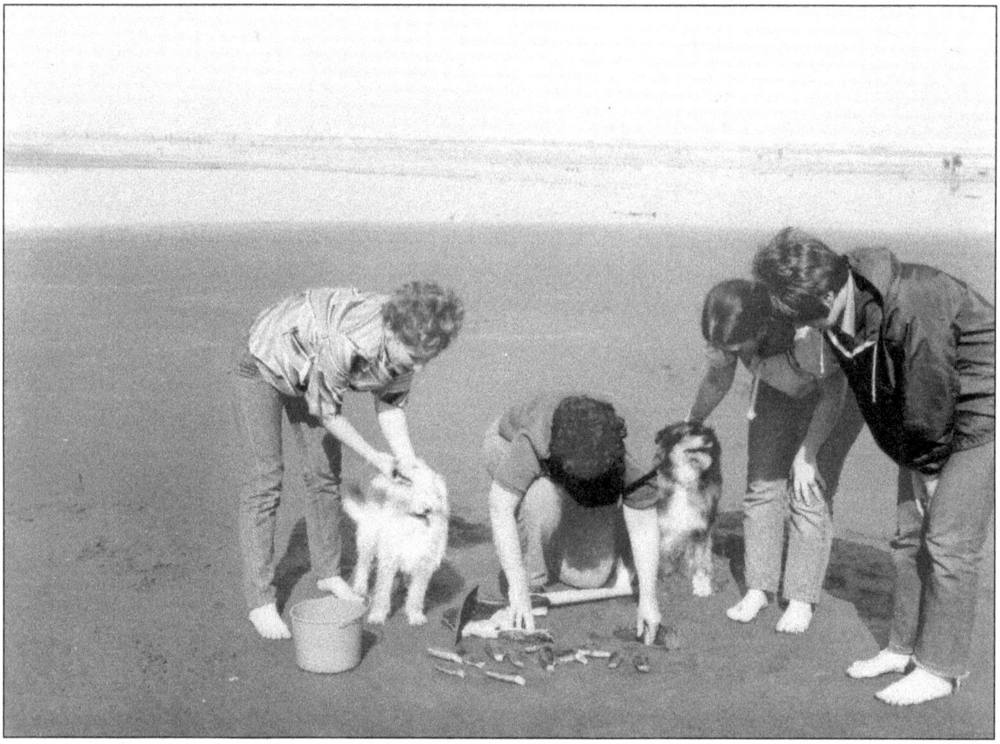

The family of Kyle and Betty Smith avidly participates in a hunt for the elusive bivalve, the razor clam, on the beaches of Ocean Shores. (CHSGWC.)

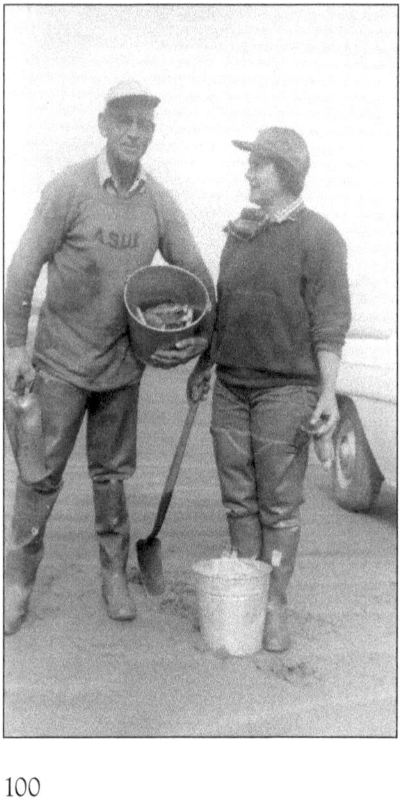

These 1950s-era diggers wear the classic gear of the day on this razor clam trip. (CHSGWC.)

Early residents of the area gathered oysters from the Usual and Accustomed places of Native Americans. The same lands are leased today by the Quinault Nation for commercial beds. (CHSGWC.)

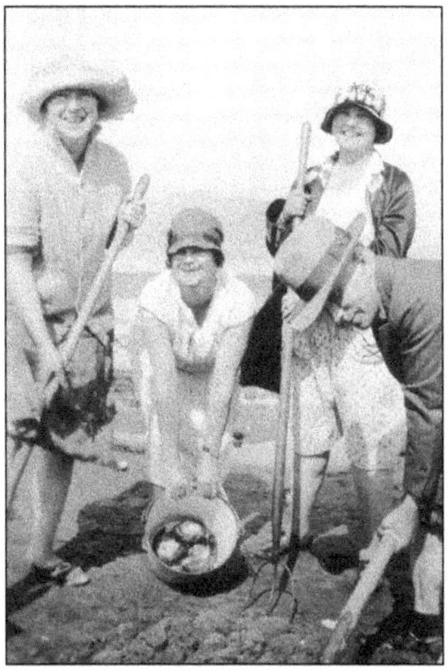

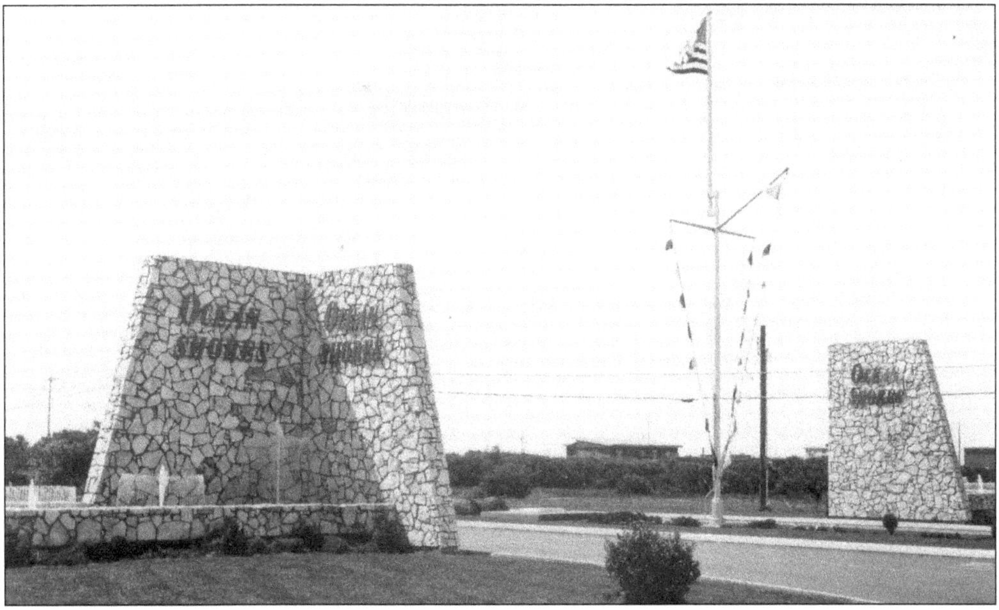

City gates of white stone with gushing fountains, in keeping with the California architecture of the development, and a nautical flag pole welcomed visitors to the city entrance and to the local business area. The first city election was held in 1969, with the new members being Paul Barbara, Al Couglin, Bill Ratliff, Jim Gray, Jerry Gifford, and George Harrison; however, they never got to hold office. A donnybrook over incorporating the city broke out that ended with the city folks voting 223 to the developers' tally of 38. After the city folks won, LaVerne McCrosky's anthem to the city, "Ocean Shores," could be sung. McCroskey had already gone nationwide with the song by performing it on the *Gong Show* in 1968. He was again a television celebrity when he sang the song to Willard Scott on the NBC *Today Show* when the city was celebrating its 20th birthday. The first council meetings were held at the Ocean Shores Inn with comanagers Cabot Dow and Dick Cushing on loan from the City of Bellevue for three months. John O'Rourke, Seattle attorney, was temporary council. The police department was contracted through the county. The National Bank of Commerce, Sea-First, and Pacific National Bank were all named official city depositories until permitted by the Federal Comptroller of Currency. (Kyle Smith, Smith Western Post Card.)

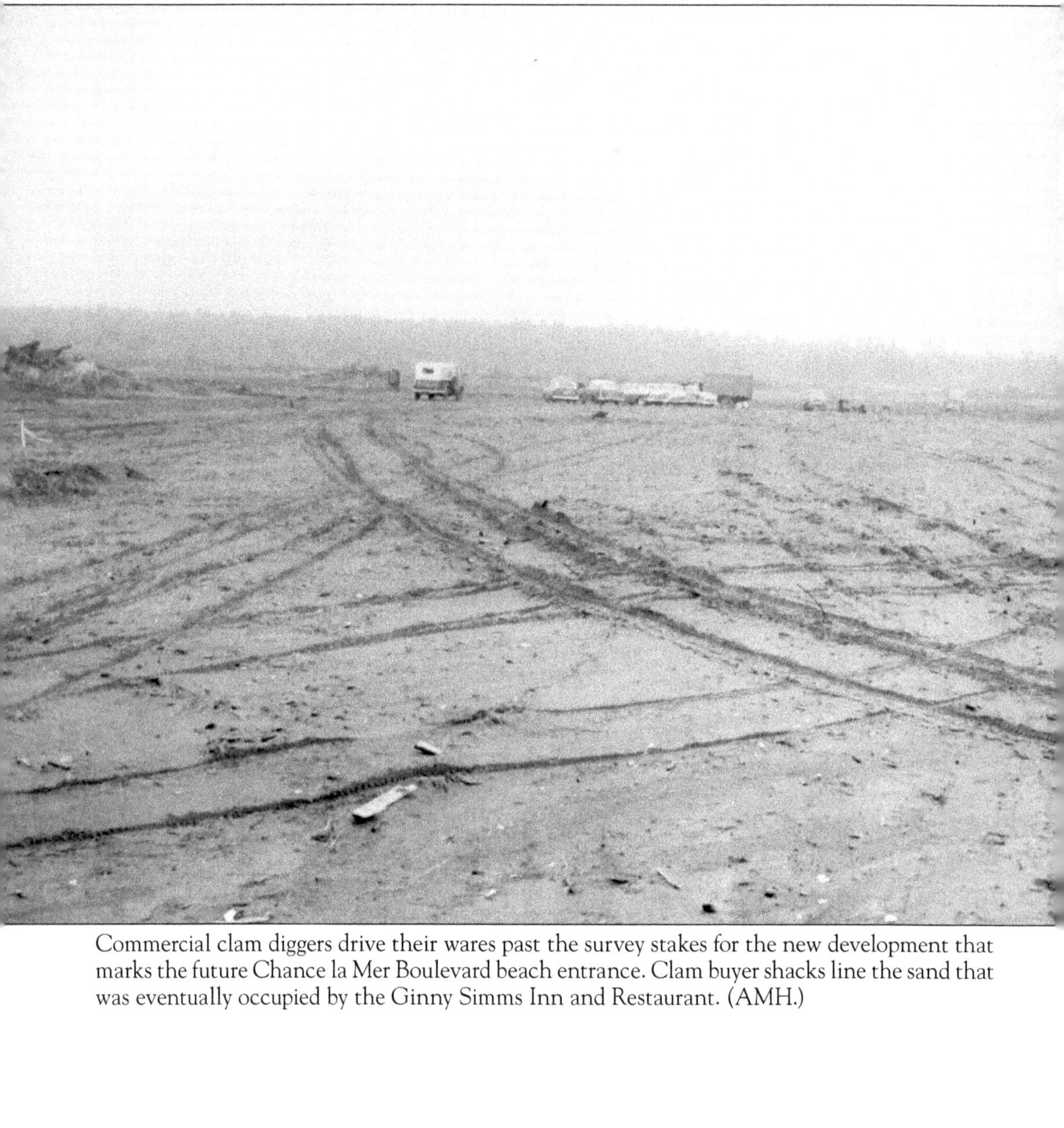

Commercial clam diggers drive their wares past the survey stakes for the new development that marks the future Chance la Mer Boulevard beach entrance. Clam buyer shacks line the sand that was eventually occupied by the Ginny Simms Inn and Restaurant. (AMH.)

Six

City Lights

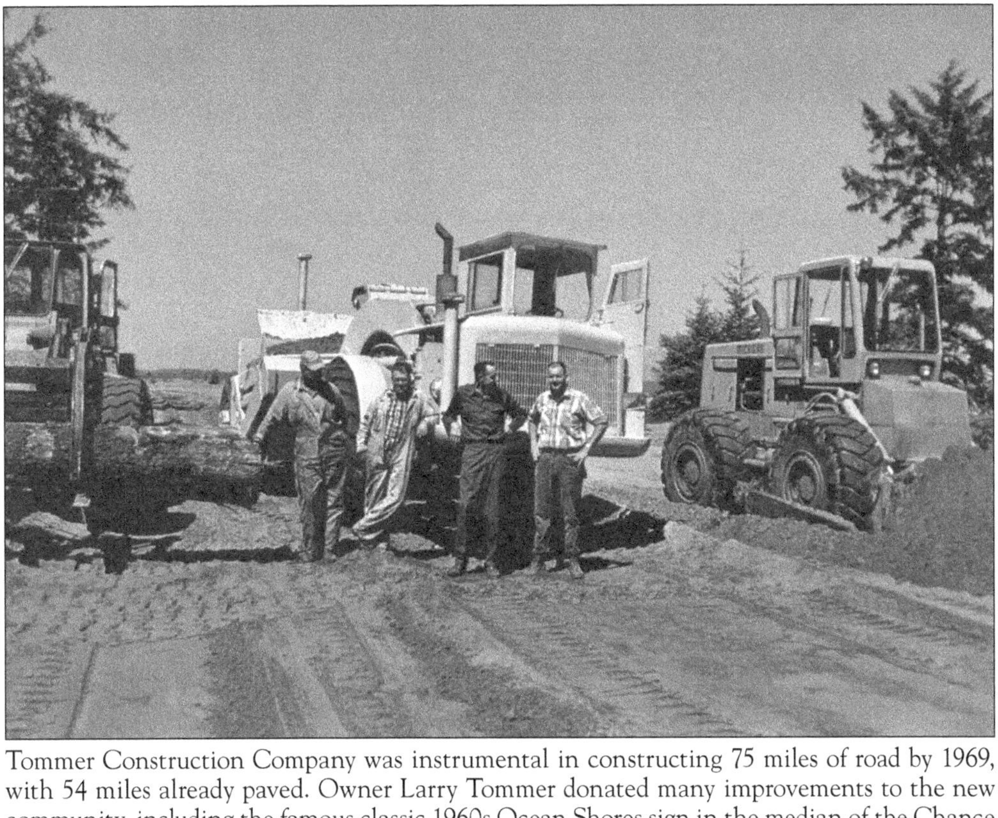

Tommer Construction Company was instrumental in constructing 75 miles of road by 1969, with 54 miles already paved. Owner Larry Tommer donated many improvements to the new community, including the famous classic 1960s Ocean Shores sign in the median of the Chance la Mer and Ocean Shores Boulevards beach approach. Perhaps the most unusual fishing exploit was the time Tommer Construction, plying their 54,000-pound Euclid self-loader in the main channel of the canal, spotted a run of salmon in the water. Revving it up, they herded the fish into a bank. Leaping up, the operator snagged a 15-pound female spawner, and nothing in the fishing regulations said anything about not fishing with a Euclid self-loader. (CHSGWC.)

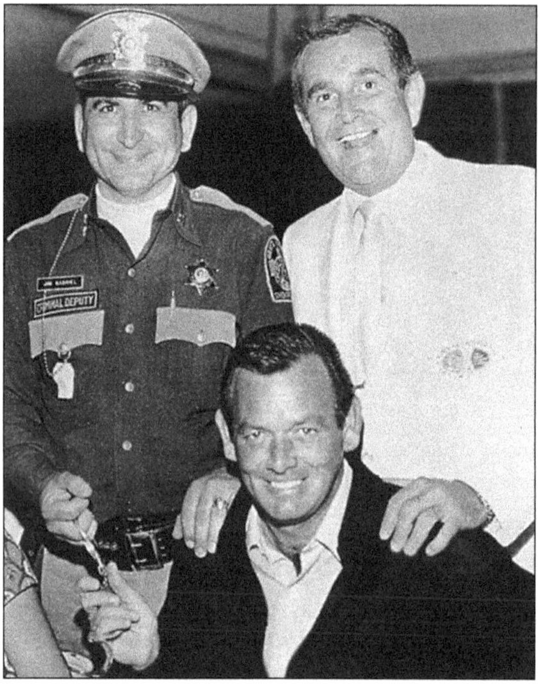

Ocean Shores–assigned Grays Harbor sheriff deputy Jim Gabriel and Pat Cox were pretty excited about being the ones to finally handcuff "the fugitive," David Janssen, during one of the Pat Boone Golf Classics. (CHSGWC.)

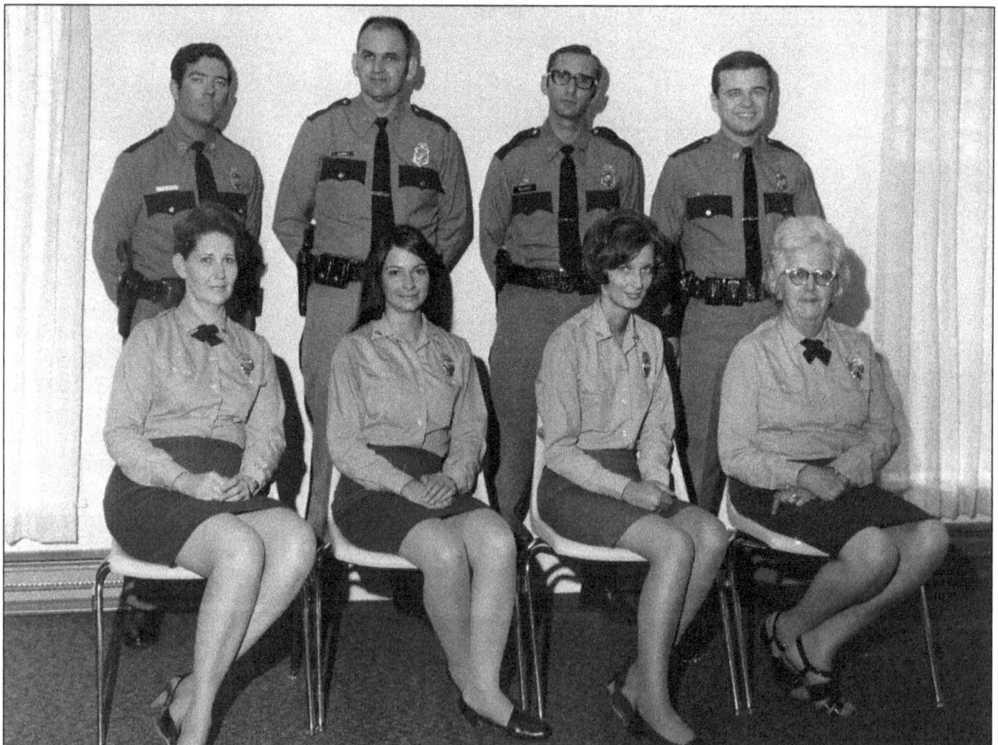

The 1972 police force consisted of, from left to right, (first row) officers Vivian Chalfant, Vicki Hollensteiner, unidentified, and Mildred Bradbury; (second row) ? Roberts, Gale Stokes, Harold Elliott, and Don Dineen. (Ocean Shores Police Department.)

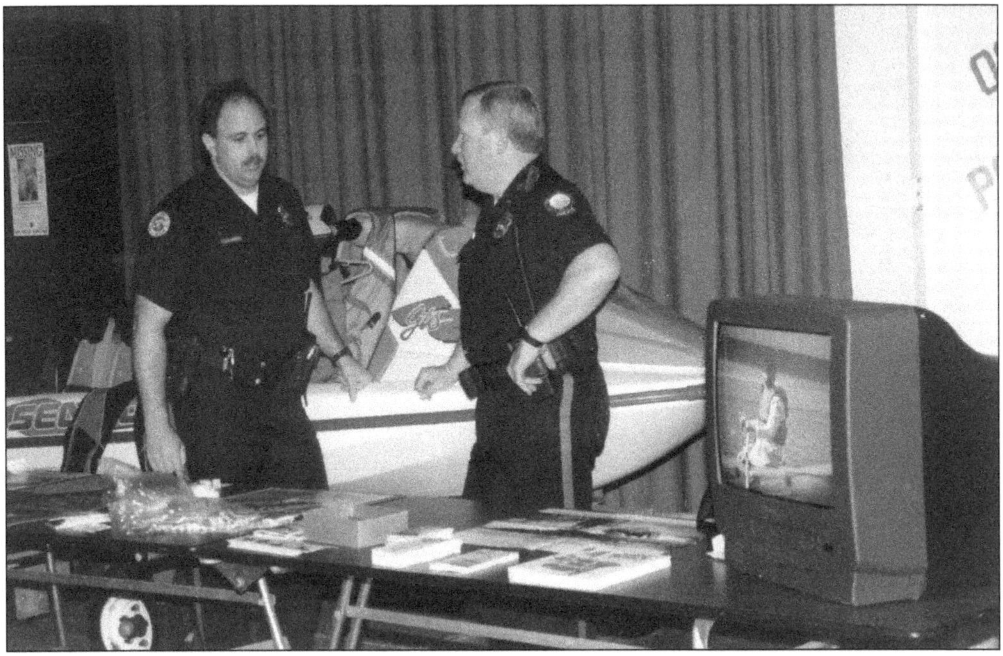

Public education by Sgt. Jim Davis (left) and Lt. Mike Styner is focused on beach safety at the March 1998 Beachcomber Fun Fair. Davis died during a surf rescue on April 26, 1998. (CHSGWC.)

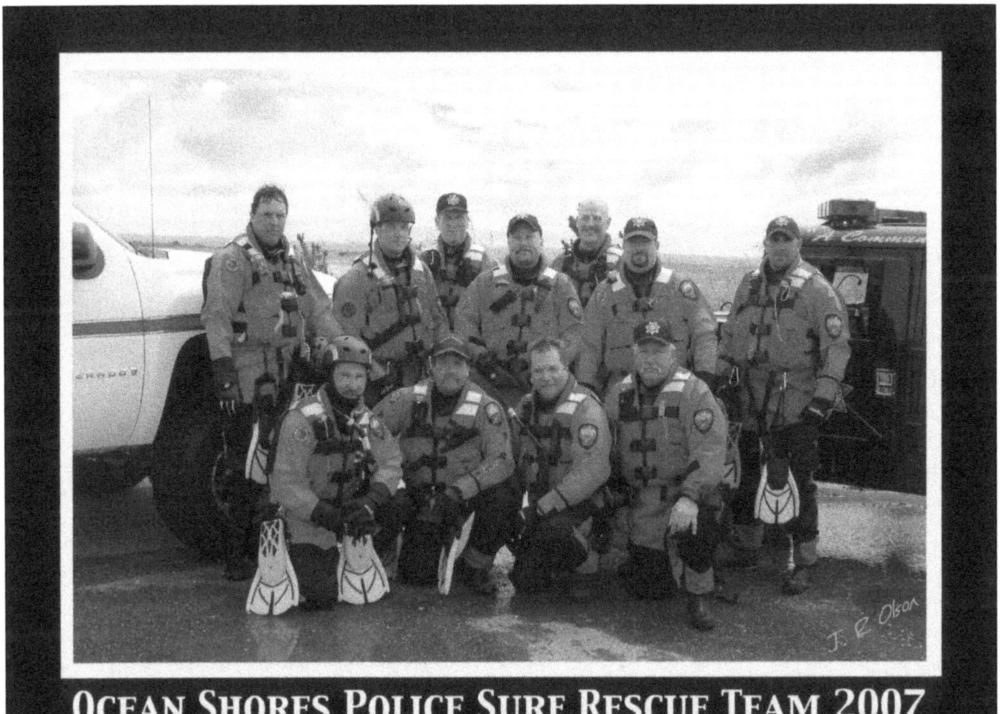

The Ocean Shores Surf and Rescue Team is on call 24 hours a day, seven days a week, to go into the pounding, cold Pacific Ocean surf to rescue swimmers and others who venture too far into rip tide areas or who are overcome by the cold waters. (Ocean Shores Police Department.)

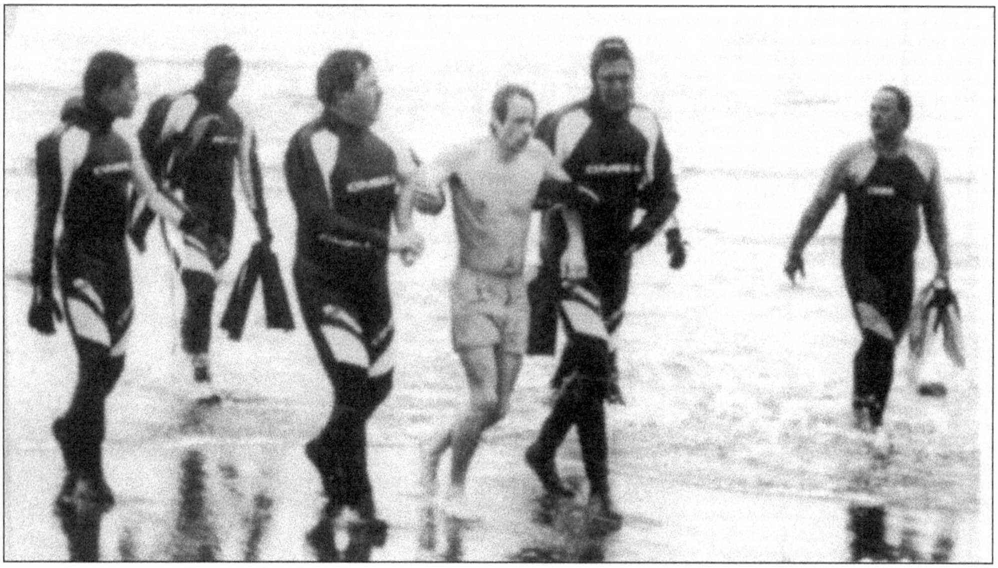

On July 30, 1989, during the first day of training for the new Surf Rescue Team, members rescued a near-drowned swimmer. From left to right are officers VanGompel, Paul Luck, Jim Davis, the victim, Lee Fundenburger, and instructor Scott Tye. (Ocean Shores Police Department.)

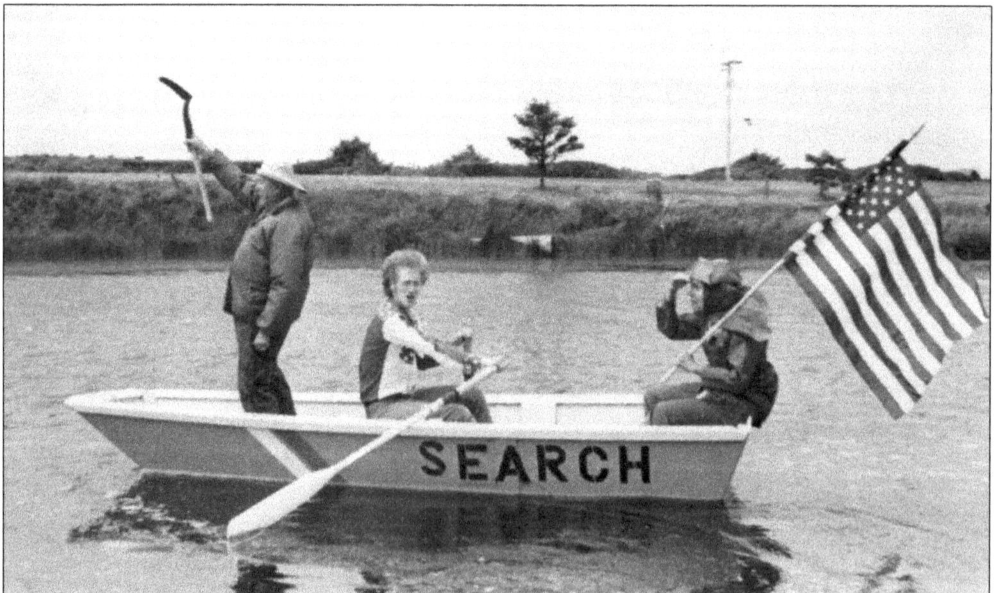

Not exactly professionals, the rescue craft was manned by Bob Ward (left), Brett Colacurcio (center), and Mayor Margaret Carlston in 1970. They must have had a premonition that tourism traffic would increase the need for a trained rescue team. (Ocean Shores Police Department.)

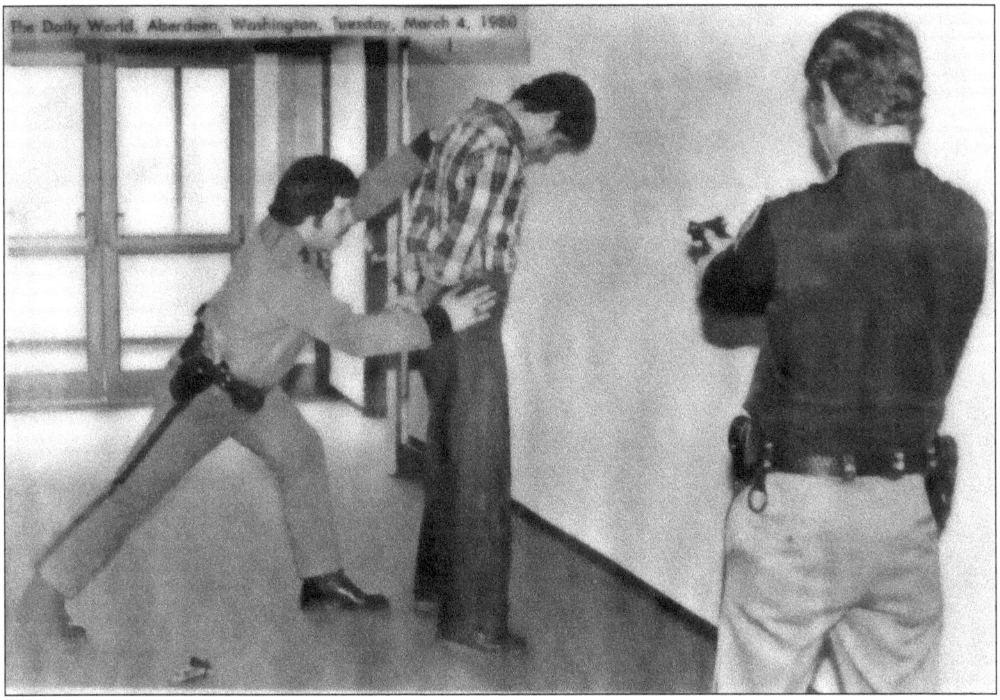

Ocean Shores policeman Mike Styner pats down a suspect (sheriff officer Kenneth Hempstead) as Ken Spencer (sheriff reserve office) secures the situation during Grays Harbor County Police Reserve Academy held March 1980 at the Grays Harbor College. (Ocean Shores Police Department.)

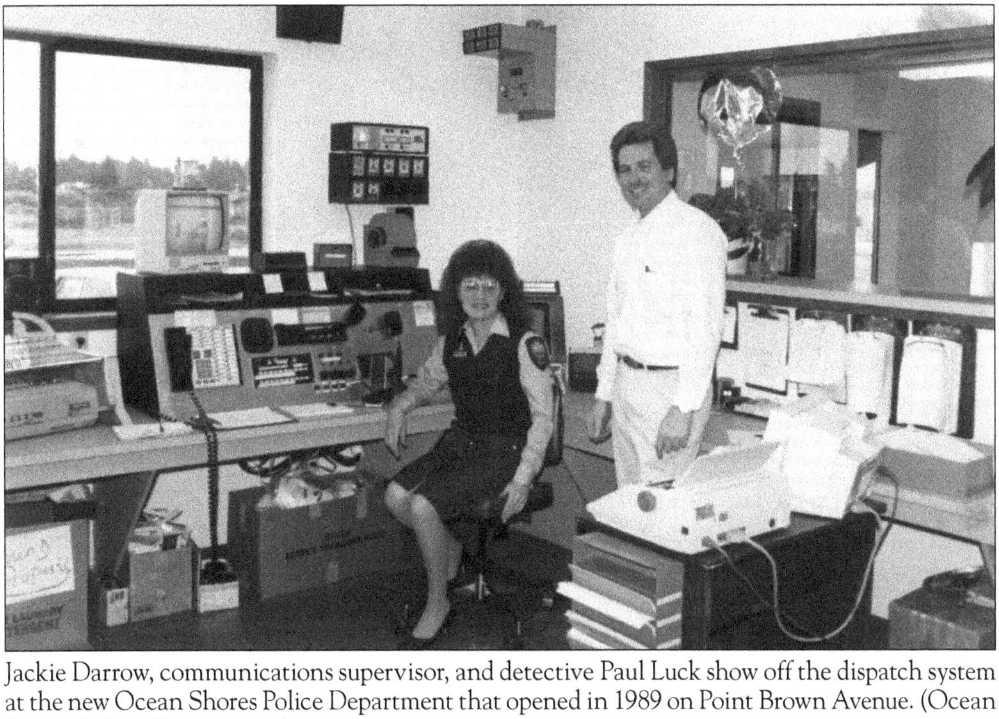

Jackie Darrow, communications supervisor, and detective Paul Luck show off the dispatch system at the new Ocean Shores Police Department that opened in 1989 on Point Brown Avenue. (Ocean Shores Police Department.)

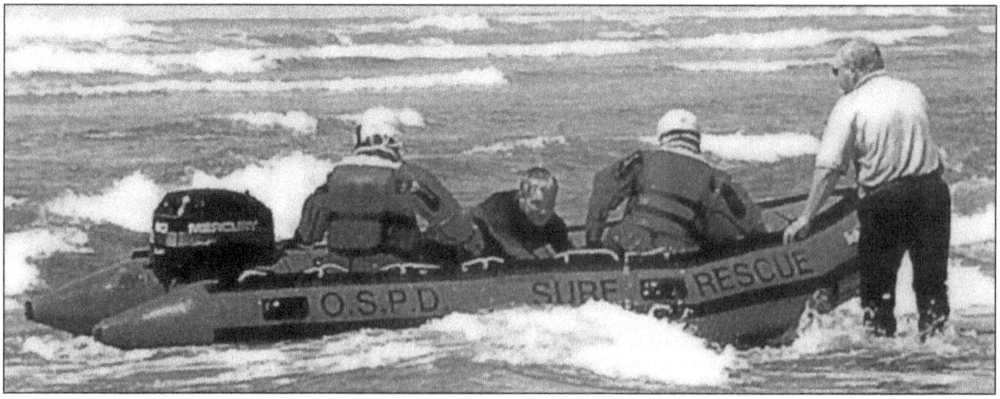

Rescue team members Paul Luck (left) and Chris Iversen (third from left) bring in a rescued surfer as Lt. Mike Styner assists on May 26, 1999. (Ocean Shores Police Department.)

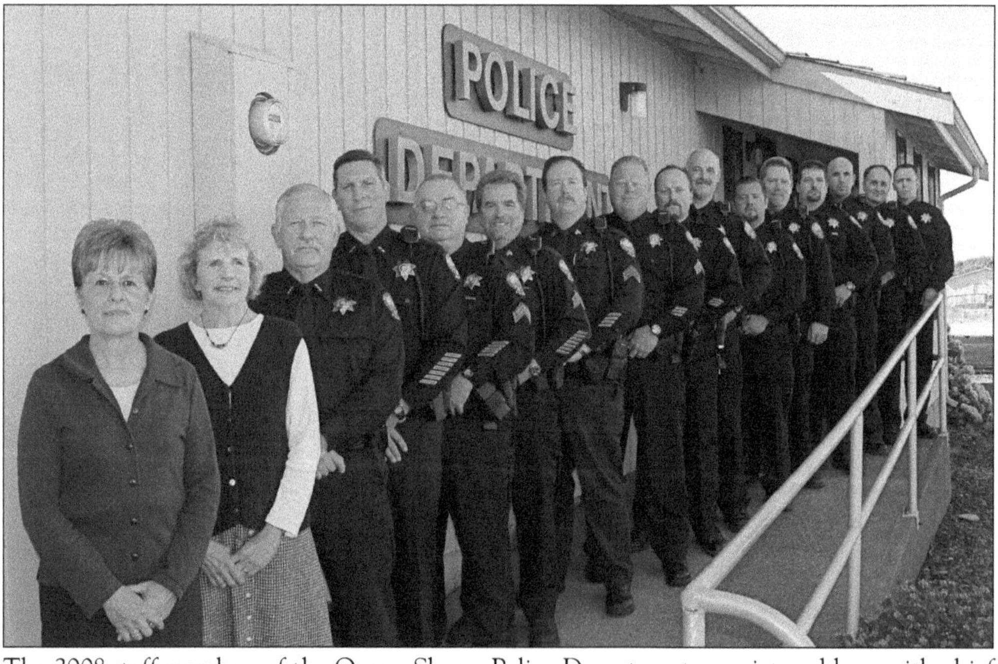

The 2008 staff members of the Ocean Shores Police Department are pictured here with chief Mike Styner, third from the left. (Ocean Shores Police Department.)

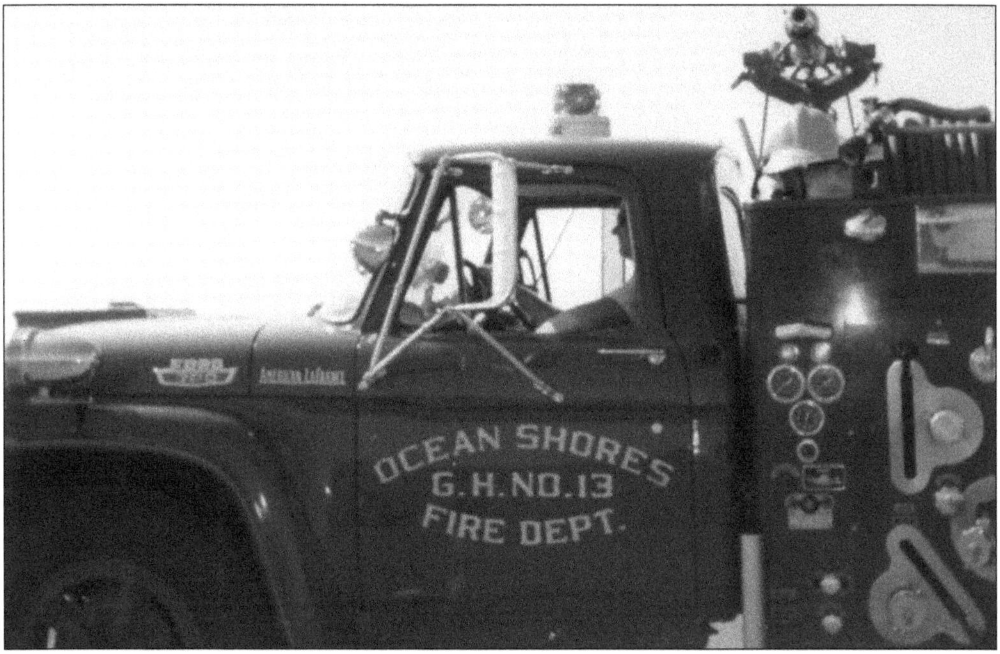

In December 1962, a fire broke out in the home of Andy Anderson. Unfortunately there was no fire department. Anderson frantically gathered up men, who ran around gathering up motel fire extinguishers to put out the blaze. Shortly thereafter, the new Grays Harbor Fire District 13 chief Don Wescott, assisted by Wes Van Blaricom, George Bertram, and Larry Tommer, built up a force of 13 volunteer firemen. It was housed in an end unit of the town's first mall. Later the $26,163, 89-foot-by-32-foot station built by Busch Construction held a fire truck, a fire engine purchased for $833 from Port Angeles, and an emergency truck that doubled as an ambulance. The Wendell-West Company financed the police and fire departments until the company was bankrupt. The bankruptcy was caused the city to raise tax funds to support the public safety departments. These photographs are indicative of the pride firemen had in their equipment, which logged many miles in various county and local parades. (Both Ocean Shores Fire Department.)

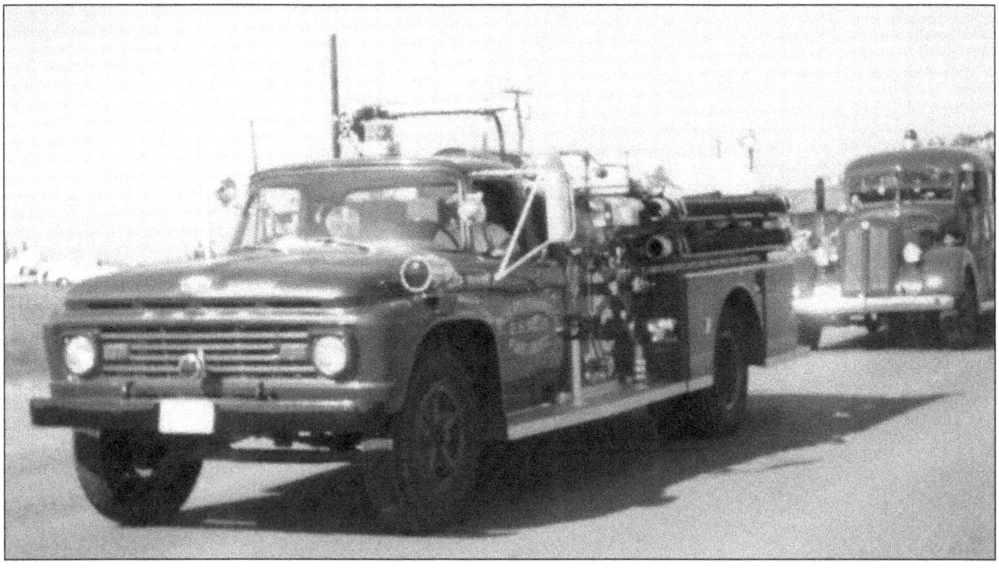

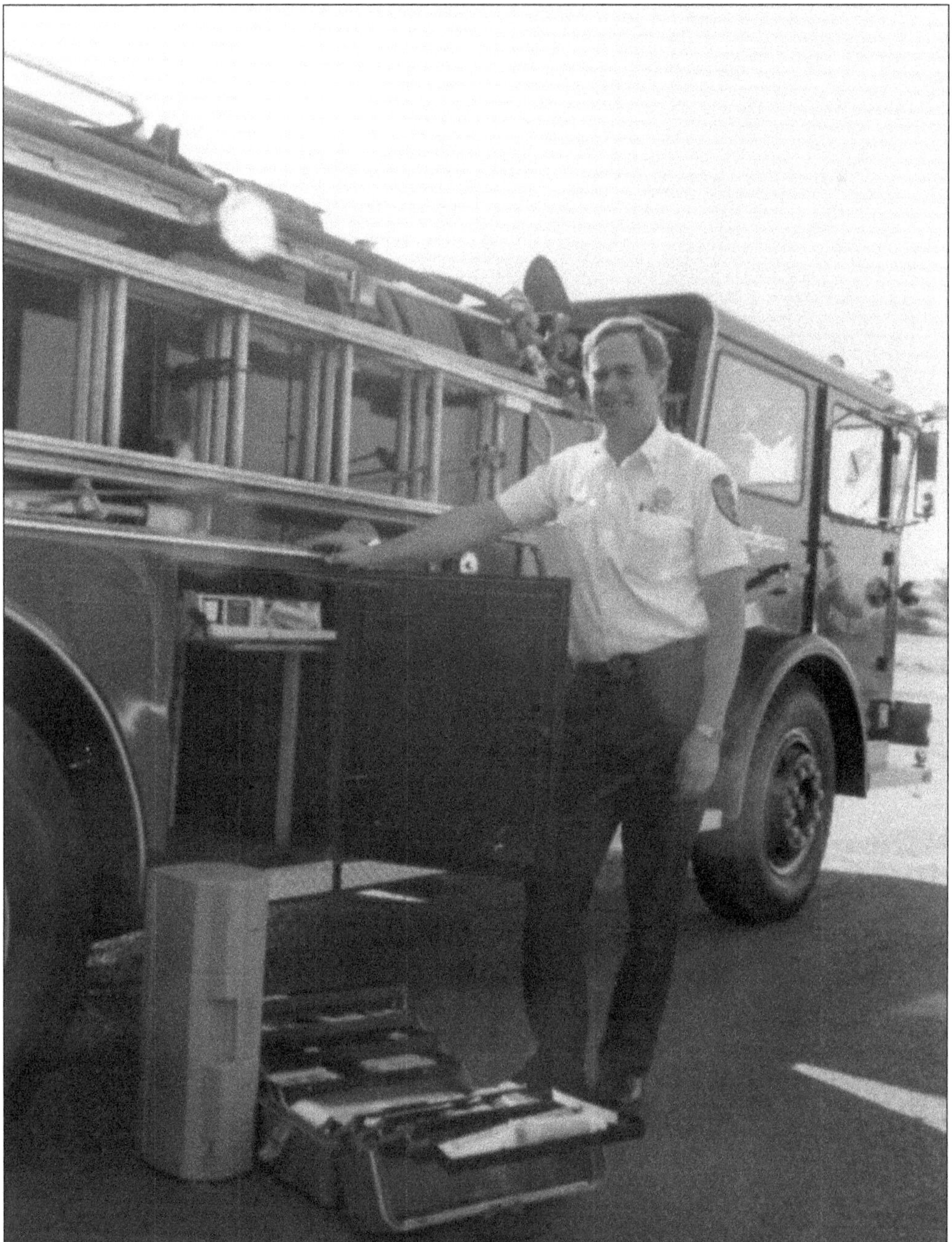

Lee Fundenburger, the department paramedic, shows the photographer the medical kit. (Ocean Shores Fire Department.)

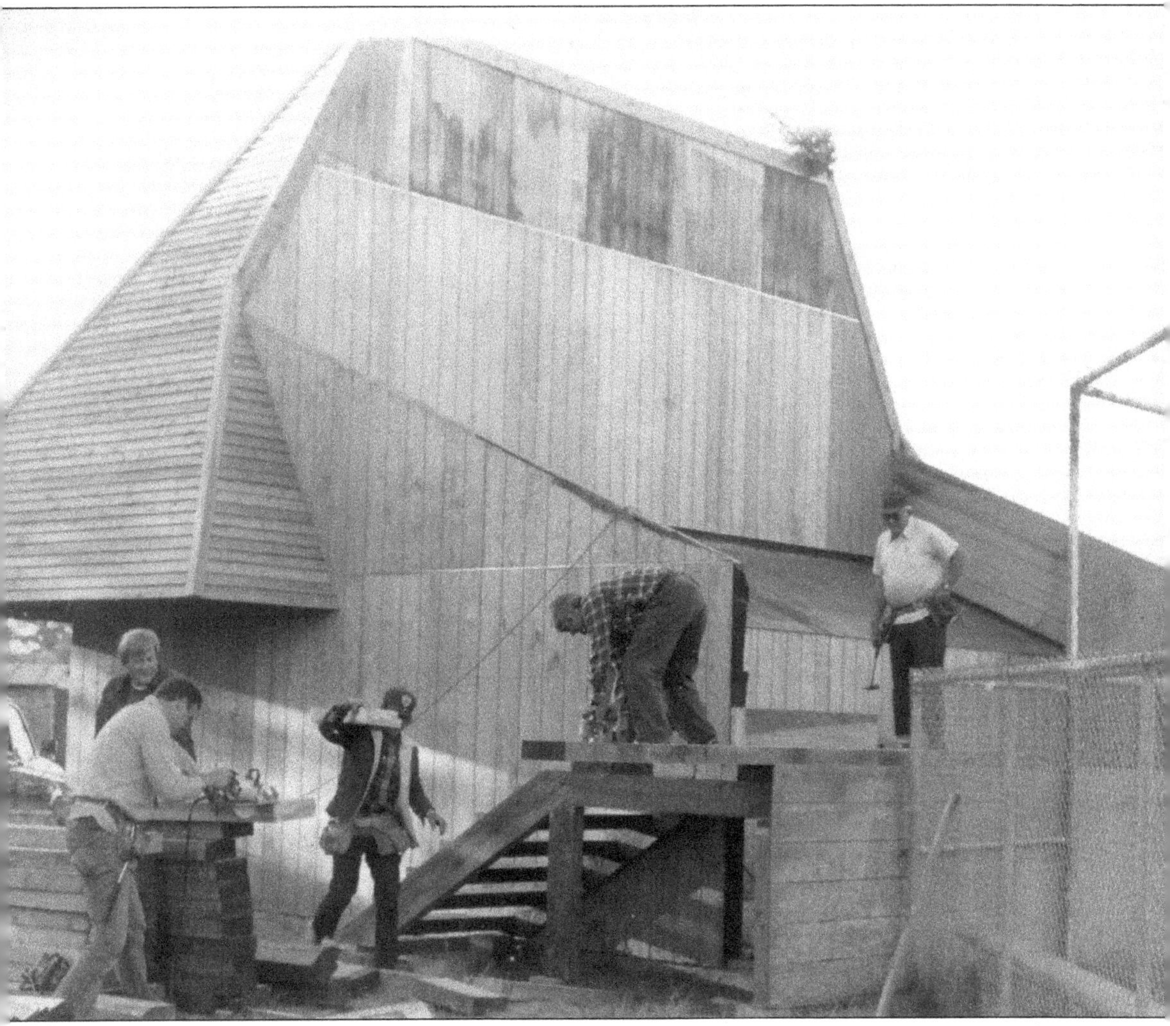

Firemen such as, from left to right, Larry Moilanen, Roy Ellis, Lynn Powell, Duane Jones, and Cy Metsker contributed to many city improvements such as this backstop for the city's elementary school and little league ball field. (Ocean Shores Fire Department.)

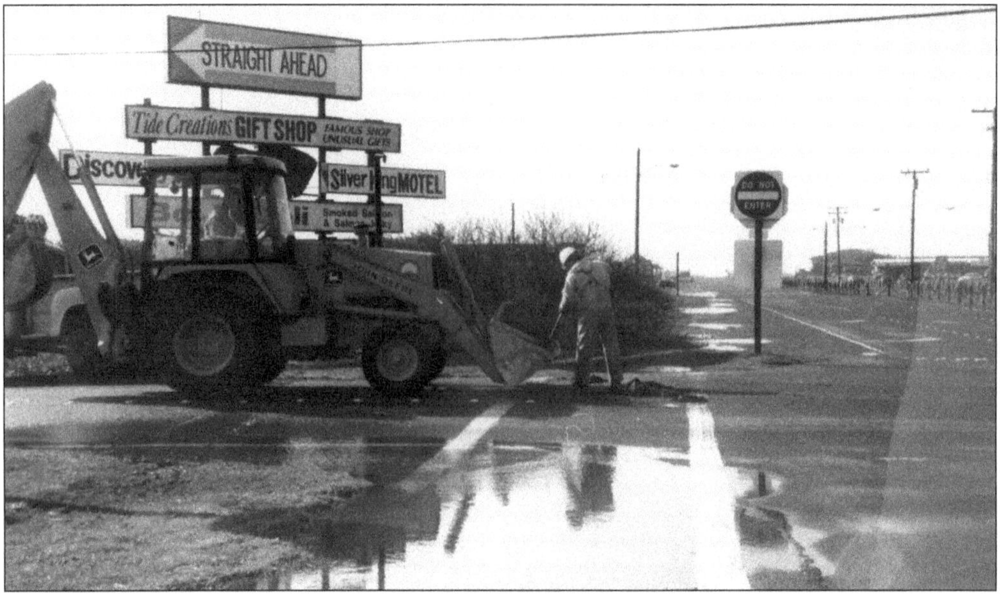

The 1994 "straight ahead" sign summed up where the city was going that decade. The sign stood at the gates on S.R. 115 and Point Brown Avenue. (CHSGWC.)

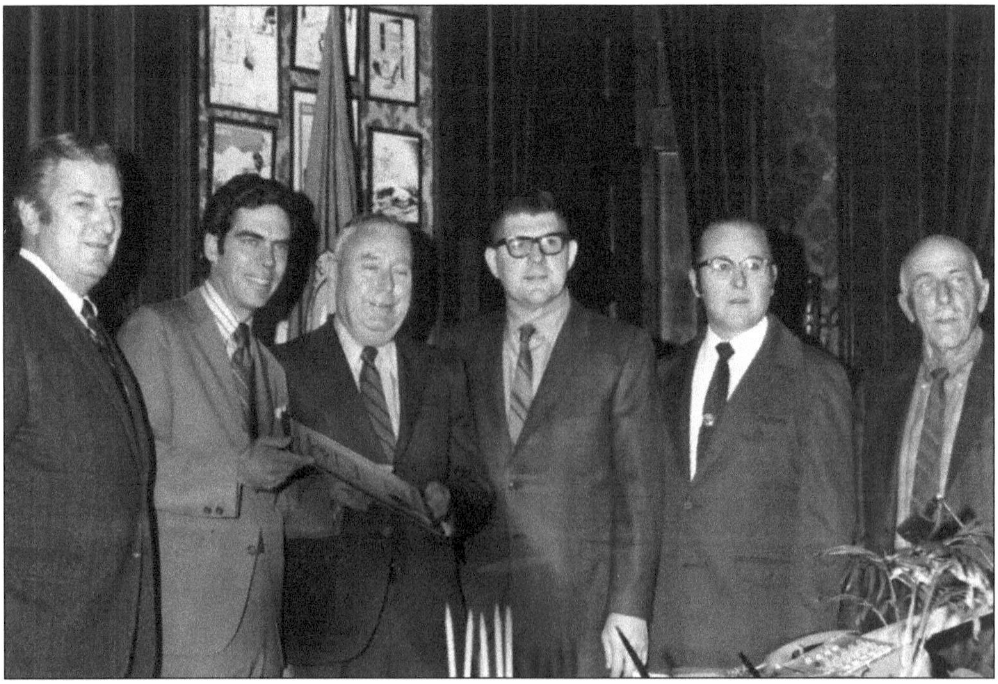

From left to right, councilman Bob Ward, Washington secretary of state Lud Kramer, Mayor Bun Lewis, councilman William "Bill" Marks, Russell Carter, and councilman W. W. "Win" Rasmussen posed after signing incorporation papers in Olympia in January 1970. (CHSGWC.)

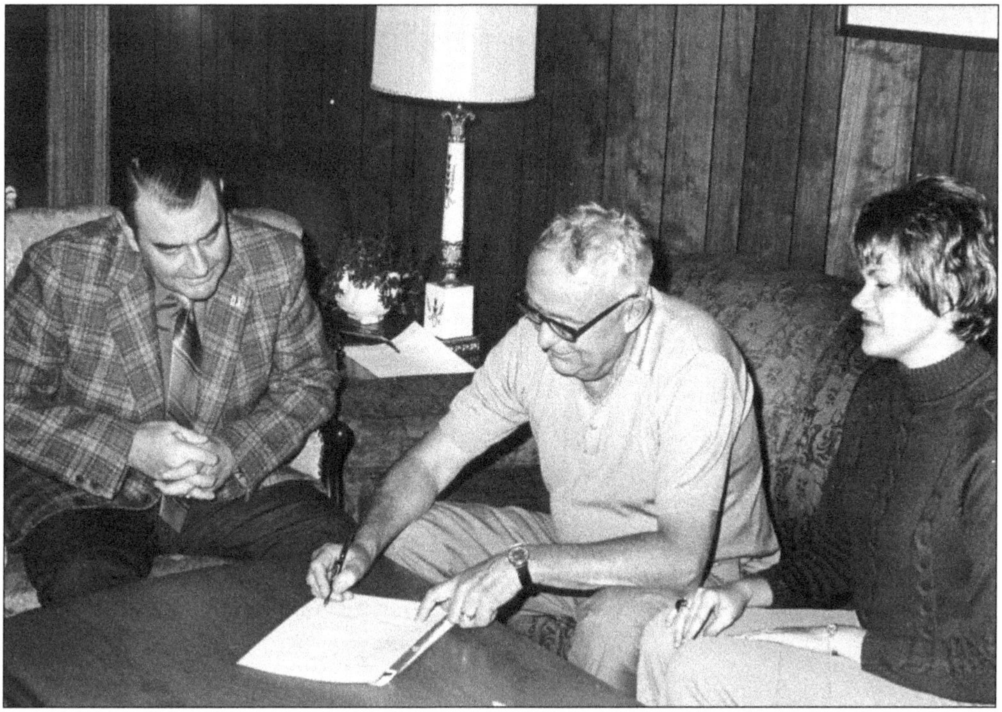

An unidentified man, Mayor Bun Lewis (center), and Joan Marks plan another Ocean Shores event. (CHSGWC.)

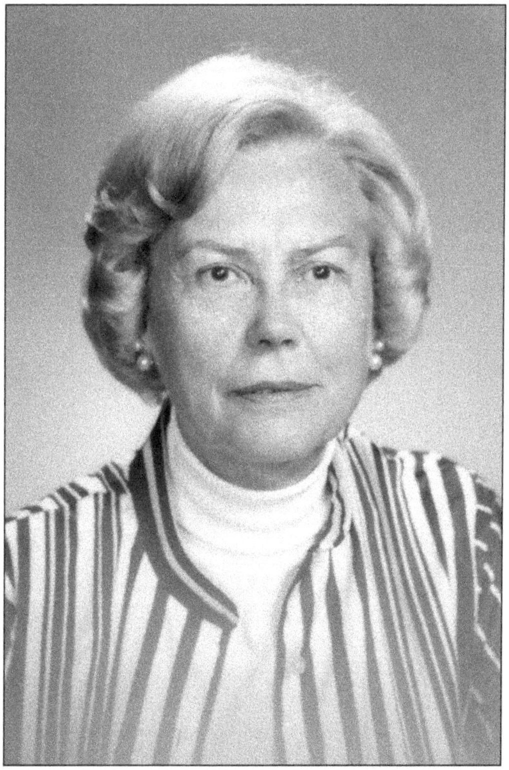

Margaret Carlston was instrumental in creating Ocean Shores' second museum housed in the convention center. Among board members instrumental in developing museum cases and their exhibits were Dr. David Daughtery, archeologist, and David Waller, well-known local artist. In 1965, Carlston was the first female mayor (pro-tem) and served five years on the council. She represented the city by serving years on the boards of Grays Harbor Regional Planning, the Tri-County and Quinault Indian Nation Council, Columbia Pacific RC&D, Grays Harbor Measures Commission, and Grays Harbor Community Concert. She had her own radio show and was active in the League of Women Voters. (Jones photograph collection.)

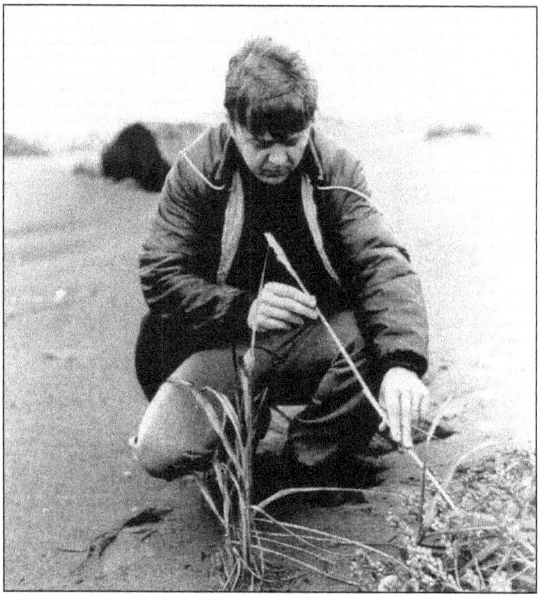

Doug Hoflin, city engineer and later city public works director, and crew planted dune grass to stabilize erosion in the jetty area in 1973 under a grant from Columbia Pacific Research and Conservation Development. Hoflin was instrumental in construction of the tide gates, planting the first shore pine trees in the downtown area, and making many other civic improvements. The first dune grass for the peninsula was imported from the San Francisco area by A. O. Damon to provide grazing for his cattle. (CHSGWC.)

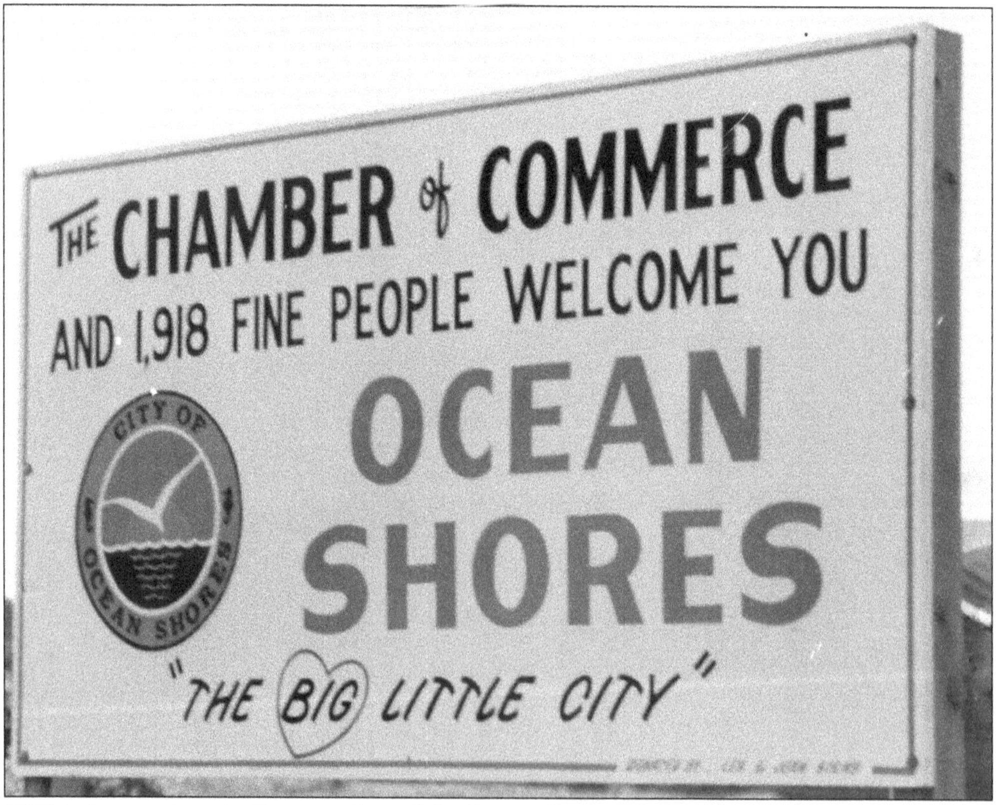

Bill Marks served as the first president of the Ocean Shores Chamber of Commerce in 1962. His wedding to Joan K. Overland was heartily celebrated by the townsfolk. The couple opened the Sea and Spice shop on April 13, 1962, the same day as the Seattle World's Fair, and sold everything a tourist required, including classy resort wear. During their first year in business, they had to enlarge the store four times. They retired from the business 22 years later. (CHSGWC.)

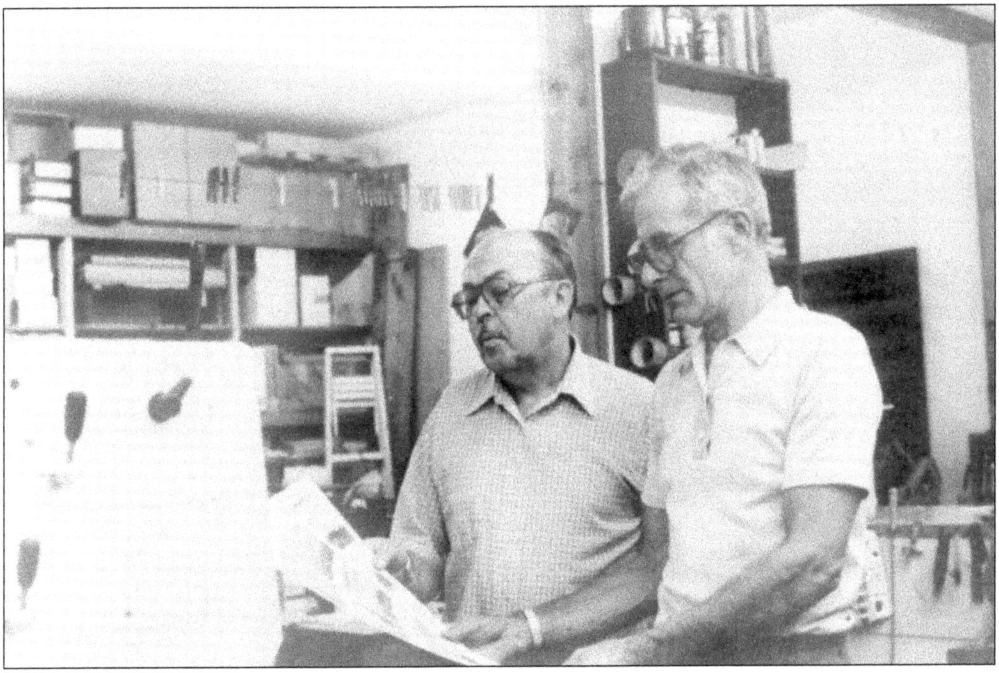

North Beach Printing Company partners Harvey Scott (left) and Andy McDougal are in their Point Brown Print Shop. Scott and J. Roy Nelson bought out their beginning partner, Tom Michaud, to operate the North Beach Print, first at Ocean City and then as one of the first Ocean Shores businesses in 1968. These Grays Harbor natives were famous for their support of the high school programs. After buying out McDougal, a later partner, Scott retired in June 1966, after 36 years in business. (CHSGWC.)

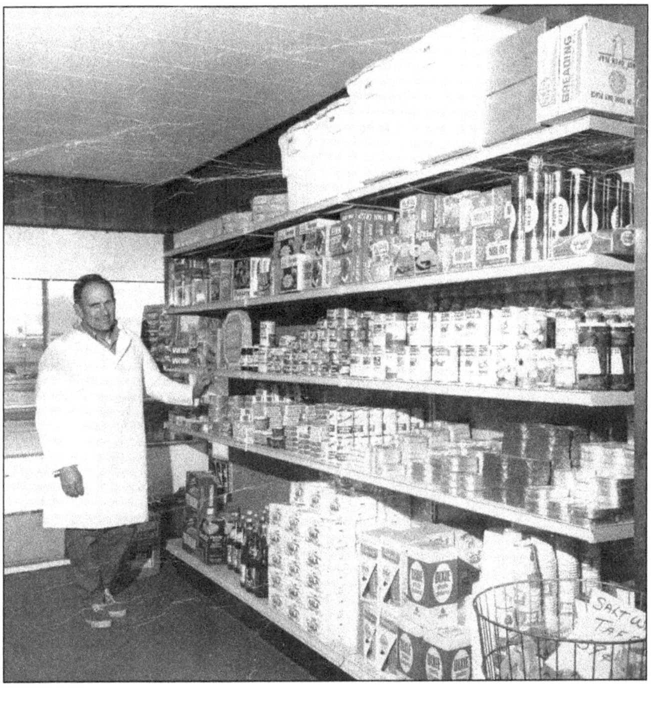

Doyle and Evelyn Miller owned the KKK, Kustom Klam Kannery, from April 1963 to April 1977, when they sold it to Arnie Jones. The family lived above the store on Point Brown Avenue, where the parents worked 16-hour days and called in the help of their three daughters during the clam season. By 1974, the crews were cleaning 1,000 limits of clams on the weekends. An amazing curio at the store was a gallon jar that barely held a monstrous, preserved razor clam. (CHSGWC.)

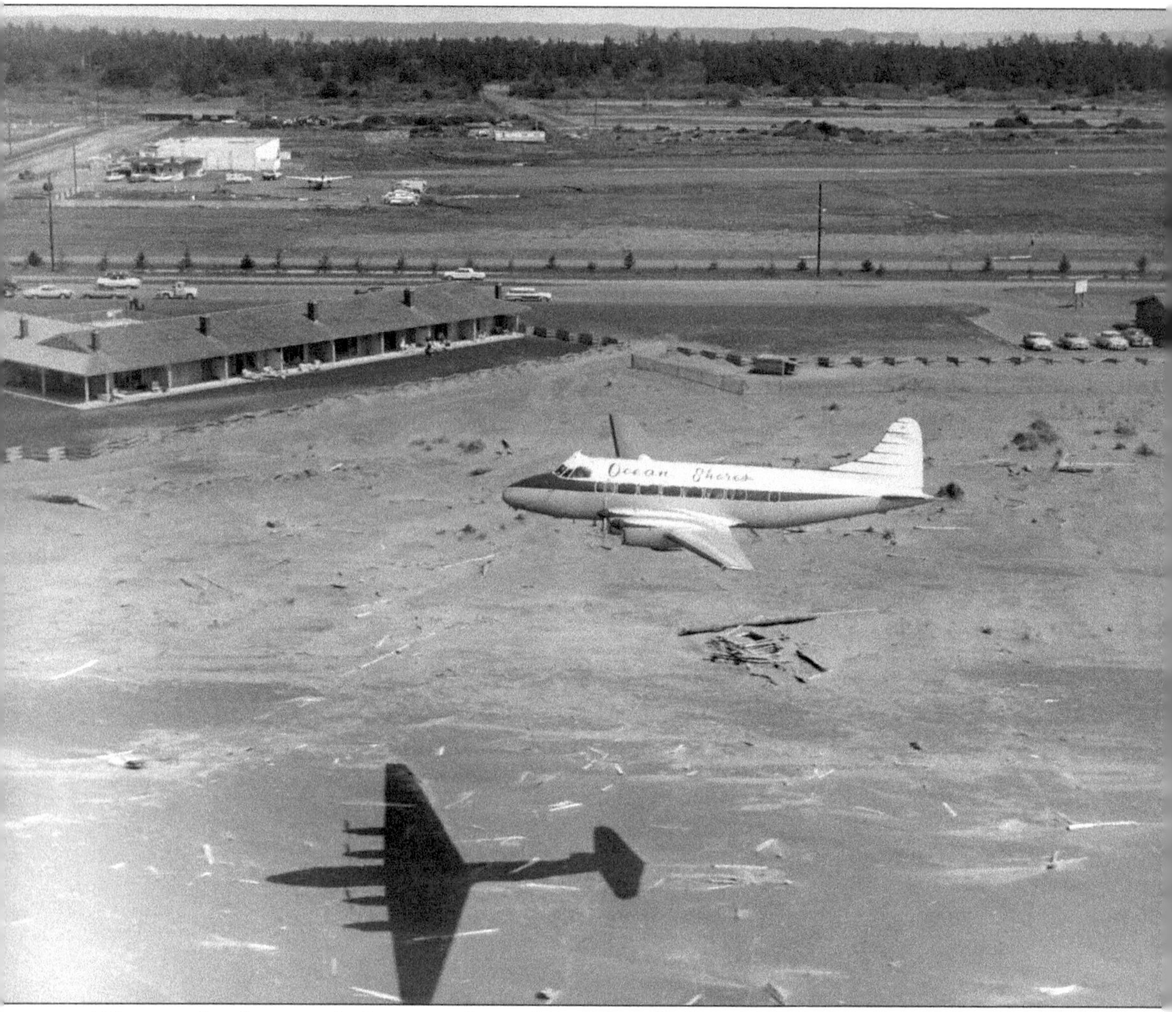

The new development had its own fleet of aircraft including a 16-passenger, four-engine Heron DeHavilland liner that made twice daily trips to Boeing Field to pick up potential lot owners. Later it was replaced by a Twin-Beech 18 and a DC-3, all proudly labeled "Ocean Shores." (AMH.)

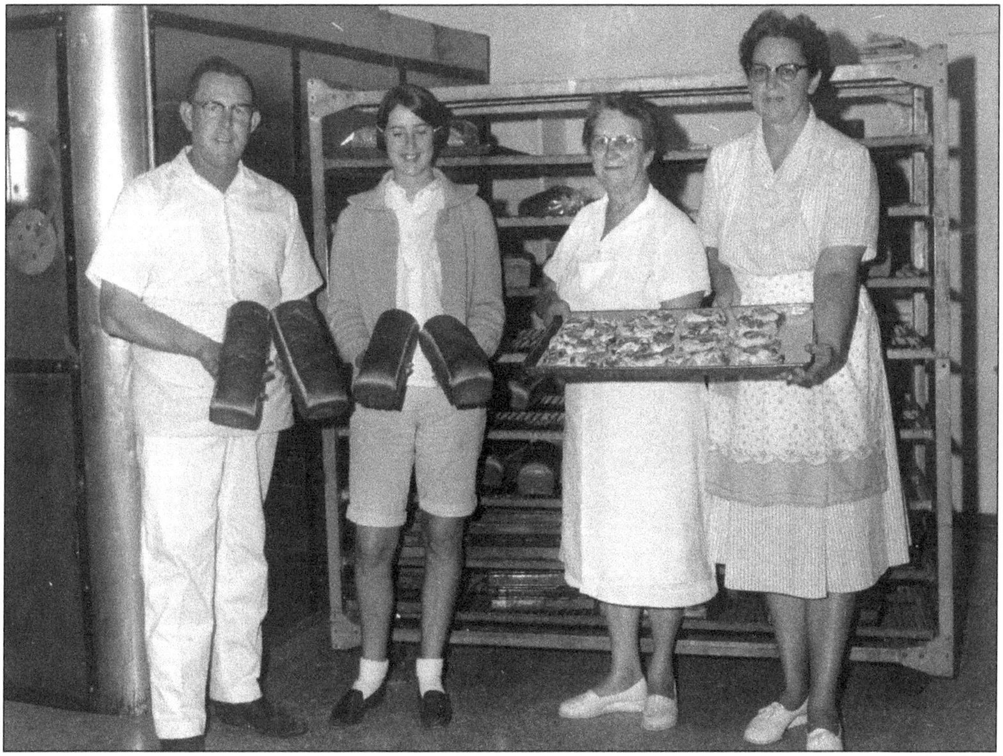

The Sand Dollar Bakery—staffed by, from left to right, Eugene Miller, Clara and Belle Rediske, and Muriel Mullen—did not lack for customers in 1967. (CHSGWC.)

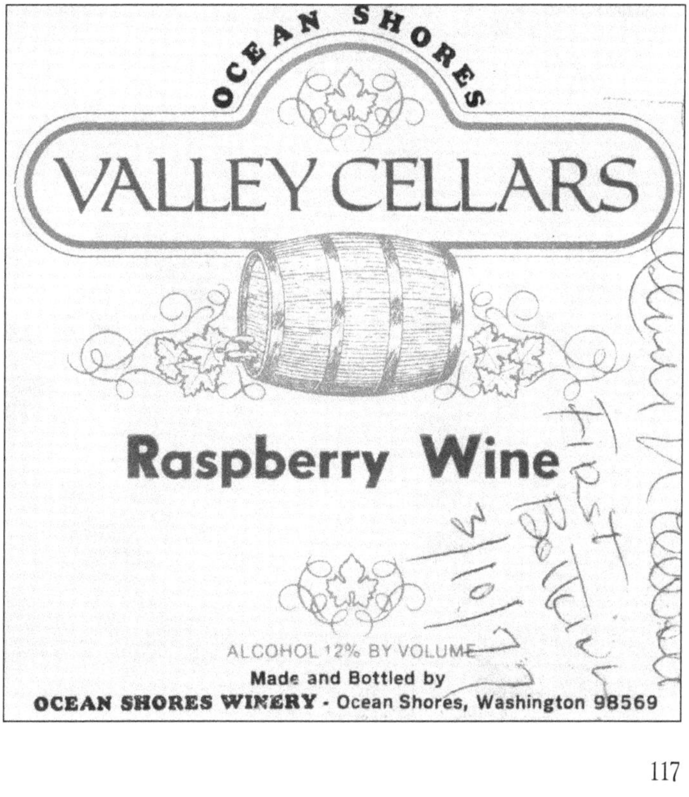

Ocean Shores Winery was a branch of the Puyallup Valley Winery that built a modern, round sales office on Ocean Shores Avenue in 1978. Erna Bench, a former newswoman, was one of the stockholders. (CHSGWC.)

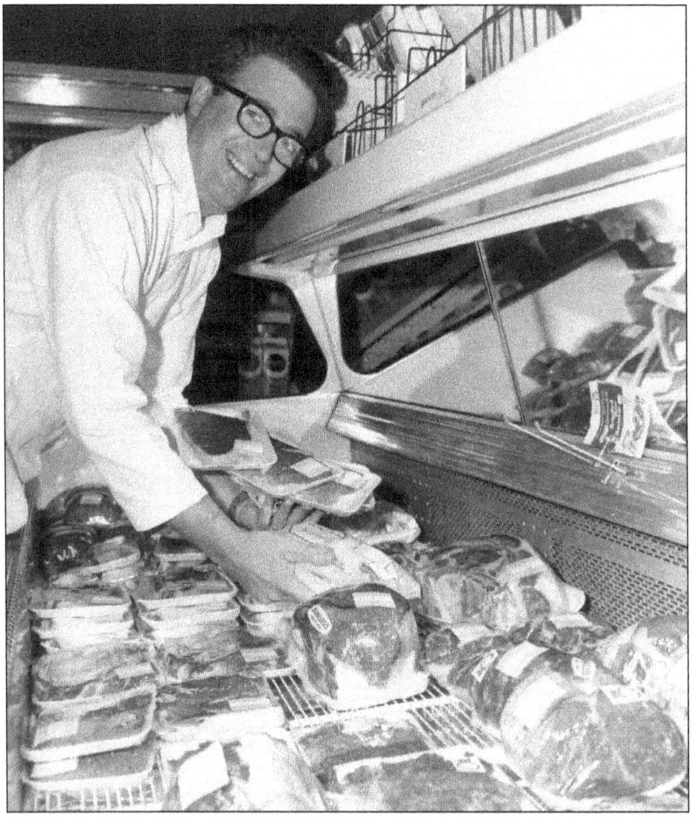

Dick Morris retired from his grocery in November 1997 after 30 years in the business. He increased his original IGA store eight times, took over the post office, a defunct liquor store, Rainier Bank, and the public restroom in the Ocean Shores Mall, later moving the store onto his own block of land on Chance la Mer Boulevard. An ardent golfer, he hosted the AM golf tournament for 20 years. (CHSGWC.)

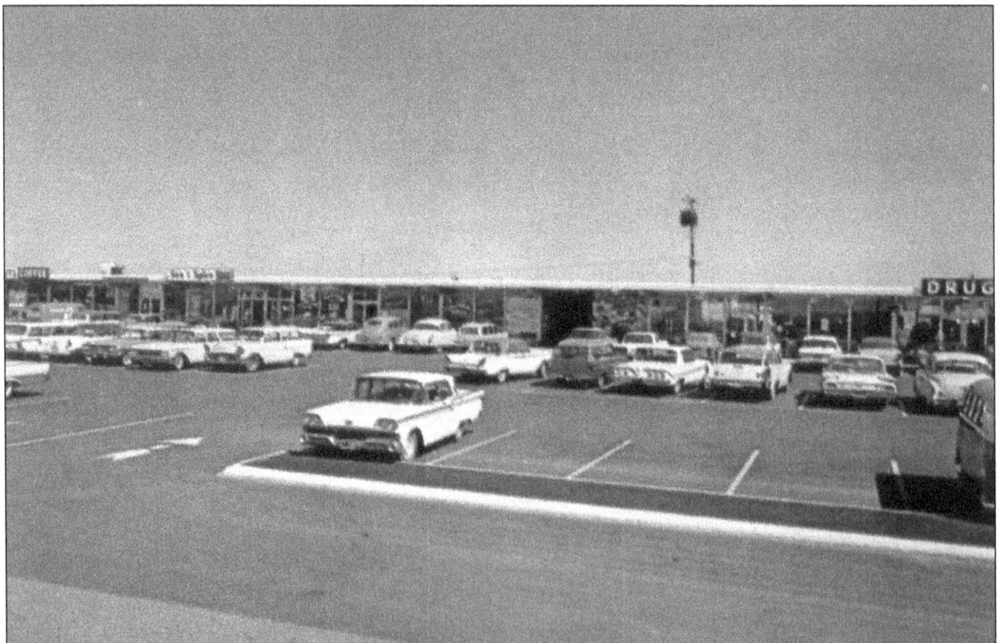

The Ocean Shores Mall was becoming a focal point for the town when this shot was taken in the early 1970s. (CHSGWC.)

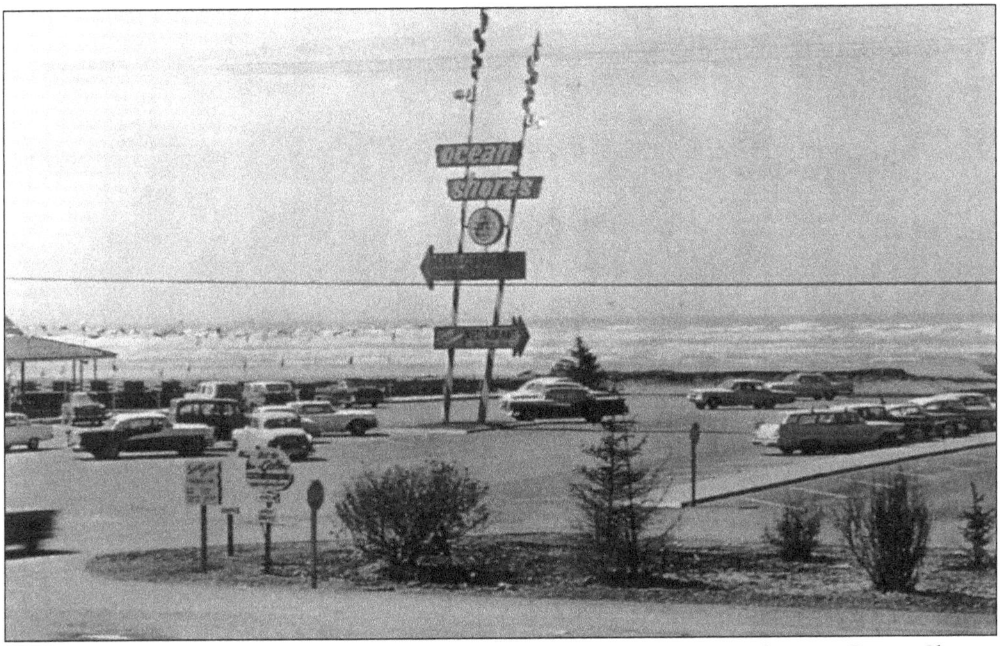

This classic 1960s signage was the place to look for when coming into the new Ocean Shores. Located in the median of Chance la Mer and Ocean Shores Boulevards, the sign could be seen from the S.R. 115 leading to the new development. (AMH.)

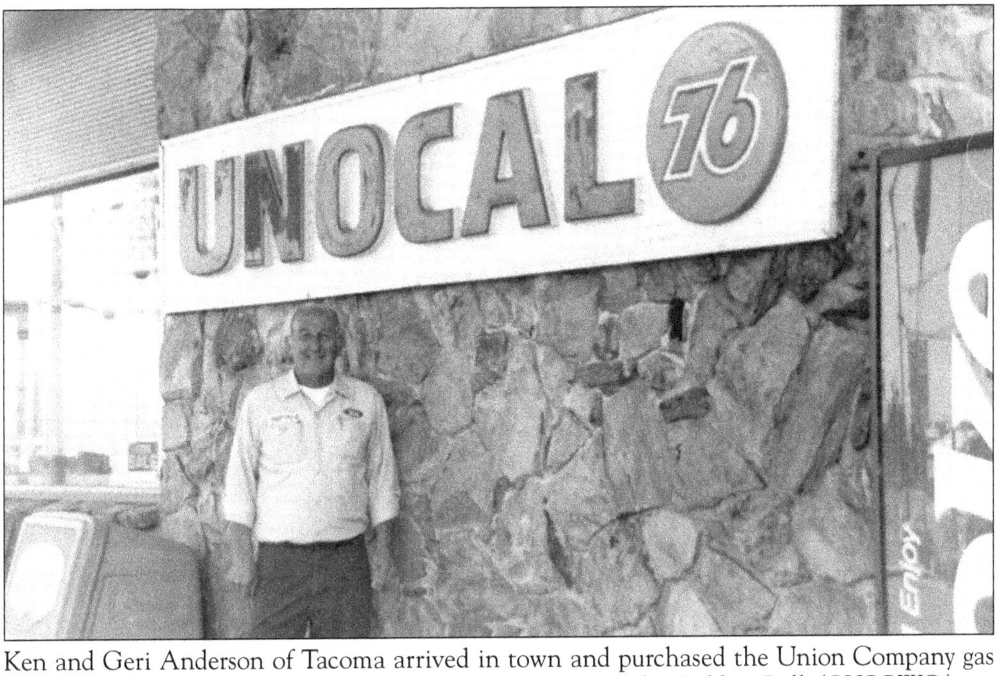

Ken and Geri Anderson of Tacoma arrived in town and purchased the Union Company gas station. Ken operated the station, and Geri handled sales at the Golden Gull. (CHSGWC.)

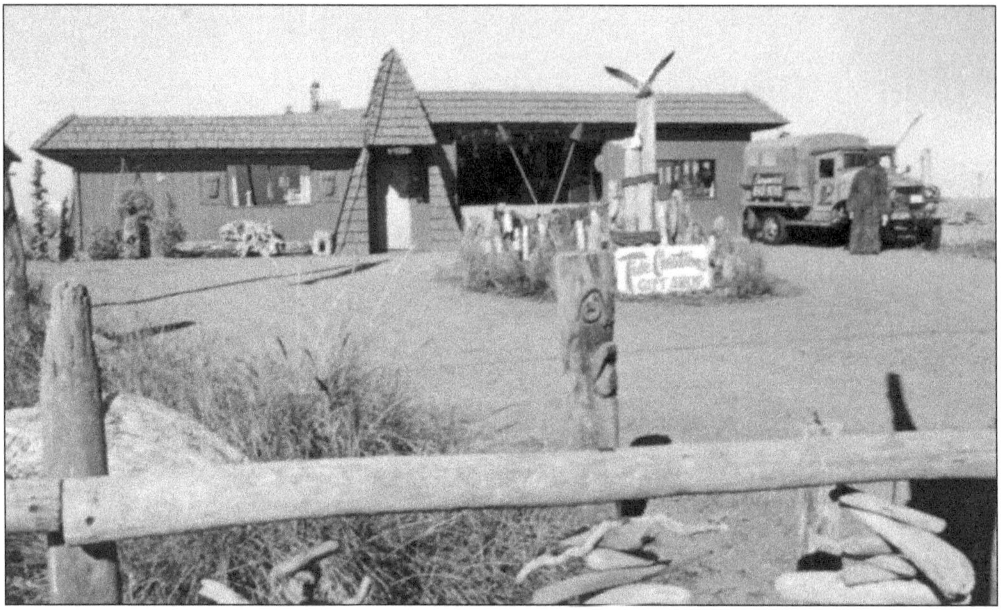

Tide Creations, operated by Erma and Doc Bedilion, opened in 1969 and was considered "the funniest shop on the beach" with its entry hall of Hawaiian Village miniatures, crazy gift items, and many varieties of homemade fudge. It was also home of the Sasquatch—the Bedilion's son, who dressed up and patrolled the beach in memory of the July 1969 sighting of the critter 10 miles east of Ocean Shores by Grays Harbor deputy Verlin Herrington. (CHSGWC.).

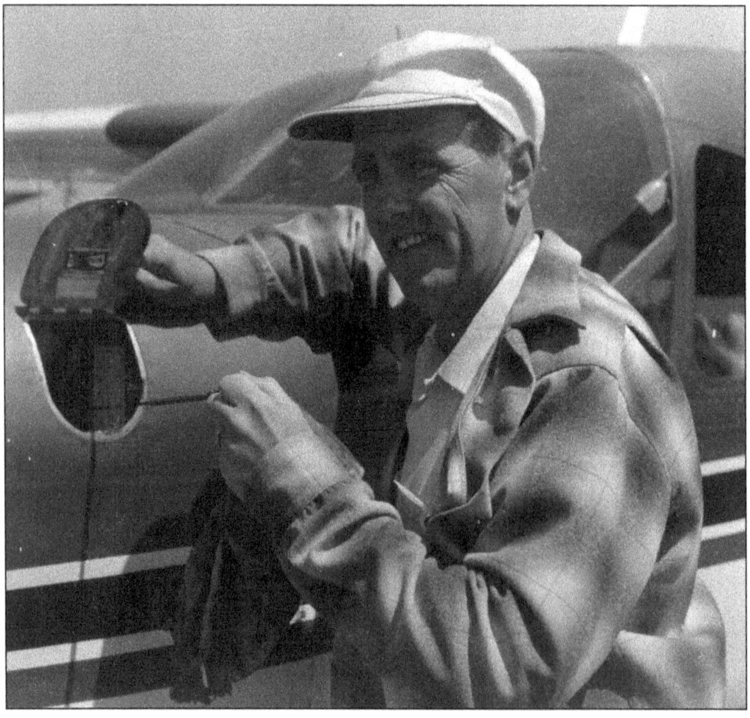

The first official Ocean Shores pilot, Jim Gray, owned Gray Air Service. A Unicom radio was installed in the downtown hangar operated by his wife, Betty. TACAN (tactical air navigation for military), DME (for civilian use), and VOR (omnidirectional range distance measuring) services for pilots came from the VORTAC (combined) range at the Sink of the Oyehut Game Refuge. (CHSGWC.)

Seven

CIVIC DEVELOPMENT

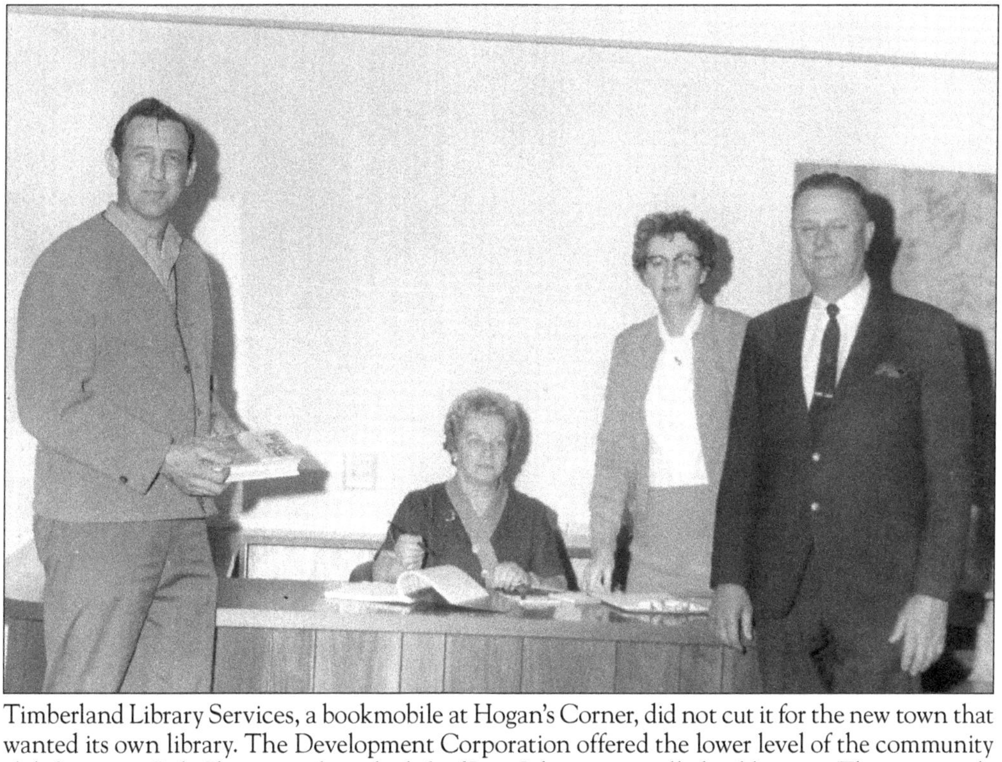

Timberland Library Services, a bookmobile at Hogan's Corner, did not cut it for the new town that wanted its own library. The Development Corporation offered the lower level of the community club for space. Bob Chase stands to the left of Jane Johnson, installed as librarian. The two people on the right are unidentified. (CHSGWC.)

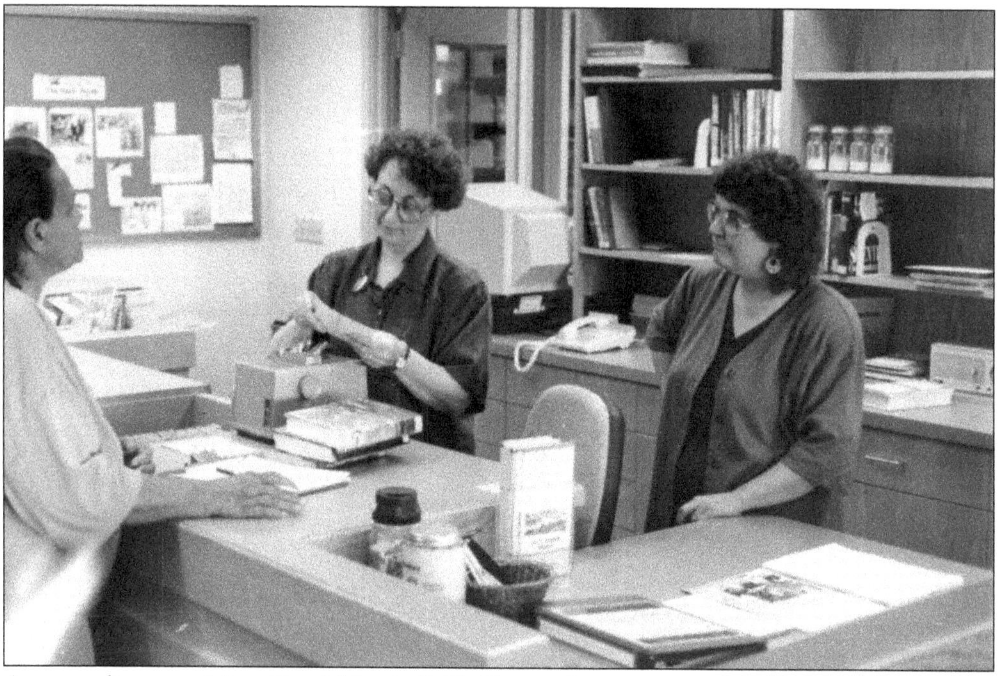

A patron listens to Nina (Ross) Morris (left), librarian's assistant, and to librarian Judy Stull as they talk about the new city library. (CHSGWC.)

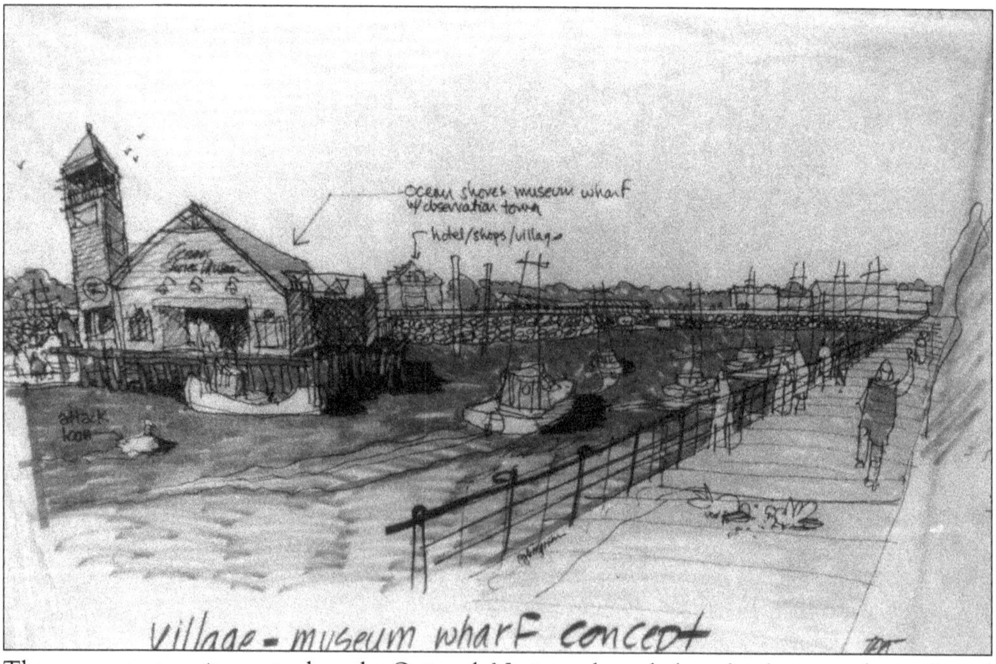

There was great excitement when the Quinault Nation released plans for the recently purchased marina area that would have included a major hotel, a cultural center, shopping, marine transportation, a working and sports marina, and a boardwalk with amenities for the local folks and tourists to enjoy the southern end of the city. A drastic change in economics and the inability of the nation to obtain federal dredging put the plans on hold. (CHSGWC.)

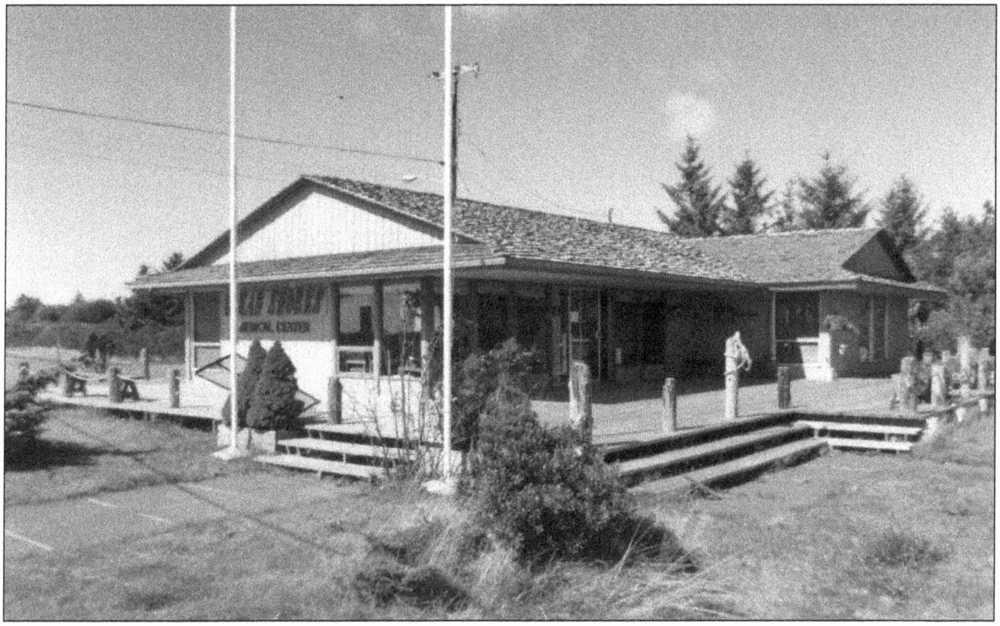

The old Wendell West south end real estate office was converted to a three-room environmental interpretive center after the NIX disease impacted the recreational clam harvest, devastating the tourism-dependent economy of the North Beach. The state developed the center to attract and inform visitors of other vacation activities. In 1994, the state closed the center. Local volunteers operated a children's summer program out of the building until the city developed the Ocean Shores Interpretive Center in 1997 with Gene Woodwick as the first director. (CHSGWC.)

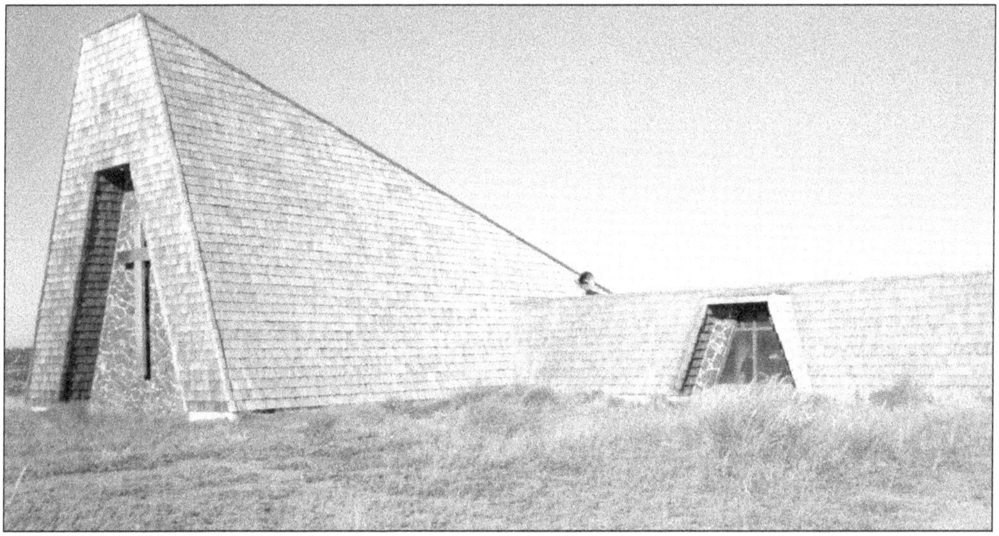

While commerce was the big-ticket item, spiritual needs were a big consideration, too. General Protestant services were held by Rev. Lewis Schultz at the old convention center on Ocean Shores Boulevard in 1964. The Galilean Chapel first held services in the Seahorse Room of the Ocean Shores Inn and the Surfside 12 convention room. Later, services moved to the old convention center (now the Bank of Grays Harbor). The first service held in their own modernly designed church was Christmas Eve 1969. In 1973, the Retreat and Youth Services building was completed. Harvey Neufeld and Orv Jacobson were the first two pastors. (CHSGWC.)

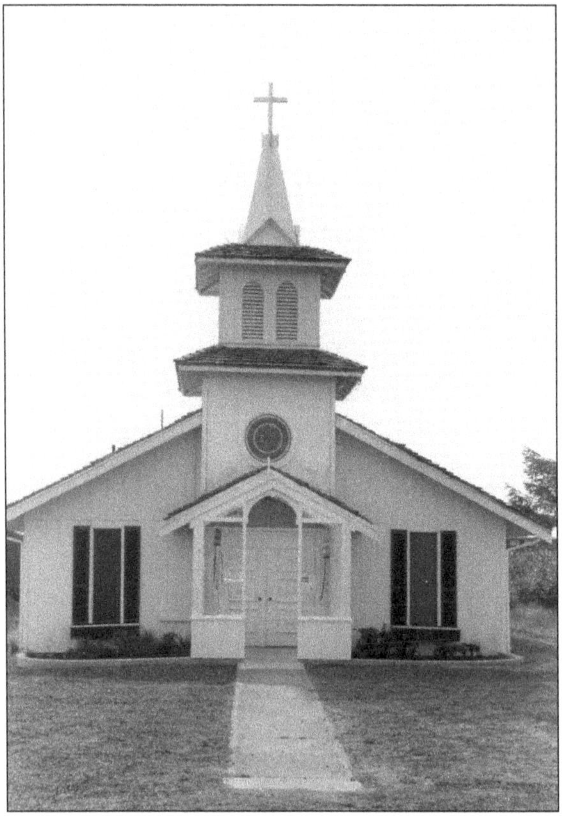

The classic little white Baptist church on Point Brown was built over the winter of 1969. The bell of a steam locomotive was donated to call the worshippers to services. (CHSGWC.)

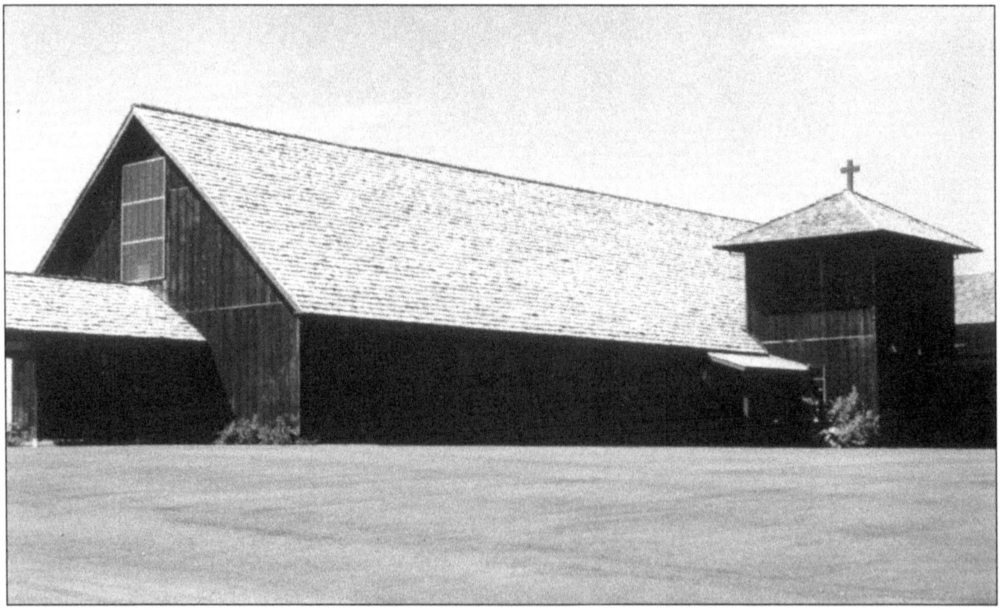

St. Jerome Catholic Church, at 5,000 square feet, was built on land at Hogan's Corner donated by Giles Hogan. Fr. Joseph A. Domenic carved the large mahogany panel *Christ On the Cross*, a foremost piece of art for the church. Fr. Peter Sand, OSB, held the first Catholic mass in the new development at the old convention center and mall. (CHSGWC.)

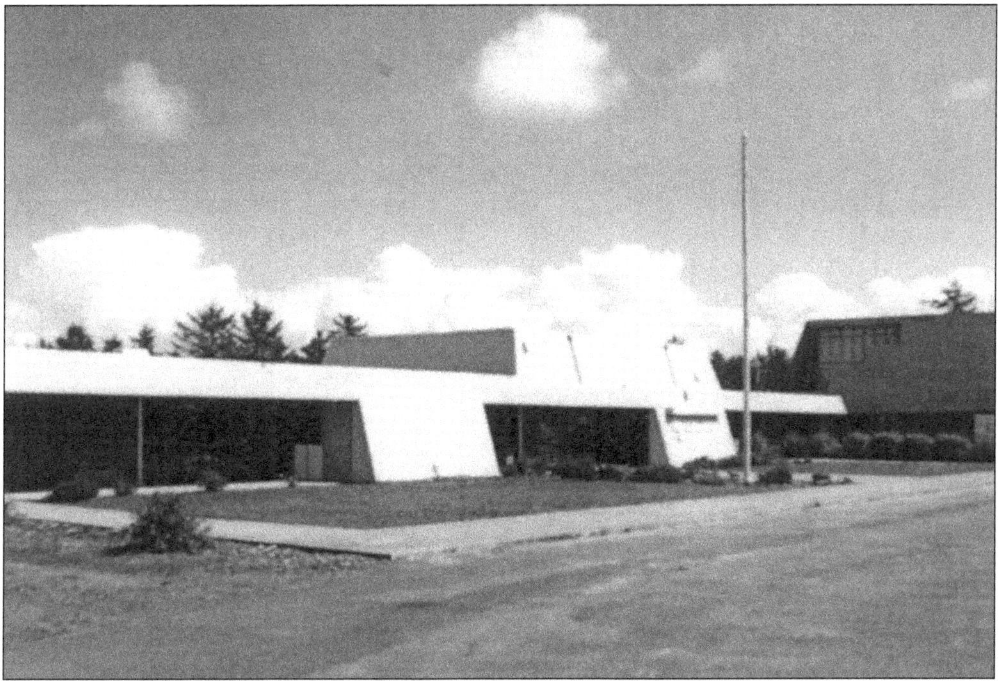

Elementary School bonds, to the tune of $312,000, were voted on by the public in 1967 with the school opening on Mt. Olympic Drive in 1971. The first classes were held on the Damon property near the dock for a few pioneer children. The first school, built nearer to Oyehut, also on Minard land, was basically a one-room shack used by commercial clam diggers' children. Emma Tanner remembers a time in the 1920s when she was the lone student and also when a class of 15 necessitated borrowing household chairs to seat everyone. The school was undoubtedly the only one in the state to have clam tides posted at the door so children would know what hours to come to class. (CHSGWC.)

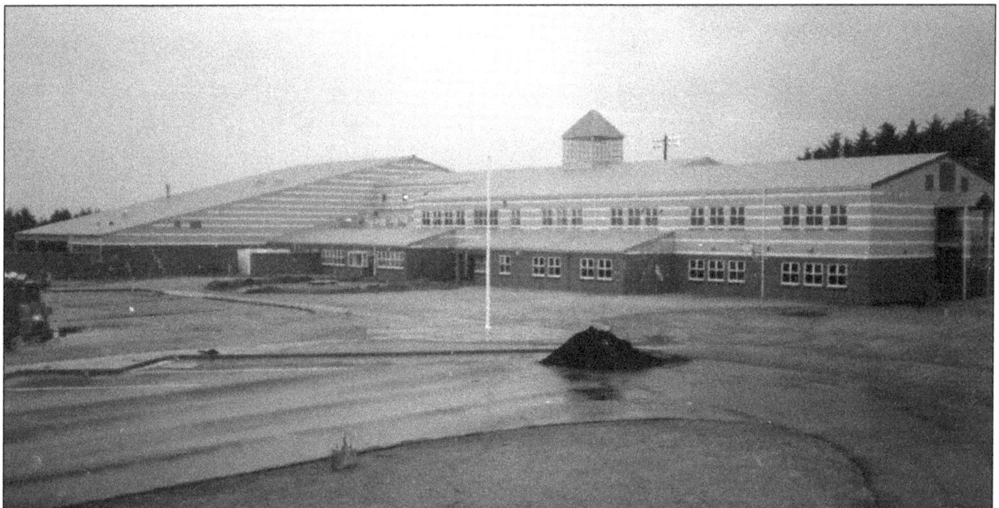

Since the turn of the 20th century, area students have attended high school at Moclips. A changing population base prompted a move to Oyehut just outside the city gates. The North Beach Junior/Senior High School opened in 1992. (CHSGWC.)

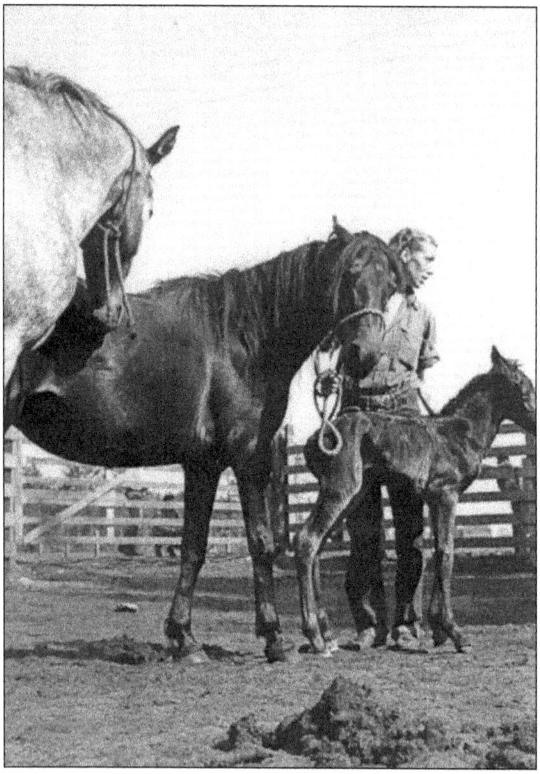

Pat (Minard) Seaman, pictured here, was known by generations of students as a bus driver for the Hoquaim and North Beach School Districts. When she was hired in 1975, she was the first female driver for the Washington Coastline's bus service. Many knew her simply as Pat when she drove the Grays Harbor County Transit Company trolley bus for Ocean Shores residents. She owned the Lazy Doctor Horse Motel boarding stable just outside the city gates. (MFP.)

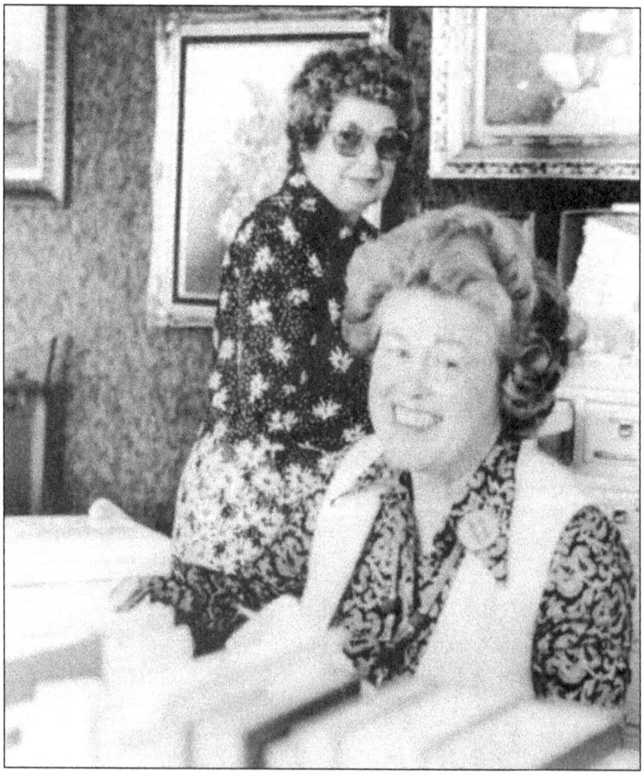

Two tireless Friends of the Library were Elsie Schneider (standing), a volunteer, and Beth Jordan, library trustee. Jordan has spent over 45 years supporting the activities of the library and was instrumental in pushing for community marine education, which resulted in the creation of the original Ocean Shores Interpretive Center, operated by Washington State prior to its closing in the 1980s. Schneider's husband, James, had kept the city on its toes at council meetings right from the beginning. However, he has always been a champion for schools and health care and has contributed greatly to many betterment projects. (The *Beacon*.)

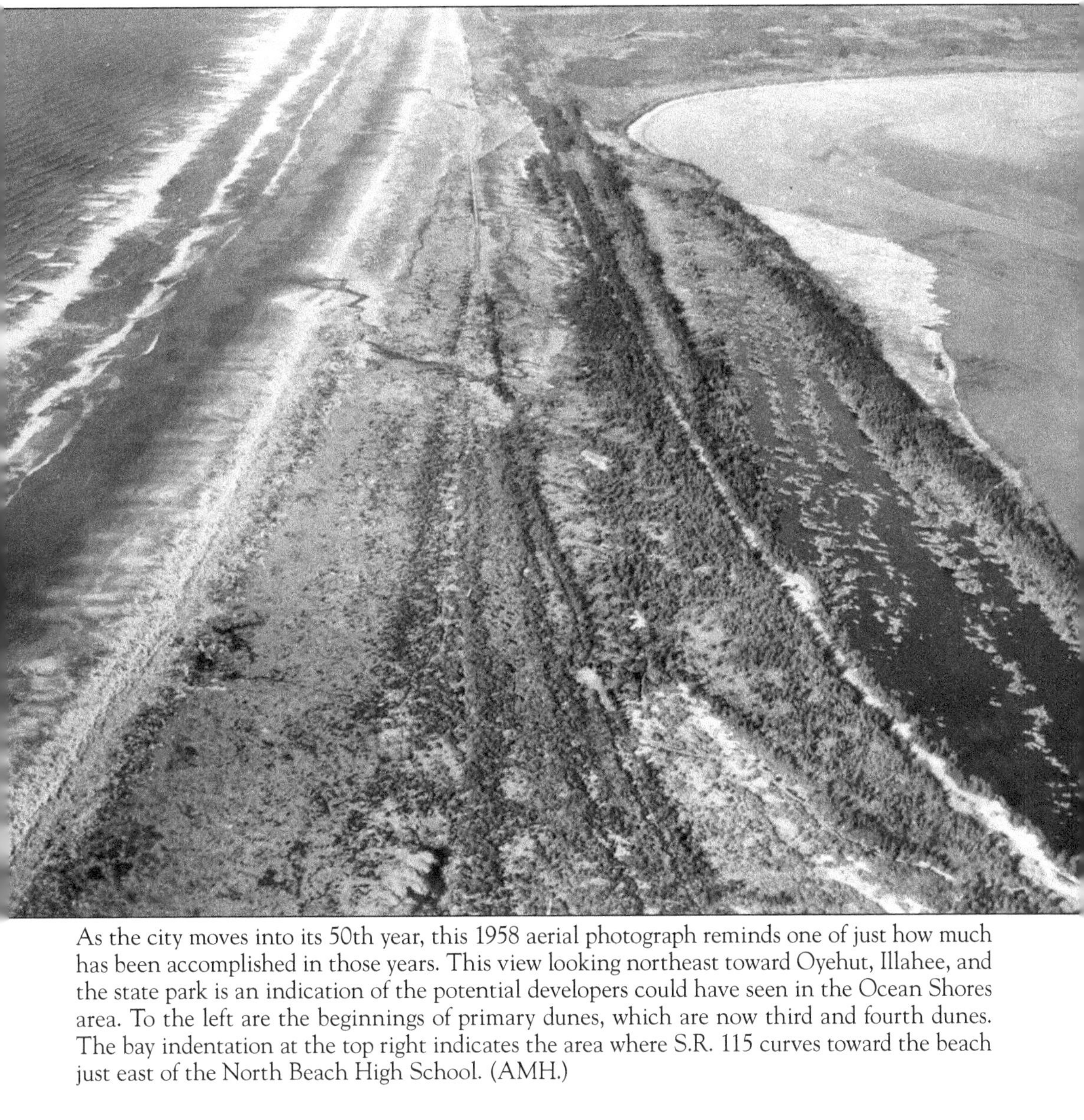

As the city moves into its 50th year, this 1958 aerial photograph reminds one of just how much has been accomplished in those years. This view looking northeast toward Oyehut, Illahee, and the state park is an indication of the potential developers could have seen in the Ocean Shores area. To the left are the beginnings of primary dunes, which are now third and fourth dunes. The bay indentation at the top right indicates the area where S.R. 115 curves toward the beach just east of the North Beach High School. (AMH.)

www.ingramcontent.com/pod-product-compliance
Lightning Source LLC
LaVergne TN
LVHW070625130926
847810LV00037B/443